Flagship Marketing

Flagships are the physical apogee of consumerism, places where brand experiences are most defined and interactions with consumers are highly refined. This book marks the first comprehensive study of the concept of the flagship, bringing together a range of scholarly insights from the field, covering issues such as consumerism, areas of consumption and experimental marketing theory and practice. The ways in which flagship projects communicate brand values, both externally and internally, form an important part of this book, and provide new perspectives on late twentieth century commercial and cultural policy and practice.

Kent and Brown offer a truly interdisciplinary approach to the concept, offering a variety of perspectives on the debates surrounding flagship function and its role as a place of consumption. Chapters focus on the development of prestigious stores, hotels and arts and cultural centres, as showcases for branded experiences and products and as demonstrations of commercial and public policy. Cases and examples include the Eden Project in the UK, automotive showrooms in Germany, hotels in Dubai and Las Vegas, and Vienna's cultural quarter. Theoretical discussion explores the tensions between costs and profitability, conspicuous consumption and the sustainability of iconic forms. The book enables readers to explore the flagship concept from different perspectives, and while a marketing approach predominates, it provides a disciplinary challenge which will open up new ways of understanding the concept.

This book will be of great interest to students and researchers engaged with marketing, fashion, and cultural studies, as well as practitioners engaged with the concept of design and urban planning.

Tony Kent is Reader in Marketing at the University of the Arts, London.

Reva Brown was the Professor of Management Research at Oxford Brookes University.

Routledge Advances in Management and Business Studies

Flagship Marketing
Concepts and places

Edited by Tony Kent and Reva Brown

Routledge
Taylor & Francis Group

LONDON AND NEW YORK

First published 2009
by Routledge
2 Park Square, Milton Park, Abingdon, Oxon OX14 4RN

Simultaneously published in the USA and Canada
by Routledge
270 Madison Ave, New York, NY 10016

*Routledge is an imprint of the Taylor & Francis Group, an informa
business*

© 2009 selection and editorial matter, Tony Kent and Reva Brown;
individual chapters, the contributors

Typeset in Times New Roman by
HWA Text and Data Management, London

Printed and bound in Great Britain by
TJI Digital, Padstow, Cornwall

British Library Cataloguing in Publication Data
A catalogue record for this book is available from the British Library

Library of Congress Cataloging in Publication Data
A catalog record for this book has been requested

ISBN10: 0–415–43602–8 (hbk)
ISBN10: 0–203–88708–5 (ebk)

ISBN13: 978–0–415–43602–1 (hbk)
ISBN13: 978–0–203–88708–0 (ebk)

The book is dedicated to Reva Brown who provided inspiration, guidance and élan in equal measure to the development and realization of this project

Contents

x   *Contents*

Figures

Tables

Contributors

Reva Brown, Professor of Management Research, Oxford Brookes University Business School

Hilary J. Collins, Senior Lecturer, School of Art and Design, University of Salford. Director of postgraduate studies, Euromed Toulon, Ecole de Management, France

Richard Coyne, Professor of Architectural Computing, Dept. of Architecture, University of Edinburgh

Charles Dennis, Senior Lecturer in Retail Marketing and Management, Brunel Business School, Brunel University

Anne Marie Doherty, Professor of Marketing, University of Glamorgan

Bronwen Edwards, Senior Lecturer, Faculty of Arts and Culture, Leeds Metropolitan University

Henrik Ekeus, Research Assistant, Dept. of Architecture, University of Edinburgh

Debi Hayes, Dean of the School of Creative Enterprise, London College of Communication, University of the Arts, London

Tim Jackson, London College of Fashion, University of the Arts, London

Tony Kent, Lecturer Principal. Reader in Marketing, London College of Communication, University of the Arts, London

Audrey Kirby, Senior Lecturer, London College of Communication, University of the Arts, London

Dion Kooijman, Associate Professor, School of the Built Environment, Technical University of Delft

Christopher. M. Moore, Professor of Retail Marketing, Heriot-Watt University

Simon Roodhouse, Professor of Creative Industries, London College of Communication, University of the Arts, London

Nicky Ryan, Senior Lecturer, London College of Communication, University of the Arts, London

James Stewart, Research Fellow, Dept. of Architecture, University of Edinburgh

Bill Webb, Senior Lecturer, London College of Fashion, University of the Arts, London

Mark Wright, Research Fellow, Dept. of Architecture, University of Edinburgh

Preface

Post-war prosperity and increasing consumption have contributed to the expansion of business and leisure in many ways. The landscape has changed through the development of shopping malls, retail and hotel chains, cultural quarters and virtual environments. Routinely used by the media to describe a variety of prestigious and usually large scale projects, flagships have found a place in our vocabulary well beyond their nautical origins.

Nevertheless, the original term 'flagship of the fleet' provides some pertinent analogies concerning consumption, commercial and design practices. In the first place the flagship has significant qualities to distinguish it from the rest of the fleet. The relationship of the flagship with other ships has to be examined; its size and position reflect its power, physically and symbolically; it provides a focus and has a communication function to other parts of the organization. The best people are needed to run flagships, and so they become aspirational places, but also ones which contribute to a sense of competition between rivals.

On dry land, flagship buildings can be determined by their style as impressive corporate buildings with an appropriate image and function and their buildings often become iconic structures. A flagship can also be thought of as a laboratory, a place to test out new ideas. It's frequently a social space and provides a location for more formal interaction, in catwalks and fashion shows. The role of designer is important for showcasing the flagship's best profile, catching the eye when cost is immaterial, and more usually when it is, and best practice in terms of its operational effectiveness, its mechanisms, and different layouts. Usually flagship stores represent the most important sites within a multiple retailer, although some are singular to define, and be defined by, their prestigious location. Locations themselves are becoming more difficult to categorize, as significant investment in websites replicate large stores and create the possibility of mixed physical and virtual flagship stores.

These ideas and more emerged from the initial discussions held by researchers from different disciplines in the University of the Arts, London, and developed through an exploratory meeting. Possible research avenues were proposed, first relating to organizations' sense of style, their design and products. A second, more specifically marketing-led approach discussed the expression of the flagship brand and its diffusion to shops and its possible cyclicality. A social perspective would engage with earlier relationships between the flagship and location and community, the role of the flagship as an icon and issues of inclusion and exclusion. This is shown in the role of nostalgia, for example memories of Biba as theatre, and development of the concept through the 1980s of flagships in different dimensions and different industry sectors in retailing. Another area to explore is how retailers themselves define their flagships, what they want exactly from them.

Subsequently, a symposium on flagship concepts and places was held at the London College of Communication in 2006, and a number of chapters developed out of the presentations. As the contributors at that event provided many different insights into the concept, so the first aim of the book emerged, which is to use different disciplines to evaluate the flagship concept and its application in commercial and cultural contexts more accurately and in greater depth than before. Since it was evident that the concept has strong associations with location, a second aim was to explore the relationship between flagship and place. It has a consumer orientation and demonstrates how flagships provide an important point in differentiating brands and places and provide memorable experiences. As such it engages with a number of theoretical frameworks situated in the disciplines of business and management, design, and history, and these provide distinctive approaches into research and knowledge about the subject.

Tony Kent

Acknowledgements

The editors have benefited from the help and advice of many people, at different stages of the project, and thanks are due to everyone who has been involved. It is difficult to single out specific names, but at critical moments the project moved forward with their advice and support. In an early developmental stage Steve Burt, Delia Vasquez, and Charles Dennis provided valuable ideas and constructive criticism. Nicky Ryan, Audrey Kirby and Zubin Sethna were instrumental in organizing the symposium, which gave rise to many of the contributions. Hilary Kamstra has given invaluable assistance throughout the project, and at every stage it has moved forward with Janice Hart's encouragement and enthusiasm. Sadly Reva Brown, my co-editor, died suddenly in January 2007. The project owed much to her incisiveness but also openness to the new ideas and research opportunities it provided.

Every effort has been made to trace copyright holders of the images reproduced in this book. If an oversight has been made, please contact the publishers, who will remedy the omission in future editions.

Introduction

Tony Kent and Reva Brown

The flagship has become part of the language of special places. It defines the visible dimensions of governmental policy and action. It has a commercial and specifically marketing function to promote and communicate, to showcase and experiment new designs, products and ways of working. It has social implications. There is an implicit creativity, which may be found in their location, architecture, use of space, products, services and technologies, and communication techniques. In the broadest sense the flagship provides an accessible point to enter into cross-disciplinary learning about society, consumption and the environment.

Flagships are found in many industries, and are widely discussed, selectively studied and to a lesser extent, researched. The contribution of flagship projects to the retail and cultural industries is of significant interest to planners and managers. Flagship stores are highly visible, as showcases for department stores and fashion businesses. They provide opportunities for food retailers to demonstrate new designs and systems. Most flagship stores are situated in major cities, and then in specific areas and streets, but they can perform an important function in smaller towns and cities too. Shopping malls can perform a flagship function to compete effectively. Even more visible and with a broader impact, flagship developments have formed the cultural centrepiece of post-industrial regeneration projects. These are museums, art galleries, and cultural centres. Many of them are found in urban locations, some, like the Eden project, in rural ones. Entire urban areas and quarters may be designated as the focus of cultural initiatives. Flagships are seen in other industries too; service industry corporates use headquarters buildings to project their organizational identities. Flagship hotels and resorts are developed to create and promote new forms of leisure and different leisure experiences. The online, virtual environment provides an alternative perspective to flagships from the physical world. Applied in new ways electronic media has the potential to create hybrid flagship environments.

The purpose of this book is to stimulate interest and thinking about the flagship concept in a marketing context. It arises from a research project and symposium held at the University of the Arts, London, in 2006. A number of chapters reflect the interests of authors at the symposium, and a conscious diversity of styles and approaches. Design, sociology, consumerism, cultural policy also find a place here, but marketing provides a cohesive theme. In addition, the flagship concept brings new insights into well-established but also more emergent fields of marketing research and scholarship. Flagship projects are distinguished by their location and differentiation. Thus they have a role in strategic marketing as the most distinctive and holistic expression of the organization's ability to differentiate itself. They exemplify the brand, indeed, may be instrumental in creating it, and demonstrate a leadership function to others, both within the organization and competitors. They have a marketing communication role to consumers, employees and a wider community of stakeholders.

The chapters explore the flagship concept through different themes and locations, each providing different and complementary perspectives. There is a strong theoretical approach within the book's chapters, which reflect the authors' own positions. For student learners, the authors' use of contrasting methodologies, written styles and their application to a common theme is instructive in itself. No particular theoretical or methodological position has been privileged. The contributors draw from marketing, using both positivistic and interpretivist traditions, and from specializations in fashion retailing and branding, but also design and design history, architecture, cultural studies, and informatics. However the purpose of the book is not to test theory but rather to introduce and explore the concept and it will be evident that a number of chapters in themselves cannot be strictly constrained within a particular disciplinary mould. It is expected that they are the more stimulating for that.

The book is structured to lead from an initial overview of the concepts and the places where flagships are found, through specific studies of the flagship and ending with a broadening of the subject. The final chapters explore cultural flagships and the opportunities provided by virtual environments. The afterword summarizes key themes and issues arising from the chapters and proposes areas for further study.

The conceptualization of flagship stores is explored in the first two chapters. In recent times, the term 'flagship store' has become increasingly popular amongst journalists, and increasingly, academic writers in the fashion sector. However as there is no accepted definition of the term, it is variously used in relation to the store size, rarity, location or site, and range of products and services on offer. Furthermore, not only is there no agreement on what constitutes a flagship store, commentators are unclear on the strategy underpinning their development and the rationale for their existence. In turn, this makes meaningful evaluation of their performance and impact almost impossible. Chapter two establishes the parameters, which define the flagship concept, to identify distinct categories of flagship store with illustrative examples, and discusses the rationale behind each type, and its role in the fashion company's business model.

Collins's chapter provides a different perspective on the flagship concept by assessing the role of the built environment and physical artefacts on its users. Dubai has seen a rapid development in its luxury hotels, many of which have represented flagships of new design and experience. Collins examines how the users of a Dubai flagship hotel, the organizational actors, adapt and change their identities in response to such luxurious surroundings. A theoretical model is developed to explain physical artefacts as expressing, reflecting, mirroring and impressing processes on the individual in the context of memorable or spectacular places.

Physical artefacts provide clear visual and tangible opportunities to create exceptional environments. It is increasingly clear though, that online environments provide rich sources of complementary or unique flagship experience. Richard Coyne's chapter explores new territory between brands, place and virtual space, by taking the flagship concept as a branded place and its role in facilitating interaction between users. It has been shown that the branded environment can influence the mood and emotions of both customers and employees, to create more satisfying work and leisure experiences. The chapter is informed by design and infomatics-led enquiry to explore the use and subversion of brand communication and space. Coyne demonstrates the possibilities through the development of mobile technologies and their impact on communication in the context of flagships as a final theme.

Chris Moore returns to the luxury theme by reviewing the nature and characteristics of flagship stores within the designer fashion sector. Based upon interviews with luxury fashion retailers, he suggests that these flagship stores can be understood using a framework comprised of three key dimensions. Their strategic purpose relates closely to the development of the brand, while the choice of location and place serves to enhance and support their premium positioning. The important status of flagship is emphasized through their position in the distribution hierarchy, and their representational significance understood from a decoding of the language of the flagship store.

Taking a broader approach to place and concept with the shopping mall, Charles Dennis explains the function of a larger scale flagship shopping development in urban regeneration. Retailing forms the heart of towns and cities in the UK and many other countries, and the health of cities is critical to that of their regions. However, modern developments challenge the role of town centres as community hubs. In many countries, particularly the US, wealthier people and their associated retail facilities have moved away from central districts. These areas have experienced physical, economic and social decline, and various strategies have been proposed and implemented to regenerate them. This chapter investigates the role of the planned shopping mall as a flagship destination. Towns often lack an organization to promote common interests, of which maintenance, and parking, but increasingly security are significant. The planned shopping mall can bring those benefits, as well as providing additional entertainment and the shopping experiences, and thus act as a magnet for business and residential development. Planned shopping malls can leverage their 'brand' to bring people, pleasure and prosperity to an area, and not just to town centres. In this way, West Edmonton Mall in Canada conjures up an image of a safe and happy environment with many shops and entertainment facilities. The Lakeside regional centre in the UK attracts other business and residential development towards these 'growth poles'. The planned shopping mall can act as a flagship for the development and renewal of community activities wanted by people.

Up to this point in the book, the focus has been on commercial flagship development. However, the next chapter turns to the role of a cultural flagship project in urban regeneration programmes. Hayes takes up the role of specific flagship development in regeneration. Evidence is emerging that post-industrial cities and regions in Europe will survive if their cultural assets are seriously valued. Cultural assets include a broad range of arts and the architectural heritage, and increasingly entertainment and leisure. Formerly seen as a difficult terrain for planners focused on the social, economic and ecological impacts of spatial development, entertainment now forms an integral part of the flagship experience. The chapter examines the cultural flagship's role as a beacon for regeneration and a signal for cultural change through a comparison between the Millennium Dome in London and Cornwall's rural Eden Project. Both projects were announced at the same time in the 1990s but thereafter their development and appeal diverged sharply. At their conception both projects were clearly aimed at and these projects physically symbolize different objectives and aspirations, development processes and operational styles. Flagship projects, manifested as museum, cultural centre or a defined geographical space, suggest that other initiatives for economic and social change will follow in their wake. However, as Hayes demonstrates, the flagship project's success factors fundamentally require a clear vision, consistently applied, with broad stakeholder support.

A second aspect of cultural flagship development engages with urban planning and regeneration in the development of cultural quarters. Cultural quarters are generally conceived as planning zones or designated geographical areas where complementary activities take place and benefit from a close proximity with each other. This model is increasingly found in cities, and is associated with the creative industries and demonstrates the influence of the Berlin Museum Island, the Lincoln Centre, and the museum clustering initiative in Hamburg. Such quarters are often identified as flagship projects for public and private stakeholders and investors. One obvious area of common interest and mutual benefit for all stakeholders is the marketing of the cultural quarter. This requires consultation between location and branding marketers, and the tenants, specific brand image/communication concept marketers, about an integrated marketing strategy.

There is a consensus that marketing the cultural quarter will increase visitor numbers for the tenants and that this growth is achieved largely through international tourists. In addition, many organizations generate temporary exhibitions and tour these shows nationally and internationally with related lecture programmes and education services, all of which need marketing. Simon Roodhouse's chapter points to both the strategic marketing and operational issues in planning a quarter as a flagship for culture and creativity; more specifically it identifies the need for collaborative working, an understanding of the benefits of mutual support for strategic partnerships and active promotion of projects. For the flagship quarter to achieve these objectives a strategy has to be developed, agreed by its stakeholders, resourced and realized.

The final group of five chapters continues the case-led approach to flagship concepts and places, demonstrated in the study of Vienna's cultural quarter. The first of these returns to the retail sector and traces the development of a specific flagship store, Simpson's, in London. Throughout the twentieth century the geographical distribution of such stores followed the principal shopping arteries of metropolitan centres such as London's West End. This area housed the flagship stores of multiple retailers, department store chains and clothing brands, often in important buildings, themselves architectural landmarks within the city. They also held a significant role within broader networks of fashion consumption, associating each brand or company as a whole with a metropolitan cachet. Edwards's chapter provides a detailed assessment of Simpson's Piccadilly store, which was explicitly intended as a flagship for the company's clothing, and a centre for a national network of clothing agents. Significantly, a striking, modern design was chosen for the store, and the building's reputation as architectural landmark swiftly bolstered the reputation and fame of the business, essential for a company which was attempting to legitimize a new kind of masculine shopping. The store's location had been carefully chosen: this was a time when the heart of the West End still had a dual, unchallenged reputation both for traditional masculine tailoring and outfitting, and for fashionable modern consumption. The chapter draws together architectural and geographical concerns to explain how stores like Simpson Piccadilly functioned as flagships within national networks of fashion consumption.

Architecture and location combine to create distinctive hotels too, which have long been promoted as flagships of individual and organizational owners, and more generally in place marketing. Their distinctiveness can be viewed from a number of perspectives including service, food, ambience and facilities, from exclusive luxurious places to functional, standardized ones. The late twentieth century saw increasing numbers of such hotels as consumers took advantage of leisure opportunities. Ryan takes the case of the hotel-casino Wynn Las Vegas, which opened in 2005 to coincide with the centenary celebrations of the city of Las Vegas. Developed by entrepreneur Steve Wynn at a cost of 2.7 billion dollars, it is the flagship development of Wynn Resorts Limited; one which, its promoters claim, will represent a new paradigm for luxury destinations that will 'revolutionize mega-resorts'. The design of Wynn Las Vegas as product and process, is contextualized within the wider development of the Las Vegas strip. The city's hotels were transformed into mixed-use spaces but also iconographically from 'decorated shed' to Disney-style themed 'architainment'. Supremely, Wynn's hotel flagship was instrumental in promoting the city and repositioning it as a luxury resort.

Manufacturers too have realized the opportunity to use distinctive buildings to communicate and showcase their products but also to create a more personal experience of the brand for their customers. In Germany, Mercedes-Benz, Volkswagen and BMW have elevated the experience of car buying, where the auto showroom has taken on a new iconic status. Kooijman demonstrates the use of flagship car showrooms as brand flagships and also consumption spaces in which the architecture and location have a significant role in expressing the personality of the brand. In this context, the Autostadt and 'car handover center'

(*Selbstabholung*) provide evidence of an experiential marketing approach that gained credibility in the 1990s as well as forming an important interactive element of the organization's brand strategy.

While luxury hotels, fashion stores and cultural buildings provide an evident stream of flagship projects, more functional buildings and less prestigious locations can provide opportunities for flagship developments. Audrey Kirby's chapter examines the concept of flagship stores in the context of supermarket brands and the visual impact of supermarket buildings. In the food sector the development of out of town superstores offered more space and new design-led branding opportunities. The first was opened in 1967 and as competition for sites increased during the 1980s, external design became more visually and contextually demanding. 'Inside-out' store design gave further emphasis to the maximization of interior sales space and gave impetus to the development of retailer brands and services. These moved beyond the two-dimensional projection of visual identity into three-dimensional retail branding combining product development, and new sensory elements from instore bakeries, fresh food displays, and cafés.

From the 1980s, fierce rivalry between supermarkets competing for prime development sites influenced not only the design of the buildings, but also the public and planners' perceptions. This was particularly evident with the four major companies Sainsbury's, Tesco, Safeway, and Asda. Competition for space and ongoing public disquiet about the decline of high-street shops placed local planners in a dominant position, and led to the imposition of planning restrictions and the demand for architectural designs and site landscaping that satisfied public opposition.

Competition also led to a new focus on store appearance and brand identity, and raised important issues about corporate marketing and the dimensions of the customer experience in the store. During the mid-1980s, Sainsbury's decided to produce a series of landmark stores to distinguish its brand from its competitors, which resulted in a portfolio of flagship buildings by high-profile architects. Several of the stores received design awards and gained Sainsbury's a reputation for architectural innovation. Subsequently Tesco, too, came to re-assess its design policy and the implications of distinctive flagship stores for its brand. These retailers turned to an extensive range of locations and design solutions in their quest for market share: from brownfield or edge of town sites, to in-fill developments on traditional high street sites. The chapter concludes with an assessment of the success of these flagship structures and their durability as an element of retail brand identity.

The virtual environment provides an extensive and dynamic environment for the replication of real life flagship stores. The final chapter examines ways in which the real life characteristics translate into the virtual world. Increased accessibility through exposure on the web is one aspect. A communications function is a fundamental feature and a transactional function has become commonplace, as brands develop online business models. However the popularity of online social networking suggests that a merged form may provide new levels of interactivity and engagement with consumers. The length of time spent by a visitor at a site or on specific pages was subject to considerable research and discussion in the earlier years of website design, in terms of its stickiness or its navigability. Jackson examines the interactive components of a flagship store and their ability to create appealing online locations. For retailers, flagship places, their location of their stores, are important. The extent to which an online location can be defined, through its links, its relationships with other retailers or the organization itself, or is even significant to real world retailers, forms an important part of this analysis.

The arguments presented in this book demonstrate the extent to which organizations communicate and interact with consumers through distinctive flagship projects. Different insights have been drawn from a range of disciplinary perspectives to open up debate and discussion about the influence and significance of flagship concepts and places. In particular, design and visual impact of different environments have been promoted, carrying with them implications for future research.

1 Concepts of flagships

Tony Kent

The flagship concept has become a well-defined feature of commercial and cultural life, bringing with it a wide range of associations with prestigious and iconic places. Flagships permeate people's daily lives, taking the form of stores, but also hotels, cultural centres, and even entire cities that allow consumption of products, experiences and processes.

Flagship projects can be used as change agents, signalling regeneration, and assuming an iconic status through which people enter a different world. They can be exclusive places, a flagship store or hotel defined by its location and position in the market. However, in recent decades some flagships have been conceived and designed as popular destinations; these are the supermarkets and shopping centres that are embedded in our communities. They are often large and imposing places but they can be small, serving a niche market in a locality. Wherever they are, elements from the flagship model diffuse into other locations in the retail or hotel chain, concepts transfer from one regeneration project to another, flagship cities adapt and create new identities.

The concept of the project driven flagship development scheme finds its origins in Baltimore in 1970 where it was used to regenerate the city's run-down urban environment. It led to the development of various centres, a marina, hotels and a variety of leisure and retail facilities. In the US re-use of old buildings, the recycling of mills and warehouses became well established. Boston's Quincy Market provided the key to Boston's downtown regeneration through its geographical location at the centre of activity in the city (Colquhoun 1995). The redevelopment of London's Covent Garden was an early implementation of this movement in the UK.

Regenerational flagship projects came to be defined as 'significant, high profile developments that play an influential and catalytic role in urban regeneration, which can be justified if they attract other investment' (Bianchini *et al.* 1992). They contain a number of elements (Smyth 1994). Each is a development in its own right, which may or may not be self-sustaining. It is a central point for further investment, through consumption but also the services it provides. It can be a marketing tool for an entire area of city, a large advertising hoarding, promoting the place for others to invest or spend. It may be part of a larger marketing approach to advertise the city, create demand for inward investment, or offer the surrounding area as one of the potential locations within the city and its hinterland. Consequently the prime purpose of a flagship is to create a development that is more than the entity in its own right. In summary, such projects combine specific regenerational functions and symbolic values (Voase 1997; Aitcheson and Evans 2003).

The concept has extended to embrace a wider range of locations and industries. Theme Parks can be considered as flagships in the context of tourism development (Dybedal 2000). Whole cities can be flagships for national or cultural projects. Governments use cultural flagships of change in post-industrial areas of which the Guggenheim Museum in Bilbao is a pre-eminent example and is at once both a flagship for the Basque country and for the Guggenheim foundation (Worsley 2004). European Cities of Culture are in part defined by the branding techniques developed through commercial and 'star' architecture strategies (Evans 2003). Airport terminal buildings continue to be seen by airlines as opportunities for positioning and branding (Leslie 2005) and the distinctive architecture of corporate headquarters symbolizes their organizations.

While economic factors play an important role in many of these projects, the focus of the chapter turns to retailing, and the development of flagship stores from a marketing perspective. In a strategic context, there is a positioning match between store and location. In the case of fashion designer-led stores location, interior design and windows, and marketing communications combine in the retailer's market positioning. Place has been an essential ingredient of the marketing mix from its inception, and especially so in the retail industry where location is frequently held to be the most important element of the retail strategy. Streets like Bond Street, London, achieve a concentration of designer fashion stores to accompany the promotion of fashion brands in terms of 'beautiful presentation on the best streets' (Moore *et al.* 2000: 920).

Department and fashion stores have traditionally numbered flagships as their most important sites, identified by size and product diversity. They can be characterized as supporting the brand's reputation. Seeing flagships as part of marketing communications for the whole chain or company explains the high levels of investment dedicated to their creation and running as a means of creating awareness and interest (Moore *et al.* 2000). Marketing communications is evident too in brand re-positioning (Moore and Birtwistle 2004) and fashion own-brand retailing in the UK demonstrates a discernable array of lifestyle images through brand advertising and promotion. In fashion stores, branding the shopping experience is defined by the 'need for fashion retailers to ensure that the own-brands' values are extended to permeate throughout the whole shopping experience' (Moore 1995: 21).

Flagship stores and their environments create memorable and sometimes spectacular branded experiences. During the 1980s, consumer research turned to experiential and hedonic consumption in retailing as well as entertainment, arts and leisure (Holbrook and Hirschman 1982). Marketers subsequently explored the significance of sensory experiences and their application to the market positioning of the organization (Schmitt and Simonsen 1997) and the primacy of the experience economy. To provide an operational account of such experiences, four realms of consumption experience were defined through the dimensions of customer participation and connectivity to the experience (Pine and Gilmore 1998; Caru and Cova 2003). Psychologically, the intensity and quality of experiences were differentiated through the degrees of challenge and skill demanded of an individual, and at their optimum, to create the most absorbing and memorable 'flow' experiences (Cziksentmihalyi 1997).

The location of retail experiences is found in the expanding literatures of store environmental research that includes retail atmosphere, consumer attitudes and behaviour (Kotler1974; Donovan and Rossiter 1982; Greenland and McGoldrick 1994; Turley and Milliman 2000), store patronage (Newman and Patel 2004) and merchandise selection and display (Ward and Davies 2004). Over a similar period of time, designers developed increasingly inclusive solutions to retail design. Store design became an integral part of clothing retailers' strategies during the 1980s, leading towards more creative interiors and exteriors. The concentration of food retailing into fewer and more powerful multiples and the transformation of store distribution and product ranges, expanded branded activity in this sector. The 'store as brand' came to relate appearance and identity to core brand values (Magrath 2005) as consumer experiences reflected the development of retail branding and store design, and their engagement with emotions and physical contact (Kent 2003). With such increasing complexity of brand themes, Beverland and Morrison (2003) propose that retailers take a gestalt perspective of brand positioning, marketing communications, in-store variables, processes and place.

The use of sensory experience has led to the store environment taking on a greater significance, providing spaces for interactivity, socialization and communication. Creating these environments places an emphasis on design, both in terms of the quality of the finished store but also the holistic problem solving approach that typifies design thinking. Retail design has to be multi-faceted by linking together art, instinct and business in a problem solving and planning process. Above all it must be creative to find or invent new environments in which space, cost and flexibility are matched to the effective communication of the retailer's brand values and the stimulation of consumer purchasing activity (Din 2000).

One result is that creativity has become more of a required organizational resource and a desirable core competence. It has become more so as consumers have become part of the retailer's value creation process, one that has moved from a product focus to individualized experience. Flagship stores operate in two dimensions, both to sustain creative design and enable consumers to be creative. Choosing and selecting food, from individual ingredients or pre-prepared meals, has become an increasingly creative process, for example 'fusion' meals with eclectic ingredients. Bookstores provide spaces for socialization but also creative thinking, enabling consumers to enter and create new thought worlds. Clothing retailers offer opportunities for consumers to create different identities by communicating fashion and style.

In this context, the flagship should be a place where customers are engaged in the environment and its experiences. The store creates memories, but such effects exist on a continuum, and can be seen with varying intensities of expression. At its most intense, the brand experience may be an essential part of the luxury flagship store, to unify the 'ultimate allure of the brand' (Moore and Birtwistle 2005). The intensity of experience in branded flagship stores has been developed and categorized by Gilmour and Pine (2002) and Kozinets *et al.* (2002). Gilmore and Pine (2002) provide a conceptualization of 'experience places', based on different sizes and locations, both physical and online (see Figure 1.1). They propose that organizations explore the possibilities of a 'rich portfolio of experiences' that flow from one level to the next, and develop a location hierarchy model to demonstrate how these can be created. The most singular experiences occur in a flagship location, one that is indelibly associated with the company, where the company 'stages the very best, most dynamic experience'. Notably Gilmore and Pine propose that manufacturers as well as retailers should engage in assessing their locational advantages to market experiences and create additional income.

Kozinets *et al.*'s (2002) theoretical framework extends Bitner's (1992) dimensions of the servicescape and the cultural associations that can play an important role to construct contemporary retail environments. Their approach demonstrates that brand related experiences prevail over functional efficiency and that experiential, spectacular and entertaining aspects of retailing are becoming increasingly important to stores. Consequently individual brands should be 'enshrined in environments built especially for them', where retailing is essentially tangible and spatial, and successfully blend virtual and real worlds. In this context, retail marketers should turn to the aesthetics of the shopping environment, where shopping and entertainment combine for consumers to make meaning out of the physical experience of the place.

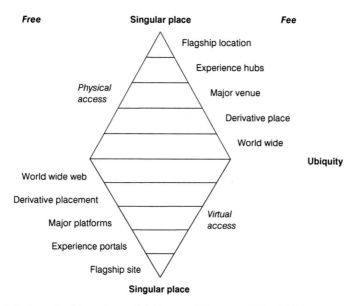

Figure 1.1   Location hierarchy model (Source: Gilmore and Pine 2002)

Their typology identifies flagship brand stores as either exclusive or non-exclusive outlets for the brand, themed entertainment brand stores and a hybrid of these two, themed flagship brand stores. This type of store promotes existing brands in a variety of outlets with entertainment as a source of income. In sum, the retail brand is seen within a context of 'entertainment-oriented services' and that brand related experiences prevail over functional efficiency. The authors extend the experiential framework, using a servicescape to classify, organize and analyse the cultural associations behind the types of fantasy elements that may play an important role to construct contemporary retail environments. They subsequently create a visual three-dimensional model to explain flagship store development through retail orientation, cultural orientation and brand orientation (see Figure 1.2). The lowest levels of retail, cultural and brand orientation are at the base of the pyramid. The higher up the pyramid the flagship store can be positioned, the more multi-dimensionally branded and more experiential it will be.

The model is open to criticism about its relativity to American consumption and its demands for consumer extraordinary or memorable experiences that may not be achievable (Caru and Cova 2003). The difficulties of positioning in the 'mindscape' dimension are illustrated by the failure of the Seibu department store in Japan. On the other hand, in developing consumer markets the servicescape dimensions may be inappropriate where a different, more practical role is required. In developing retail markets, flagships undertake different roles; in China clothing manufacturer wholly owned flagship stores act as their own factory promotional events and as a role model and even a service point for other stores (Cassill *et al.* 2004). Nevertheless the framework provides a useful basis from which to examine retail flagship stores in the UK.

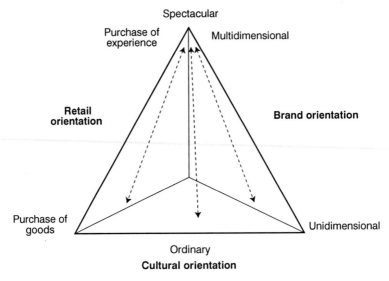

Figure 1.2   Dimensions and forms of flagship brand stores (Kozinets *et al.* 2002)

Analysis of flagship store references in the media from 2004–2005 demonstrates that the term is used very loosely. At its most general, flagship is synonymous with novelty or 'newness', to create interest in a new development. This may be purposeful on the part of the retailer or adopted as part of their communication strategy through PR. The majority of references refered to by sector concern clothing and footwear (see Table 1.1).

One consistent theme that emerges, is the consistent use of flagship stores to thoroughly combine elements of the marketing mix (see also Foxell and Kent 2006). The basic elements of the mix promotion, place and product assortment, and to a lesser extent, price, are carefully planned and controlled in the flagship store. The complexity of these stores lends support to the extended mix approach (7Ps) as the physical environment and people are particularly important elements.

More specifically, and purposefully, interviews with key participants in retailing, design and property management demonstrate the use of the flagship, in all cases, as having a retail branding function. Retail flagships are more than stores; firstly they are positioned to communicate corporate and brand values to customers and employees, competitors and communities. Marketers use the terms 'beacon' and 'lighthouse' to describe this aspect. In their bricks-and-mortar embodiment, they can be considered as constituting, in addition to a retailing sales function, three-dimensional forms of advertising and promotion. Increasingly they provide opportunities for two-way communication and interaction, and co-production with their consumers. Thus the function of a flagship can be understood within a marketing communications strategy, the benefits of which transcend that of the store itself. It gives the brand exposure to different audiences, demonstrates confidence and expresses interest, and at a more emotional extreme, excitement.

Closely related to this theme is that of the 'ideal'. The flagship, at the very least, is the best example of the retail brand and can be understood as the 'purest

Table 1.1 Distribution of flagship stores by retail sector

Sector	Number of references
Clothing and footwear	70
Food	11
Health and beauty (including chemists)	4
Other	24
Electrical and computer	4
Department stores	32
Variety stores	0
Furniture/carpets	10
DIY	2
Non specific/multiple/different categories	22
Total	178

Source: UK printed news media, March 2004–March 2005

expression of the brand' to internal and external stakeholders. Products, service and environment combine to provide leadership and best practice, as a prototype for the store group. Flagship stores are where customers and visitors 'see the diversity of the product and the background as well' and stores are differentiated from others through the quality of their staff and services. However, the 'ideal' takes on different meanings in different retail sectors. In the clothing sector, the flagship is defined by their function to showcase their best profile, effectively to catch the eye, and where cost may not be a prime consideration.

Clothing retailers' flagships are clearly determined by 'style' and interactivity, both with products, and socially with other people, in which interior design plays a significant part in the experience. At Top Shop's Oxford Circus, London flagship, the design avoids structure and aims to create an impression of the fashion industry's constant change, an eclectic environment employing colour, product design and display. Zones, rather than departments merge into each other, showcasing individual labels, fashion themes and product groups from catwalk ranges to retro fashion. In the basement a popular café is adjacent to a large video screen; the topical music is an important facilitator to the shopping experience.

By contrast, flagship stores in the food sector are defined by best practice in the operational environment, the mechanisms, technologies and different layouts of stores. These are places where experience is premised on 'food as fashion', showcased through presentations and demonstrations. But fashionable food retailing requires a closer understanding of the fashion industry, in which competition from other retailers is relentless, and timescales for product development and the selling season itself, are short. Moreover these aspirations contrast with the long-term implications of building maintaining corporate brand identity. For grocery retailers the flagship store equates to power; they reflect the size and importance of the organization. Tesco's re-use of the Hoover building in West London creates viable sales opportunities through its location and catchment area but also in its arresting identity.

In a retail environment characterized by the consistency and sameness of multiple retailers, these stores typically offer a greater choice of products and services. Flagships provide the opportunity to experience these within distinctive, often memorable and in places unique, physical environments. It is an ideal store for the latest manifestation of the brand, embracing a holistic approach to showcase distinctive experiences. The content of the showcase varies by sector. In the food sector latest practices, layouts and technologies define flagship stores as the newest large store, one that will be replaced by the next large-scale development within a relatively short timescale. Clothing sector stores demonstrate a complex mix of product and service experiences, enhanced by investment into a comprehensively designed store environment, to endure over a longer timescale.

'Designed space' forms the third theme. Food retailers' flagship stores tend to be determined by space availability; the stores may contextualize spacious semi-rural sites, the 'superstore', but as Tesco's Hoover building, and Sainsbury's Camden store demonstrate, planning constraints may force them into anonymous urban locations. For other retailers, location can define, and be defined by the flagship store. Harrods in London and Jenners in Edinburgh typify distinctive local positions. In London but more especially in Birmingham, Selfridges plays an important role in defining Oxford Street and the Bullring shopping area. Selfridges creates a distinctive, monumental presence to define the start of an experience of shopping on Oxford Street: it is the first building to stand out from the western end of the street's postwar development. As well as defining the street, Selfridges is also defined by the street, in that it can never aspire to Knightsbridge, or the select and smaller scale of Bond Street. It occupies the more mixed and accessible world of the non-exclusive retail chains' flagships, of Marks & Spencer, John Lewis and HMV.

Regent Street's central location and architectural integrity create an environment for memorable experiences before entering the distinctive worlds of Liberty, Hamleys, and more recently Apple. The street is deliberately planned to create a differentiated environment from the competition created by neighbouring Oxford Street and nearby Bond Street. The landlord, the Crown Estate, has taken the opportunity to act in two ways. First to upgrading the physical fabric of at least some parts of the street, and as restrictive tenancy agreements expire, provide retailers with improved facilities and retail designers more opportunities. Predictably this found retailer support, after many years of under-investment in the 1970s and 1980s, in a comment that 'there's been a lot of investment in recent years in the real estate provision and the infrastructure and environment in Regent Street. Now everybody who is fashionable will want to be in Regent Street'. The emphasis here is on fashionability, and the dangers of not keeping up with fashion.

Second it has implemented an explicit strategy to attract flagship stores to Regent Street, to differentiate it from Bond Street or Oxford Street. This does not necessarily distinguish Regent Street, because in the words of one local commentator, '... we all know where the fashion flagships are; they all tend to be in the same place, Oxford Street, Regent Street, Bond Street'. Nevertheless a single landlord was seen to give unilateral power because it's 'all the same landlord, it's all the Crown Estate so they can do that'. The street demonstrates that store size is not always a critical factor. While it is often synonymous with prestige, proximity to other similar stores can provide a comparable halo for smaller stores.

Avoidance of internal structure, and carefully designed spaces are evident in flagship stores. The Apple flagship store has succeeded in a two floor open-planned space of 20,000 square feet behind a stone faced façade. London's Regent Street will create larger store spaces to replace the small sites designed in the 1910s–1920s. Zara in the first wave of new flagship development, introduced its first standalone store in the UK and some nine other retailers have followed suit. Habitat offers a parallel to Apple, with the same use of a central staircase leading to a mezzanine floor, café overlooking the street, product display designed for interaction and a pedagogic element in its presentations and talks about interior design. More modestly, food retailers too have explored the use of space in their flagship superstores, extending upwards into mezzanine areas, and re-organizing spaces for non-food products.

Table 1.2 Location of flagship stores

Flagship location	Number of references
London – general	12
London – West End	62
London – Covent Garden	8
London – Knightsbridge	8
Total UK	179

Source: all news reports, 31 March 2004–31 March 2005

Size and scale often distinguish flagships, where extravagance is part of the experience, and historical reputation may be a significant part too. Such stores can be destinations for an entire sector in London. Hamleys showcases toys; Niketown is a showroom for the product, price and knowledgeable staff. The authoritative design and layouts communicate to the customer, but the purchase may then be made online or at a warehouse location. However, the flagship is not necessarily the largest store; some flagships can be smaller and quirky, being distinctively different from the surrounding environment. One flagship store was carefully identified as such in South London suburbia, Clapham Old Town. Some locations can accommodate smaller, more specialist retailers; Covent Garden and its fringes provide opportunities for fashion retailers seeking a flagship store defined by its proximity to a large target market and compatible competition. Lingerie specialists Agent Provocateur created a new genre of upmarket erotic retailing from its Soho store. London's central retailing locations provide opportunities for retailers to find suitable sites within a concentrated geographical area.

Market research and the opportunity to develop strategic marketing form the fourth significant theme, and one that is distinct from a marketing communication function (see Figure 1.3). Flagship stores provide feedback from customers and staff about the 'ideal' retail brand, and in this sense can be seen as part of a customer relationship strategy. They can be defined by their relationship to other stores, to transmit new ideas to other stores in the multiple group as part of an organic process of internal communication. Marketers identify the stores' role in setting standards of service to staff as well as products and layout. These are locations where new products, services and concepts are trialled and if successful, adapted for other stores. Flagship food stores demonstrate the latest developments and are superseded by the rate of change in technological advances; in the words of one respondent, 'ideas and thoughts might actually go forward and be developed in other stores and branches'. In addition, flagship stores provide a capability to be creative, to extend or replicate the brand online, opening up possibilities for both physical and virtual flagship stores as well as creating hybrids combining virtual elements into store environments.

The preceding analysis focuses on flagship brand stores and provides an explanation of their marketing function from a UK perspective. Elements of

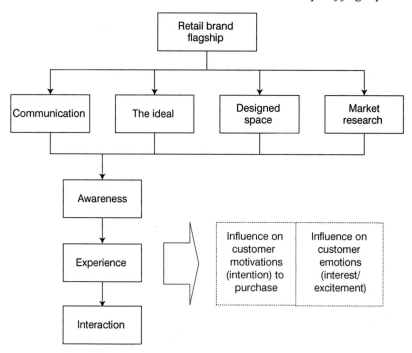

Figure 1.3   Flagship store branding

Kozinets's flagship brand stores model are evident here and point to other marketing opportunities. With reference to the model (Figure 1.2), cultural orientation is well represented at the higher end of the scale with large and grandiose stores. The architecture and design from the nineteenth and early twentieth centuries in terms of scale and their ornate 'otherness', have an external sense of presence that creates inspiring locations. These sites are largely but not exclusively in central shopping areas and are typified by department stores. But re-use of other sites such as cinemas, factories and warehouses can fulfil the same role. Internally such buildings provide opportunities to use their space in new and different ways that in the case of London's Apple store, is distinctively inspirational.

At the other end of the cultural continuum, Kozinets's proposals for Landscape Themed flagship brand stores within a mundane or ordinary environment require adaptation in the UK. The proposition that retailers will find opportunities to market 'natural' experiences appears well founded. However with less space and higher costs, the scope to create such environments is diminished, with the implication that flagship operators will have to develop smaller scale solutions. At the most mundane Kozinets's proposal to expand factory-tour-type operations is evident within a context of the UK's heritage activities. These mix 'factory-tour as retail branding' enterprises with the regeneration of disused sites, for example, in the mining experience in Rhondda (see Figure 1.4). However, in the UK limitations of space and the longer heritage of many sites and in some

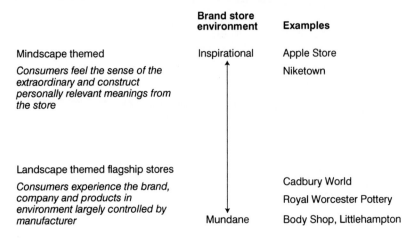

Figure 1.4   Cultural orientation of flagship brand stores

instances their iconic status, play a significant role in the perception of flagship stores. A further consideration concerns the role of governmental organizations in developing large-scale themed areas, particularly in regeneration programmes, where private enterprise might be expected to take the lead in the US.

Retail orientation is reflected in stores both at the lower end of the scale, encouraging and emphasizing short-term sales and those with a longer-term brand building orientation. A characteristic of the UK retail industry is the highly developed multiple retailer sector, with its strong portfolio of own-brand merchandise. The retail brand, 'the manufacturer' consequently has a higher profile than in the US. Marks & Spenser and Topshop resemble GAP and Old Navy in the US as exclusive, or largely exclusive, flagship brand stores, but ones in prime shopping locations that generate high turnovers and an expectation of high and consistent profits. Brand orientation is reflected in the one-dimensional elements of these exclusive brand flagships compared with the multidimensional ones of Niketown and Topshop.

However the 'stores that tell stories' to enable consumers to make meanings from place are not necessarily the creation of brand store designers. Department stores by virtue of their location, reputation and prestige often possess long-established flagships. Memorable experiences can be also achieved within the confines of smaller sites than those envisaged in America. Nevertheless stores must engage with customer emotions to attract new customers and retain the loyalty of existing ones. This may be in the sense of providing spaces for shared cultural values, meaningful communities in the store, and being continually sensitive to local cultural needs, in essence following a theme Kozinets defines as marketscape. When the sense of immersion in the flagship store is at its most intense, when in one respondent's view, it is 'like going to church', stores can position themselves at their most extraordinary, experiential and multidimensional as mindscape flagships.

Conclusion

This chapter demonstrates the ways in which the flagship concepts have become a significant part of the language of branding and promotion. Flagship stores can make a significant contribution to the visibility of UK retail brands and are valuable as showcases for products, and practices as media for communication to internal and external stakeholders. They provide opportunities to demonstrate leadership with new designs, products and experiences. Interactivity and change, the need to offer new experiences, 'a grand day out' for sensory consumers, are features of the most successful environments.

In terms of Kozinets's flagship brand store typology, this research has ranged more widely over the concept of 'flagshipness'. These are department stores and food retailers that do not strictly fulfil their flagship brand store definitions. Nevertheless these flagships make important distinctions between US and UK retail industry structures, and extend our thinking about the appropriateness of the concept. In its exploration of flagships both in their luxurious and iconic forms and in their expressions as places for everyday shopping, the research findings point to a diversity in branding that frequently does not match the intended marketing aims. This is indicative of the experiential and evolutionary nature of the flagship. As such this chapter charts a phenomenon that is in transition and that has yet to establish rules of behaviour and orthodoxy on how things 'ought to be done.' This analysis implies that retail innovation in the future will look to the integration of marketing strategies with design strategies and of operational cultures, especially in the food sector. These will be directed towards deeper empathy with the customer and to demonstrate greater interactivity. The compatibility of the physical flagship with the growth of online shopping raises further issues of classification. Merging the spaces of the virtual world with physical ones remains a creative challenge.

Running through these disciplinary perspectives has been an exploration of creative processes and practices, in product and fashion design, interior and exterior concepts and their realization. Design elements in the flagship environment have become increasingly integrated, and flagship stores can be significant design statements. The Hershey store in New York, the Louis Vuitton store in Tokyo, the Prada stores in both cities and Niketown stores in general, provide instances of flagship stores that have become a monument as much to their architects as to their merchandise. Less spectacular places, too, provide a symbolic and material environment in which consumers engage with the brand. This is creativity and innovation manifested in cultural and social events, located in the external environment, and constructed through interaction between producers and audience (Csikszentmihalyi 1999); a prized activity of this century demonstrating the 'new and valuable' as well as the 'original and useful' (Pope 2005).

Creativity and change in the future point to more clever environments, possibly more intellectually demanding and certainly more consumer responsive. We may see stores as magazines or stores that metamorphose; increasingly hybrid uses of space will blur the distinctions between places of consumption, between different types of store, hotel and cultural centre, and on a larger scale, areas and quarters.

2   A classification approach to flagship stores

Bill Webb

Introduction and definitions

The chasm between academic and commercial worlds of retailing has never been better illustrated than over the topic of so-called 'flagship stores'. Hardly an issue of the UK's weekly fashion trade paper *Drapers* is published without a news report of some little known brand opening an often short-lived 'flagship' outlet in London. One such example is the 'Covent Garden Flagship for Dune' (March 25th, 2006) which describes a new 140m² shop 'large enough to showcase the whole range'. Stores themselves promote their new shops in the same way, for example the Swedish brand GANT took a full page in London's Evening Standard on October 14th, 2004, to announce the opening of its new 'Flagship Store', which turned out to be a modest shop in Richmond, Surrey. As Ryan (2005) observes, 'retailers are notoriously prone to exaggeration and one of the most commonly used phrases is "we opened another flagship last week".' From the media coverage alone, it could be assumed that 'flagship' is most often used as marketing hyperbole to glamorize the latest store opening in a retail chain.

Ryan raises a further problem relating to the number of flagships evident in multiple retailing. When Admiral Lord Nelson was satisfied with a single flagship for his fleet, it is not clear why so many brands appear to require multiple examples. A case in point is the American luxury accessories brand Coach, which was reported to have opened 'its seventh Coach flagship store in Japan' (Resnick 2004). This represented the total number of stores in the country. Not to be outdone, Louis Vuitton has evidently opened 'its twelfth and largest flagship (Chinese) store in the capital city Beijing' (Olson 2005); again each of these is a flagship store as they only operate twelve outlets there.

By comparison with the media, academic research has largely ignored the phenomenon. Influential textbooks on retail management have all been mostly silent on the topic. To find some mention of flagship stores, researchers can fall back on the Macmillan Dictionary of Retailing, published in 1991, which describes them as:

> The major shop or outlet in a chain, usually located in capital cities, which is larger than the other outlets and carries a wider range of merchandise. It

carries the flag for the chain and maybe the trial ground for new ideas. The store is usually furbished to a higher standard than the others and may have its own unique identity in the chain.

(Baron *et al.* 1991: 82)

Tucker (2003) takes a similar view, stating that a flagship store can be defined as the large or dominant store in a prime location, which often acts as a 'brand monument, ultimately creating a 3D environment of all that their brand is about … these places are about selling a lifestyle and giving customers something to aspire to' (Tucker 2003: 28–30). Moore and Docherty (2007) extend this analysis with a focus on the luxury fashion industry and the function of the flagship store as an integral part of the internationalization process of designer brands.

Although flagships are often distinguished by their size relative to other stores in the same chain, they still may not have an outstanding local physical presence. Reviewing a new 'flagship' branch of the Warehouse fashion chain in Oxford Street, Tosh (2005) took the view that, as it was somewhat smaller than its neighbours, its flagship status must have more to do with its location than its size. Nor is an enhanced design concept a precondition of a flagship. Reviewing a new 'Firetrap Flagship' in Covent Garden, Lewis-Barclay (2005) found few features to distinguish it from nearby non-flagship stores. Bold differentiation was less significant than being 'a member of the same trendy club in a happening part of town'.

For premium brands, a further dimension of 'flagshipness' is frequently found in the use of famous architects or designers to create iconic buildings. Future Systems' work for Selfridges or New Look, Rem Koolhaas's controversial high-tech environment for Prada in New York, or the shops created by John Pawson and Nigel Coates for Jigsaw and projects completed by Renzo Piano, Ron Arad or Herzog and de Meuren are frequently cited examples. Most of the luxury brands employ well-known designers for their flagship stores, believing in the added kudos and press coverage that they will receive, and perhaps also in adding the value of 'a three-dimensional work of art' to their capital assets.

Stores such as these can cost as much as $100 million to plan, construct and fit out, which is in itself a highly effective barrier to prospective new entrants into the luxury fashion sector. An outstanding recent example is the 6,000m² Armani Tower opened in November 2007, alongside Gucci and Hermes in Tokyo's Ginza district. This new built emporium is eleven stories high and includes a spa as well as restaurants and the full range of Armani personal and home fashions. Many luxury brands, including Burberry, Polo Ralph Lauren and Armani have reported a sizable swing in turnover from traditional wholesaling to sales through their own retail stores, as they seek to gain these advantages, retain their margins and protect their brand environments. Floor (2006) however, points out that in tough trading times, when expenditure needs to be reduced, these expensive flagship stores are often the first casualties of budget cut-backs.

Profit centre or brand building?

Some experts on retail branding, such as Aaker, have identified the flagship store as a means of 'immersing customers in brand experiences' (Aaker and Joachimsthaler 2000: 182), moving the retail branding concept on from two-dimensional brand identity to three-dimensional brand experience. Mikunda has described large branches of Zara as 'a three dimensional advert – a lifestyle magazine that you can walk into' (Peneder 2005). This aspect has been picked up by those interior designers and architects like Rashid Din, involved in creating these spaces. Din writes of flagship stores:

> Flagship stores are a relatively new phenomenon, emerging in the last ten years from retailers' desire to make a larger-than-life statement about their companies and their brands. This is the most dramatic statement a brand can make: space will be used to impress, and furniture and fittings will be of the highest quality. Such stores will generally be located in prime sites. Financed jointly from a company's development and marketing budgets they are ... expected to be loss leaders – their value is as a billboard for the brand.
>
> (Din 2000: 20)

Flagship store design is becoming an increasingly specialized and important discipline. Another retail designer, Nicholas Zalany, believes that:

> As retail store designers, we ... [believe that] what makes the flagship level store different from typical stores, beyond increased space and merchandise, is the opportunity to place more emphasis on communicating brand. The flagship store serves to excite, inform and connect with its audience.
>
> (Zalany 1998: 1)

Floor (2006) believes that in flagship stores, sales and profits are subordinated to communicating the brand identity, a view of the store's brand – building role. This brand perspective is echoed by Varley and Rafiq in their assessment of retail stores, that:

> Flagship stores are those stores regarded as the pinnacle in the retail chain. They are usually large and located in high footfall, prestigious locations. They offer a full range of merchandise, with an emphasis on the more expensive, high quality and high fashion lines. The role of the flagship store is essentially about retail brand building and reinforcement rather than profitability. The media coverage that flagship stores attract adds to the communications process. When entering new international markets, retailers often begin with a flagship store incorporating the latest store design, to test the reaction to the retail concept.
>
> (Varley and Rafiq 2004: 167)

Such views accord with the development of emotional branding theory that evolved during the late 1990s. From this perspective, emotional engagement with a brand can be deepened through exposure to the visual and sensory features of a 'brand space' (Gobé 2001; Shaw and Ivens 2002). Schmitt and Simonson (1997) coined the term 'marketing aesthetics' to discuss how brand image is communicated via the holistic visual appeal of the brand experience, as exemplified by the flagship store. Very often the largest outlets of leading fashion and lifestyle retailers in major cities will include a panoply of additional products and services, and be supported by extravagant promotions to heighten the positioning of the brand. Selfridges and Topshop in Oxford Street are good examples, but so too are FNAC, Sephora or Galleries Lafayette in Paris, KaDeWe in Berlin or the impressive Peek and Cloppenburg 'Weltstadthaus' in Cologne, Germany (Horbert 2005).

A few retailers attempt to take this strategy one step further by using the flagship store as a tool to re-position a brand, rather than merely to enhance and revitalize its existing position. The trade journal *Drapers* reported that Diesel opened its London flagship in Bond Street as part of its upmarket repositioning (Anon 2006). Levi's flagship denim store for women in the Rue de Rivoli, Paris, is another example. However, Ritson (2006) believes that most such attempts to reposition historic brands are misguided as they ignore the brand's heritage. Clegg (2006), quoting Kasriel, agrees with this, maintaining that flagship-style experiences only work when they build on a brand's existing values and 'act as a showcase for something that is already there'.

The desire to engage customers more fully with the values and experiences of a brand has also been a powerful stimulant to non-traditional retailers to open 'flagship' stores. Perhaps the French term for the concept 'Magasins Phares' (literally 'Lighthouse Stores') more accurately describes the desire of these businesses to make their brands more visible and more tangible. This can be achieved on two levels. On the level of physical experience, customers can engage with ubiquitous small products like mobile phones (Samsung), watches (Swatch) or computers (Apple), creating a tactile and three-dimensional relationship that is hard to replicate on the screen or printed page. The second level concerns brand communication, through the ripple effect of media exposure, viral marketing and WoM (Word of Mouth) endorsement that flagship stores can generate.

Discussing the much lauded new Samsung flagship store in New York, Pegler (2005) explains the interactive opportunities with the product created by the retail space that invite visitors to handle, play, manipulate and interact with the various products. Its commercial role is not paramount, but rather Samsung uses the store and specifically its very large spaces, to enhance its brand image. This is essentially the strategy behind the 'Experience Centres', launched by Samsung's competitor, Nokia, the most recent of which has opened in São Paulo, Brazil. The origins of such brands are most usually manufacturers like these mobile phone companies or others such as Apple, Nike, Levi or Swatch, but can equally easily be mail order companies like La Redoute or Boden, or most recently retailers with a direct marketing background like Bravissimo (UK) or Coldwater Creek (USA). Their common concern is how to give a three-dimensional experience to what is essentially a two-dimensional brand identity communicated electronically or via print media. Commenting on the opening of the new Apple flagship in London's Regent Street in November 2004, Stuart Elliot of the *New York Times* wrote, 'don't call it a store, call it an ad with walls', continuing to discuss how 'the store itself has become one of the key elements of the marketing mix'.

Floor (2006) supports this argument for the flagship store as physical manifestation of the brand identity in which manufacturers can determine the store environment surrounding the branded product. The store concept becomes a three-dimensional advertisement for the manufacturer's brand, through which the consumer walks and the store itself becomes the brand experience. Furthermore the manufacturer's flagship store allows the brand to showcase its entire range, and to obtain direct feedback from customers as a result of first-hand contact with them. These developments had been identified over a decade earlier when Thrift (1997) claimed to identify a new trend which she described as the 'new phenomenon of unusually lavishly designed shops' which serve as 'three-dimensional ads ... to promote a brand name which the public associate with a single product or range'. She cited examples of the Original Levis Store, the Dr Martens Department Store (now closed), the Ray-Ban store and Niketown. She concluded that these new 'brand flagships' have developed out of the realization by manufacturers that the branding initiative had passed to retailers and that key producers had to regain command of the 'brand space'.

Eight years on, Kiley and Berner (2005) made much the same point when describing how brands such as North Face, Coach, Liz Claiborne and Lacoste had all opened flagship stores in New York, having become disillusioned with the visibility given to them by their traditional department store stockists such as Bloomingdales. As was noted above, while the department store sector worldwide consolidates, so clothing suppliers have increased their share of sales going through their own stores. In order to minimize channel conflict with their remaining wholesale accounts, they have tended to confine their retail development to major city centre 'flagships' whose role is overtly 'to promote the brand for everyone' and provide a venue for trialling new products and illustrating display and visual merchandising ideas for the benefit of their stockists as well.

This strategy critically requires the brand to occupy or create highly impressive and visible landmark buildings. Commenting on the development of its ninth global flagship store in São Paulo, Brazil, Nokia's Retail Development Director, Jeremy Wright (2007), described Nokia's flagship store programme as 'targeting major shopping destinations in buildings that stand out from the crowd'. The stores' distinctive design has been widely acclaimed, achieving the award of Most Innovative Retail Concept of the Year. Each flagship store should contain innovative features for customers and these should be evident in the very high quality interiors. Plans for the Nokia Flagship in Regent Street, London, include a 'media lounge' where shoppers will be able to learn more about the features of Nokia equipment at their leisure (Ryan 2007). Turning to the exterior, the façade of the building will mark out the site as a true flagship store. Location is a critical element as Nokia flagship buildings must not only be the best in terms of appearance but also located in prime shopping areas to maximize their visibility. In this respect, size of store is less significant than the visual impact of the building (Bathurst 2007).

Many fashion and lifestyle brands have also used the flagship strategy as a means of entering new geographic markets. In the current scramble for market share in the developing countries of Asia, especially China, expansion via 'concessions' within department stores is often the most practical route. However, the creation of one or more local flagship stores establishes presence for the brand and communicates to potential host stores that you are serious about the market – making concession negotiation much easier. This strategy is not confined to emerging markets. Hall (2007) reports that the UK fashion brand, Karen Millen, is looking for a flagship store in Paris to support a concession roll-out in the Galleries Lafayette department stores in France. In the same report, Karen Millen's International director draws on the trading evidence from existing concessions in Galleries Lafayette to support the decision to open a flagship store. The aim of the store is explicitly stated to support expansion in France and to raise the brand's profile. Being seen in the right location once again is specifically discussed; the fashionable Rue St Honoré shopping street provides Karen Millen with an appropriate image as a global brand in the minds of French consumers. Rather differently, conversations that the author had with management from Dunhill some years ago suggested that a London flagship store was necessary for the credibility of the brand in the eyes of Japanese visitors to London on whose custom, back in Japan, the business was heavily dependent.

The creation of a highly visible icon for the brand has the effect of raising its awareness and credibility for customers, media and partners alike. Discussing Uniqlo's initial failure to trade profitably in the UK, their UK CEO explained that one of key issues that led to massive financial losses was the absence of a flagship store (Coble 2007). In this case, issues of location and visibility had not been reconciled since one of its first stores to open in the UK could well have achieved flagship store status. However it was located on the fringes of Knightsbridge, in London, and although the area has a reputation for exclusive designer brands, this was unable to compensate for the relatively weak position of the store. Commenting on the opening of Uniqlo's new flagship store in Oxford Street in London, the company's chairman believed that the new flagship would change the way people perceive Uniqlo, and increase its brand recognition in the UK (Czerny 2007). The company subsequently announced that its next flagship would be in Paris (Fitzpatrick 2007).

The role of retail flagship stores in raising awareness and loyalty to the brand has sparked the recent debate about the sustainability of the concept if their business model is not directly linked to making a profit. Essentially this debate pits the marketing community, who look for a long term return on investment to accrue across the entire brand performance, against the financial community who expect the stores to be revenue and profit generators in their own right on a financial reporting period basis. Niketowns were perhaps the first examples of stores which depended on the so-called 'halo effect' to raise the brand profile and market share of Nike products on a regional basis. Tucker (2003) states that for flagship stores, 'there is product and sales, but these are often secondary concerns'. This very point was made by Hollander three decades earlier, and has been more recently supported by Moore *et al.* (2000). Flagship stores can be managed as part of the retailer's communications activity, on the grounds that the store is creating awareness and interest. As such, the store can be considered to have an advertising function, and losses which arise from maintaining the flagship are financed from the corporate communications budget.

Further assessment of the business models of the flagship stores was undertaken by Rasch *et al.* (2005) of The Boston Consulting Group, through their research into vertically integrated textile groups in Germany. This suggests that whereas standard shops in a chain make an average positive contribution of 6 per cent, for their flagship the figure is a net loss of 9 per cent. As well as higher property costs as a percentage of flagship store sales, staffing costs and depreciation of expensive fittings and equipment are also greater (see Figure 2.1). Allegra Strategies (2005) point out that, because of their prime locations and high footfall, flagship stores need to be refurbished more frequently than regular branches, adding significantly to cost.

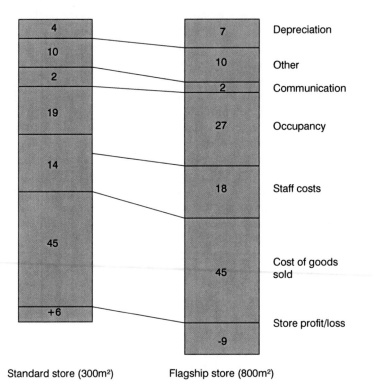

Standard store (300m²)   Flagship store (800m²)

Figure 2.1   Retail profit model of standard and flagship retail outlets (%) (Source: Rasch *et al.* (2005) translated by the author)

In times of recession, the sustainability of all marketing expenditure tends to be questioned, and so it has proved with the concept of the brand flagship as a marketing expense. The demise of the Dr Martens store in Covent Garden has already been alluded to. In fact, Central London has witnessed a constant attrition of expensive flagship stores in premium locations such as Bond Street, Regent Street and Knightsbridge, whose owners have become disillusioned with the drain on corporate profitability for which they have been responsible. Examples would include outlets of Tommy Hilfiger, Allders, Marc Cain, Guess, and many more. Sometimes these outlets appear to owe their origins rather more to the egos of their owners than any credible marketing or commercial strategy. Writing of the new Asprey in Bond Street, Ritson (2006) believes that it fails both as a brand icon and a commercial machine. He describes how 'Asprey blew millions on its flagship store, but there isn't a single person in the place'.

For publicly quoted high street retailers, unprofitable flagship stores are seen as an indulgence, and the role and business model for them is seen rather differently. In Tucker's (2003) assessment, the Topshop store at Oxford Circus is one of the best flagship stores as it makes plenty of money, is distinctively differentiated from the other stores, and is a well-defined destination in itself. It frequently features in fashion and London-based media, with one report describing how the retailer uses this store to promote special ranges in terms in a 'frenzied free-for-all', in one instance selling one thousand special edition designer label garments in six minutes (Foster 2006). The author's discussions with Topshop management have revealed that the business uses its flagship to test new designer ranges, and also to identify 'winners and losers' from its 'own-bought' stock as much as four months in advance of their general release.

Clements (2000) also believes that flagships have to be financially viable, describing French Connection's new store in Oxford Street as 'possessing a cool design confidence similar to Niketown, but while Niketown is largely a temple to the brand, French Connection must make its flagship work commercially'. Middle market companies, especially those with public limited company (PLC) status, stress that a flagship store should exhibit 'best practice' retail trading skills in order to drive the company forward, and maximize return on investment. An anonymous retailer cited by Allegra (2005) states that the retailer's flagship store is a centre of excellence to develop best practice, and that the flagship store should have a dual function both to showcase the brand and generate profit.

Allegra Strategies, in a detailed review of flagship stores in London in 2005, identified twelve critical success factors, which they believe underpin the sustainability of the concept. Clearly the relative significance of each factor depends on the merchandise segment and trading level of the flagship operator. Elements like The Third Space, a concept initially devised by Howard Shultz of Starbucks, and opportunities for entertainment explored by proponents of experiential marketing, notably Pine and Gilmore (1999) and Gobé (2001) relate to the leisure role of flagships. However, a potential pitfall for the high street multiple retailer, arising from the development of flagship stores, is their inability to replicate the experience – or to justify the cost of it – across their retail network

Table 2.1 Critical success factors in flagship store sustainability

Prime site/location	High operating standards
Full merchandise range	Superior customer service
Sufficient size	Events and entertainment
'Third Space' facility	Uniqueness
Store design	'Wow' factor
Superior shopfit	Intelligibility and navigation

Source: Allegra Strategies (2005)

(Clegg 2006). This can lead to a divergence of brand image and disappointment amongst provincial customers. Allegra demonstrate that the development of flagship stores can have negative effects on a core retail business, beyond the potential costs and losses associated with the store itself. These relate to negative brand association caused by the failure of a flagship or of experimental aspects within it, and also the disappointment felt by customers in smaller branch stores, when their shopping experience fails to match that encountered in flagship stores of the same brand that they have visited.

Analysis

This review of academic and commercial literature has served to highlight the diverse origins, characteristics and objectives of the retail 'flagship' concept. An attempt to define any type of retail format invariably runs into difficulty. A concept as old as a 'department store' is variously defined by international and national associations in terms of its size, number of floors, product range and service method. A 'hypermarket' is usually considered to start at 1,200m² in Germany, 2,500m² in France and 50,000 ft² in the UK. With these discrepancies arising in relatively well-understood concepts and formats, there seems little chance that a consensus will be achieved for a definition of 'flagship'.

The starting point must be to identify from the literature, academic, expert and from the retailers themselves, those dimensions that can be considered universal and relevant. Allegra's suggestion is that a flagship must be linked to the concept of a retail destination and thus cannot apply to markets, which trade in commodities or for which shopping is routine. This chapter has identified eight pertinent definitional aspects, most or all of which apply to any flagship store. First, the store should be located in a large metropolitan market. Then it should be large in relation to standard stores selling the same product groups. It must occupy a prestigious, high footfall site. Preferably it should make use of an iconic building or incorporate impressive new architecture. Such stores should also employ an innovative retail interior design concept, often created by a 'big name' architect or designer. They should be able to accommodate a full or extended range of products, services and experiences and exhibit 'best in class' operating standards; and finally they should benefit from supportive marketing and promotion, and be designated as 'flagships' by their owners. This is, in part, 'self-definition'. The relative importance given to each aspect will depend on three things: the market context (country, region, city) in which the store is operating, the type of business running the store, and the operating company's specific objectives which are, to a large degree, linked.

In terms of a classification of businesses, which make use of flagship stores, fashion companies clearly lead the field. These need to be subdivided into brands which are principally manufacturers or suppliers, those which are retail chains, those which are one-off independent stores, and those which had their origins in catalogue retailing or e-commerce. It is probably best to separate out the luxury brand businesses for which the flagship concept plays a rather different role. These can be fashion or accessories based, but examples are also found from the fields of footwear, jewellery, watches, cosmetics, haircare and homewares. A third category is department stores, which should be sub-divided into one-off stores such as Harrods or Au Bon Marché, and the largest branches of department store chains such as Macy or Kaufhof. A fourth, and rapidly growing category, are flagships developed by technology based brands retailing computers, mobile phones, games and gadgets. At a higher level are the prestigious automotive showrooms. Lastly, there are leisure and lifestyle brands operating in the sports, toys, entertainment and foodservice sectors.

It should also be possible to identify the relative importance of different objectives of businesses operating flagship stores. These are closely associated with the types of business, can vary over time, and can co-exist with different priority weightings. They can be ranged on a scale from highly strategic (for example, brand positioning) to fundamentally operational, with a focus on maximizing sales and market share or identifying winners and losers. The following have emerged from the review carried out in this research (see Figure 2.2).

Based on these criteria, the author suggests that it might be possible to develop a classification of four types of 'flagship' store:

- The destination flagship: this type of store is epitomized by the largest branches of department store chains such as Galleries Lafayette, El Corte Inglés, or Debenhams which offer an exceptional shopping range and experience. As Ryan (2005) observes, it is debatable whether a single store can be considered a flagship, which returning to the naval analogy questions where Nelson would have been without his fleet, but conceptually a Harrods, Liberty or Bergdorf Goodman also fall into this category.
- The selling machine flagship: second, the largest branches of chains like Topshop, Next, New Look, River Island, GAP, or Peek and Cloppenburg are often designated 'flagships' by their operators, but are actually in essence the most important outlets in their chain. They need to maintain the integrity of the parent brand and typically demonstrate its core characteristics in a deeper and more profound way, in order to optimize potential trading in the largest and most competitive markets.

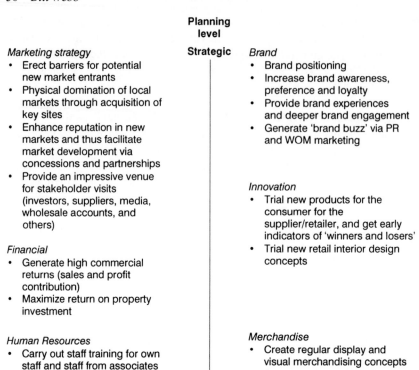

Figure 2.2 Business objectives for flagship store retailers

- The brand reputation flagship: this term refers to the store which represents a business which has not traditionally retailed its own merchandise on the high street. Thus these outlets serve the dual purpose of physical presence to the brand and generating sales. Many of the stores mentioned in this chapter (Levi, Niketown, Firetrap) fall into this category, as do most of the luxury brands (Armani, Louis Vuitton, Gucci). Outlets operated by sports teams such as Manchester United (which are especially large in Asia) also fit in here. The balance of objectives is very varied between operators, and when their role is not clearly defined and agreed the stores often run into trouble.
- The showroom flagship: lastly there are flagship stores who aim to sell little or no product, but exist mainly as a marketing tool to generate awareness, reputation and product familiarity. Those flagships showcasing 'high tech' products such as motor vehicles, computers or mobile phones are mainly in this category. Leading FMCG manufacturers, like Nestlé and Coca-Cola, are demonstrating this tendency by opening 'brand spaces'.

As with 'information only' websites, the temptation is to extend them into 'transactional' sites.

Conclusion

In the age of multi-channel retailing, flagship stores are with us to stay. From the exploratory investigations in this chapter, it would be useful to refine the four classification elements which have been suggested. It would also be interesting to carry out marketplace audits to see how well these classifications apply in practice. Further insights could be gained from in-depth interviews and case studies of a sample of brands operating flagship stores in an attempt to validate what are, in most existing literature, little more than impressions. Research with property companies could reveal what market rental premiums are commanded by typical flagship locations, which would give some insights into their value. It could also reveal the longevity (or 'success rate') of flagship outlets in key locations and sites.

3 Emotion and identity in flagship luxury design

Hilary J. Collins

> Hotel client: 'This place makes me feel as if I've succeeded. I couldn't have afforded to come to a place like this at home so by being here in this environment it reminds me how far I've come. What a fantastic place this is.'

This chapter is set in the context of the architectural interior design of flagship hotels. Little attention has been given to the effect of our perception of spatial design, which is generally considered a specialist area belonging to architects, interior designers and engineers. However, these specialists frequently have little knowledge of the future uses of the building. Sometimes very little communication takes place between the managers or employees who will occupy the building and the designers who create it. Designers may also have little understanding of how the physical setting and our interpretation of it can affect how we as users perceive ourselves and how we react.

I would argue that commissioning of architectural spatial design for a flagship hotel project is in response to a strategic plan, one of the aims of which will be to obtain flagship status for the project. The designers' role as creator means that although they may use information from managers and users to create a design concept, they cannot fully realize how we as users of the building will interpret that design. This is partly because we interpret the environment from a multiple identity perspective and from different situational contexts.

When a designer is commissioned to design for a flagship hotel project, the design will probably be required to fulfil a number of functional, aesthetic requirements, which also may consider the image and identity of the organization. On completion of the building, the users will take their place and may interpret their environment differently from the intended design concept. A process of sense-making of organizational life will begin within various changing contexts, but is it in line with design and managerial expectations?

Our most basic understanding of perception tells us clearly not; so what can this chapter tell us that we do not know and how can we use this information? We need to consider that physical symbolic artefacts are frequently subject to multiple interpretations and can have both intended and unintended consequences, which go from extremes of us being oblivious to, or incensed by them, further complicating the matter. Given the spiralling cost of real estate and the consequent financial investment in flagship hotels it is important that these designs are perceived as intended.

The purpose of this chapter is to describe a framework which has been developed for conceptualizing the process through which actors, within a luxury flagship hotel in Dubai, adapt and change their identities as a result of interpreting their built environment and compare this with the image the hotel may have as a 'flagship'. Conceptually and empirically, I have followed Rafaeli and Vilnai-Yavetz's (2004) assertion that there is a relationship between physical symbolic artefacts: and emotion and this emotion arises from three conceptually distinct aspects: instrumentality, aesthetics and symbolism. In this context, the definition of physical artefacts includes layout, material objects, logo and building design and are symbolic when meaning is constructed. My claims were built from research undertaken within a luxury 'flagship' hotel in Dubai, which was undergoing changes to the built environment. Dubai has been the centre of media attention in recent years because of its investment in a range of flagship development projects not least in the hotel industry.

The study involved using methods of observation, photography and interviews with organizational actors and hotel clientele within this luxury flagship hotel aiming to understand how they defined and responded to their physical environment. This study was used to generate models to illustrate how organizational actors and hotel clientele related with this built environment and the physical artefacts within it. I employed the idea that organizational actors have identities, which include self, group and organizational identities and are altered or influenced over time. Adopting a social constructionist epistemology, I support the concept that identities are in a constant flux and a permanent state of becoming rather than being (Thomas and Linstead 2002; Svengisson and Alvesson 2003). Therefore identity is 'constantly being reconstituted in discourse each time we think or speak' (Weedon 1987). In our engagement with the 'other,' organizational actors construct or alter their identity (Thomas and Linstead 2002). This draws on an ontology which promotes the processual view of the world (Chia 1996) where 'how an actual entity becomes constitutes what the actual entity is … its "being" is constituted by its 'becoming' (Whitehead 1929: quoted in Chia 1996). Meanings derived from this social constructivist perspective are then not fixed but are negotiated.

I focused on incidents arising from an organizational management of change involving organizational actors, hotel clientele and physical facilities, which were a starting point for interpretation of physical symbolic artefacts and identity-forming processes. Some of these issues are emotional in nature and can affect individual and group processes and can stimulate different types of responses from those that are less emotionally charged. To understand these phenomena it was useful to examine the symbols themselves, identity and how it is formed and the extent to which the literature documents the use of artefacts and symbols in this process.

Symbolic artefacts

The meanings of physical symbolic artefacts are socially constructed and the use of physical symbols is a routine activity that is taken for granted and conducted, consciously and unconsciously, by organizational members (Pratt and Rafaeli 2001). Physical symbols can represent multiple meanings, one symbol having different meanings in different contexts. Symbols can be interpreted to give meaning not only about the physical object but about the relations of the people involved. For example, a large desk in an office will tell you the person behind it has status in the organization and a meta message is that this person can tell you what to do. The intent of an actor using a symbol may be misinterpreted so when, for example, management introduces open plan areas to promote communication these layouts can be interpreted by others in the environment as an infringement of privacy. When we are engaged in conceptualizing a design concept it is highly relevant that we, as designers or managers, have an understanding of the eventual interpretations of our work.

Identity and how it is formed

Identity is the act of forming, engaging and repairing our constructions to give a sense of coherence and distinctiveness (Alvesson and Svengingsson 2003). Identity involves asking, 'Who am I?' or 'Who are we?' (Pratt and Foreman 2000). Identity though, is not singular as we acknowledge the existence of multiple identities within the same individual. Organization identity has been defined as comprising those characteristics that members perceive are fundamental to (central) and uniquely descriptive of (distinctive) the organization and that persist within the organization over time (enduring) (Pratt and Foreman 2000). The aspect of 'enduring' has caused some discussion since its introduction by Albert and Whetton as 'stable'. This chapter adopts the more recent definition: 'It is a process in which individuals create several more or less contradictory and often changing managerial identities (identity positions) rather than one stable, continuous manager identity' (Alvesson and Svengingsson 2003).

Research has also been undertaken to understand our workplace identities (Elsbasch 2004a). This chapter uses the definition of workplace identities which incorporate self, group and organizational identity. Individuals can alter organizational identities and the relationship between individuals and organizations is reciprocal just as organizational identities can influence individual behaviour, individual behaviour can influence organizational identities (Pratt and Foreman 2000). The Hatch and Schultz (2002) model explained the identification process as comprising four aspects as follows:

Expression refers to how the organization expresses itself and this is done through symbols such as architecture, advertising and dress. Expressing is the process by which culture makes itself known through identity claims. Mirroring is the reflection of an organization through the opinions and judgements of others and links image to identity and this part of the identity is constructed through social construction. Reflecting is the process by which identity is embedded in cultural understandings. It is the process by which organization members understand themselves and the result of how organizational members perceive themselves. and this manifests itself in the organization's history and makes an organization's values and assumptions explicit.

Impressing refers to the images of an organization that are projected to the environment and is done through various outreach and PR publications. This model has suggested that the use of physical symbolic artefacts is restricted to the expression aspect of the identification process. I will explain later in the chapter how the role of physical symbolic artefacts is more extensive than previously anticipated.

Process by which physical symbolic artefacts are interpreted

Boje (2001a) proposed that we understand the social situation, in its complexity, through multiple lines of narrative through which the actors in the situation, and we as researchers, make sense of, and attribute meaning to, events, the self and others. It is proposed in this chapter that physical artefacts are in fact an extension of language in that they fulfil the same documented roles in the organizational life. Language can be imprecise and it could be argued that the symbolic significance of artefacts is even more imprecise. However, viewing symbols as a language provides insight by reminding us that meaning could be found in individual physical symbols (words) and patterns of physical symbols (sentences). These patterns, or language, could be useful in realizing complex and subtle relationship issues, such as those involving ambivalence or plurality (e.g. Pratt and Barnett 1997; Pratt and Dutton 2000). Physical objects can be a communicative tool, being interpreted, manipulated and altered by actors in the organizational built environment. They can be a call to action, mobilizing and directing (Straati 1998), gaining commitment (Edelman 1977), exerting control and power (Bourdieu 1991), communicating (Girin 1987), and controlling perceptions and creating meaning (Pondy and Mitroff 1979), and a political object and resource (Wilson 1992).

Becker (1990) posited that a variety of components in the built environment can give information to users. This supports the view that users may utilize external environmental cues either to categorize or make inferences about the organization. Other researchers have focused on the effects of specific stimuli upon behaviour such as colour (Bellizzi *et al.* 1983) or music (Bruner 1990). Research into organizational dress has established that colour may carry symbolic information: blue; for example, can convey dignity red may convey affection (Burgoon and Saine 1978); and dark colours convey power (Joseph 1986). Pratt and Rafaeli (1997) proposed that dress attributes act as a symbol of core organization values. Fussell (1983) proposed that the purity or naturalness of dress materials determines the attributions. Synthetic fibres (such as polyester) are proposed to convey lower class and status than pure fibres (such as silk) and that purity of materials is an important symbol in organizations. In organizational interior design the pureness of the fabrics specified can be used to denote stratified roles. Csikszentmihalyi and Rochberg-Halton (1981) and Wallendorf and Arnould (1988) wrote that home interiors contain a wide variety of objects that hold special importance for identity. Such objects are meaningful because they remind people of their pasts, travel experiences, achievements, close friends or because the objects are symbols of religious or ethnic identities. But the individual-level self is not the only one that may be conveyed through such objects. In analysing individual differences in favourite objects in the home Cikszentmihaly and Rochberg-Halton (1981) detected a dimension of 'differentiation' and 'integration' involving the choice between symbolizing self (differentiation) and symbolizing others (integration).

Current research has examined the role of identity and interpretation but there is a gap in the knowledge in connection with the organizational built environment. This could be significant because understanding the role of physical artefacts in flagship environments could assist our understanding of how our identities are adapted using our interpretation of the buildings and artefacts around us and how this relates to the image of the flagship by stakeholders. Artefacts, using the metaphor of a language, allow us to form, affirm or influence our identity within the daily fabric of organizational life. Increasing attention has been given to the role of symbols and identity but the context of using physical artefacts as a language metaphor has been underestimated. As Rafaeli and Vilnai-Yatetz (2004) state, a gap exists between the extent to which artefacts are used by organizations and the theoretical understanding of the roots of this use.

The literature has not directly addressed *how* actors construct their identities and with *what type* of physical symbolic artefacts and how this relates to the image of the organization and the buildings they occupy. In order to understand the relationship between physical artefacts, identity and image in this context I focused on finding out the process and the extent by which organizational actors and clientele within a luxury hotel interpret physical symbolic artefacts in this built environment and how the information obtained from interpreting physical symbolic artefacts is used by actors to influence/affirm actors' perceived threat to identity, identity affirmation, or identity change. Finally, I asked how this process related to the notion of the hotel being a 'flagship'.

Pratt and Rafaeli (2001) have viewed symbols as a language for enacting relationship issues within organizations and defined the type of symbols by portability and instrumentality but the extent, use and process by which this occurred was not researched within complex identity relationships. I used the Rafaeli and Vilnai-Yavetz (2004) proposition, focusing on the relative importance of the different dimensions of instrumentality, aesthetics and symbolism and combined this with the Hatch and Schultz (2002) concepts of mirroring, impressing, expressing and reflecting as identity formation concepts. I applied this to the process of interpretation of physical symbolic artefacts to understand how they impact or are used to alter or construct identities and how these interpretations relate to the image of the hotel as a flagship.

This leads first to a proposition that we have an emotional reaction to physical artefacts and interpret meaning from them and this reaction is then used in an identity forming/influencing or altering process and our reactions, as actors within, or stakeholders outside, a built environment are intrinsically linked to the activities in which we are engaged and socially constructed from the interpersonal interactions in which we engage. Second, that the role of physical artefacts in the built environment is used within four, rather than the previously envisaged one, aspect of identity and image creation, and there is a relationship between our identity forming processes and the image of the hotel as a 'flagship'.

Following on from this I developed three typologies based on the Hatch and Schultz (2002) organizational dynamics model. Typology 1 (see Figure 3.1) illustrates that emotion, which results from the interpretation of physical symbolic artefacts, and informs the identity formation process. The Hatch and Schultz (2002) model places identity within the context of culture and image and this research has found that the interpretation of physical artefacts plays a role in all four of the identity processes explained in the Hatch and Schultz model, namely, expression, mirroring, reflecting and impressing.

The proposed typologies which follow illustrate the variance in the resulting different types of identity derived from the interpretation of different dimensions of the artefacts interpreted in varying contextual situations. Previous data have demonstrated that all three different dimensions of the artefacts are used in the interpretation process and that people in different circumstances and contexts interpret physical symbolic artefacts differently and this affects which dimensions will be used and whether or not all, two or one dimension is used. These typologies

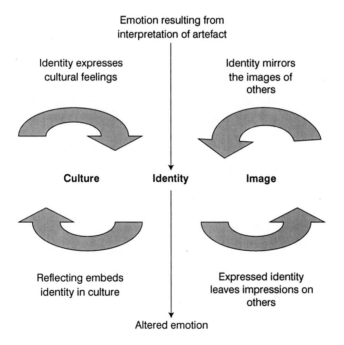

Figure 3.1   Typology 1: Use of emotion from interpretation of physical artefacts in identity formation

illustrate that the process of mirroring, reflecting, impressing and expressing are used in the formation or alteration of identity subsequent to the interpretation of physical artefacts. The research implies that when there were negative issues concerning status, respect, power and legitimization, identity fragmented into group and self-identity. Typologies 1 to 3 go on to elaborate in more detail the micro processes involved in identification using symbolic artefacts.

Typology 2 is perhaps the most interesting typology. It illustrates the results on identity of interpretation using the negative symbolic dimension of a physical artefact. When participants were triggered by a negative emotion and interpreted the symbolic dimension this produced a high level of emotion, and identity split off into organizational identity. This organizational identity, over time and under the same circumstances split into group identity, which, if the same circumstances remain, split into self identity. This would indicate that this splintering-off process takes place over time.

Data vignettes recorded from participants across the case study show how, when participants interpret the symbolic dimension negatively using physical symbolic artefacts in the built environment, the resulting identity processes fragment over time. The initial data illustrated workplace identity: 'We are supposed to be all together in this. The leisure club is supposed to send a message to the community that we care but no one cares about what happens within the hotel' and then gradually over time this fragmented into organizational identity:

> The leisure club is supposed to symbolize the hotel's involvement with the community but wouldn't it be better to look forward to industry not to kids. All the while this crap is going on we don't even know if we've got a job or where we'll be allocated.

As the same contextual circumstances continued, this organizational identity fragmented further into group identity as illustrated in this vignette:

> The leisure club has had all that press put out about it, but what does that mean for the gym group? We've had to drop everything and get the staff to work on it, while all these changes are taking place and we are getting moved around to new workstations.

Eventually this fragmentation continued and resulted in self identity illustrated in the following statement:

> Alpha talks about the transitions project but I had to come out and sit in the hotel while a few rich kids decided they wanted to camp out. They even had maids with them who brought their food. My kids were left with a babysitter and I still had to rearrange my desk because I've been reallocated a new space.

All four processes of identity formation are used to influence or change the identity and this identity, gradually over time fragments from a workplace, through to an organizational, into a group and then self identity. The following data vignettes illustrate all four processes in use with respect to organizational identity only but data was collected which confirms the use of all four processes.

Expressing, referring to how an organization speaks about itself is evidenced in the following: 'The leisure club is supposed to symbolize the hotel's involvement with the community but wouldn't it be better to look forward to industry not to school kids. All the while this crap is going on we don't even know if we've got a job or where we'll be allocated.' This example illustrates the fragmentation down to organizational identity (as previously quoted) through the expressing process.

Reflecting, the process by which organizational members understand themselves as an organization and the result of how organizational members perceive themselves, is evidenced in the following:

> All the staff are the same. Some hotels are better than others but at the end of the day we are a replaceable resource. They invest in buildings, they invest in facilities but where is the investment in staff, where are the professional development funds? Nowhere.

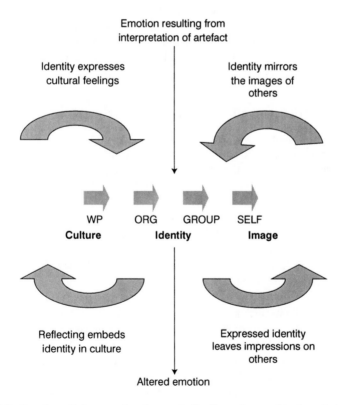

Figure 3.2   Typology 2: Interpreting the symbolic dimension positively and the instrumental and aesthetic dimensions negatively

Mirroring, the reflection of an organization through the opinions and judgements of others and that links image to identity, is evidenced in the following:

> There is not much point having industry discussions here because we can't change the character of the place and the guests are our products. The opinion of industry says a lot about our role here, and it's not good. What it really means I don't know.

Impressing, which refers to images of an organization that are strategically projected to constituents, is evidenced in the following: 'The hotel gets a lot of publicity for stuff like "transitions" but at the same time no one wants to have our guests but they have to.'

Typology 2 is the one typology where it is difficult to predict reaction to a change to the built environment because participants relate the change with an element of the artefact that holds a personal symbolic meaning either to them personally, their group and their organization. Therefore these interpretations and resulting identities can be different from what may have been envisaged and managerial intentions.

This typology is the result of interpretation of all three dimensions of the physical artefacts within the hotel built environment. These are, interpreting the symbolic dimension positively, interpreting the instrumental and aesthetic dimensions negatively – all three of which produced the same results in terms of the affect on the identity formation processes.

Interpreting the symbolic dimension negatively

When organizational actors interpret this, this typology illustrates the results on identity of interpretation when we interpret the symbolic dimension of a physical artefact. The influence of the management of change process in this typology produced a negative emotion. When a participant was triggered by a negative emotion and interpreted the symbolic dimension this produced a high level of emotion. As a result of interpretation of the physical artefact within the incident, and the resultant meaning this had for participants, the workplace identity split off into organizational identity. The participants identified with the hotel but saw the hotel as separate from a workplace identity, which would have incorporated the self, group and organization.

Again data vignettes from various participants in the hotel show how the interpretation of physical artefacts was used in all four processes of identity formation but also illustrate how over time the organizational identity split off from the workplace identity. This fragmentation continued into group and self identity. For example, using the impressing process, this organizational actor discusses the brochures while embracing a workplace identity: 'The brochures all contain photos of the buildings and the interiors and they are only designed to impress our potential guests and potential contractors.' Again under the same circumstances and within a relatively short period of time this had fragmented down to an organizational identity: 'We use our buildings to advantage. That's why they are on the website banner and several hotel publications. The organization is trying to prove its place amongst other hotels.'

> The process of identity formation, interpreting the instrumental dimension negatively had the same results. This illustrates the results on identity of interpretation using the instrumental dimension of a physical artefact. The influence of the management of change process in this typology produced a negative emotion. When a participant was triggered by a negative emotion and interpreted the instrumental dimension, this produced a low level of emotion, but the workplace identity split off into organizational identity. This data vignette illustrates the expressing process resulting in workplace identity: 'The hotel does spend a lot on facilities and buildings but they never seem to get it right. If it works it's the wrong spec and no one knows how to operate it or the stuff breaks down after three months and no one repairs it.' Some time later expressing results in organizational identity as identity starts to fragment: 'The facilities are old fashioned, we don't seem to have much. The work stations are old and tatty. The computers don't work half the time.' These, unlike the interpretations through the symbolic dimensions are fairly predictable.

These data vignettes show how when participants interpret the instrumental dimension negatively, using physical symbolic artefacts in the built environment, all four process of identity formation are used to influence or change the identity and that this identity splits off into organizational identity over time. There is a low level of emotion displayed throughout this process.

Interpreting the aesthetic dimension negatively

This typology illustrates the results on identity of interpretation using the aesthetic dimension of a physical artefact. The influence of the style of leadership and management of change process in this typology produced a negative emotion. When a participant was triggered by a negative emotion and interpreted the aesthetic dimension, this produced a mid-level of emotion, and the workplace identity split off into organizational identity.

The process of identity formation, interpreting the aesthetic dimension negatively, again results in fragmentation from workplace identity to organizational identity and again uses all four processes. This is an example of reflecting within a workplace identity: 'People outside the hotel view us as traditional because of the style of the buildings and this is a negative attitude because we are supposed to be geared to the future of the hotel industry.' This then fragments in the same circumstances and over a relatively short time period to organizational identity: 'We saw ourselves as being high tech but all our external visitors are worried about coming here because they think of traditional constraints when they see the building.'

These data vignettes were recorded from participants across three 'flagship' hotels and show how when participants interpret the aesthetic dimension negatively, using physical symbolic artefacts in the built environment, all four process of identity formation are used to influence or change the identity and that this identity splits off into an organizational identity over time. There is a mid level of emotion present throughout the process.

This typology is the result of two categories of interpretation. These are interpreting the instrumental and aesthetic dimension positively, both of which produced the same results in terms of the effect on the identity formation processes.

Interpreting the instrumental dimension positively

This typology illustrates the results on identity of interpretation using the instrumental dimension of a physical artefact. The influence of the style of leadership and management of change process in this typology produced a positive emotion. When a participant was triggered by a positive emotion and interpreted the instrumental dimension this produced a low level of emotion, and the workplace identity remained intact. For example, in expressing:

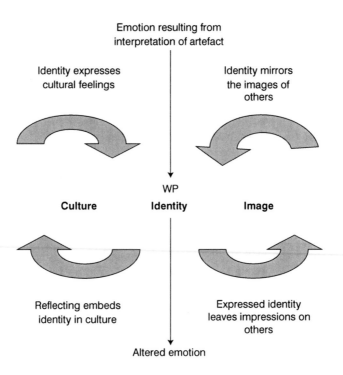

Figure 3.3   Typology 3: Interpreting the instrumental and aesthetic dimensions positively

The hotel expresses its position in the community by its investment in the hotel and the facilities. They are of high quality yet functional and that's what we are about – high quality and function. The web and the brochures tell what we are all about; they show how high the standards of the grounds and the facilities are. It's all high quality stuff here and no mistake.

In impressing: 'The web and the brochures tell what we are all about; they show how high the standards of the grounds and the facilities are. It's all high quality stuff here and no mistake.'

These data vignettes were recorded from organizational actors and clientele and show how when participants interpret the instrumental dimension positively, using physical symbolic artefacts in the built environment, all four process of identity formation are used to influence or change the identity and that this identity remains stable as a workplace identity over time.

Interpreting the aesthetic dimension positively

This typology illustrates the results on identity of interpretation using the aesthetic dimension of a physical artefact. The processes through all six typologies are the same. The influence of the style of leadership and management of change process in this typology produced a positive emotion. When a participant was triggered by a positive emotion. and interpreted the aesthetic dimension, this produced a mid-level of emotion, and the workplace remained intact. This is illustrated in the following data vignette showing the expressing process: 'The buildings and the interiors are beautiful, it is a massive investment and we all proud to be part of it, it says a lot about us and who we are'. This is shown again in the reflecting process: 'Most people I speak to think this must be a great place to work, fabulous facilities, amazing design – look at the sports and leisure facilities, we are really lucky here.'

The data vignettes were recorded from participants and show how when participants interpret the aesthetic dimension positively, using physical symbolic artefacts in the built environment, all four process of identity formation are used to influence or change the identity, and that this identity remains stable as a workplace identity over time. There is a mid-level of emotion present throughout the process.

Data from all processes revealed that participants interpreted artefacts through the dimensions of aesthetic, instrumentality and symbolism and that this produced emotion which concurs with the Rafaeli and Vilnai-Yavetz (2004) findings. Rafaeli and Vilnai-Yavetz (2004) proposed, within the confines of their case study, that these reactions are conceptually and empirically distinct from reactions to the activity in which individuals are engaged and from the interpersonal interactions in which they engage. However, my data revealed that within this different context, with both types of participants, the reactions observed and analysed were directly linked to the activities of the actors and to the interpersonal relations they experienced. Data revealed that the participants held views of their collective self that were central, distinctive and to an extent enduring but that when issues of insecurity, respect, status and power were apparent these aspects where changing. Data revealed that during the changes when issues of respect, power and status were apparent, the identity split into an 'us' and 'them' and organizational identity was viewed separately by the participants to workplace identity which then became a self and group definition. Data provided empirical support for Hatch and Schultz's (2002) process model of organizational identity both with regards to the organizational identity and the workplace identity (self and group) in connection with the aspect of different types of processes being used. Data, however, revealed that physical symbolic artefacts were interpreted to provide information for not only the expression process as indicated by the authors but also mirroring and reflection processes.

In addition it was found that in specific relation to context, different power relations affected the process of interpretation and consequently the change process. Logically perhaps the hotel clientele used the interpretation of physical symbolic artefacts to influence their self and group identities, and organizational actors used the interpretation of physical symbolic artefacts to influence their organizational and workplace identities as well as self and group. During times of uncertainty, workplace identity split into two categories, self and group, and second, organizational, as participants ceased to identify with the organization's identity.

Second, the role of physical artefacts in the built environment has been found to be used within four, rather than the previously envisaged one, aspects of identity and image creation and these were expression, mirroring and reflection processes.

Finally, the findings suggest that the reactions observed and analysed were directly linked to the activities of the organizational actors and hotel clientele and to the interpersonal relations they experienced.

Implications for flagship hotels

To conclude, the role of the built environment and the physical symbolic artefacts within it is extensively used within identity forming and influencing for both organizational actors and less frequent occupants such as hotel clientele. Importantly, the use of expression and reflecting in the identity formation process had to balance the evaluation of mirroring and expressing used to evaluate the image and the concept of being a 'flagship' in order to maintain this exclusive image. When these processes were not balanced, the perception of organizational actors and clientele was that the image of being a 'flagship' was eroded. However, when these processes are balanced, the image of the flagship is enhanced. This is a process that can be monitored and controlled to ensure that the required image is maintained.

The process of interpreting physical artefact using the symbolic dimension negatively had far reaching implications. This is the one process which designers or managers cannot control or predict with any accuracy and has the greatest influence on the identity forming process and the subsequent image of the hotel. This may mean that if users interpret physical artefacts in this way it will lead to the erosion of the image of the hotel as a flagship. If this aspect of the process is a concept we cannot control, then is it something we need to understand and monitor to avoid negative consequences?

The symbolic physical artefacts within this luxury flagship hotel were used extensively, and future research may consider a longitudinal study to evaluate the extent to which these phenomena can be generalized to other geographic regions or other examples of 'flagship' and whether this occurs in less prestigious environments.

4 Virtual flagships and sociable media

Richard Coyne, Mark Wright,
James Stewart and Henrik Ekeus

In this chapter we address the relationships between the flagship concept and networked digital media. Our investigation draws attention to the social, or sociable, aspects of flagships. The flagship is primarily a meeting place, a landmark around which people and activities gather, in physical spaces and now the spaces of new media.

The identification, advocacy and creation of flagship buildings has increased even as businesses apparently reduce their dependence on physical, localized places. Globalization implies an apparent diminution in the significance of place, and a growth in the importance of communications, digital networking, e-commerce and global capital (Brauer 2002; Kozinets *et al.* 2002; Jencks 2005). The flagship seems to operate in the age of information as a means of providing controlled and exaggerated physical presence to placeless commerce. In providing physical place, the flagship also affords a means of bringing people together in ways not easily accomplished by communications media. For all their putative sociability, sophisticated communications abet, but are insufficient for the needs of people to meet together in physical places. It seems that flagship buildings, stores, and installations serve as physical foci, as gathering places, to otherwise distributed, diffused and virtual businesses.

The flagship is a physical showcase, but as such it also conforms to the role of the landmark (Lynch 1960). For Lynch, a landmark is a 'simply defined physical object: building, sign, store, or mountain' (p. 48) that primarily assists in wayfinding, but it is also a site of pilgrimage, excites the interest of the commercial tourist, and serves as a meeting place: 'I'll see you under the clock tower.' Physical structures draw visitors in ways that invisible systems and organizational infrastructures cannot. Their procurement, cost, role as venues and status as foci for events serve to gather participants and celebrities, and as such invite media attention. People might visit a flagship building not only because of the formal qualities of that place, its functions, commodity and opportunities to browse and buy, but because other people go there. They are aspirational meeting places, drawing trend setting lead consumers. Popularity and publicity sustain one another in a spiral of attraction. The Apple stores in New York and London are well known examples of buildings that serve as lures for social activity and as publicity machines. Though its products are available in the high street, and can be purchased online, Apple seeks to draw attention to a few well-placed physical flagship sites that provide opportunities for visitors to interact with experts and other devotees, to eavesdrop and to observe others.

Digital media feature prominently in displays and systems in flagship buildings, and as such are emblematic of flagship functioning. A flagship is usually conspicuous, reputedly experientially rich, up-to-date, forward looking, and sometimes deploys the latest communications devices and media. Rem Koolhaas' (OMA) Prada flagship store on Broadway in New York City was designed with changing room doors that incorporate liquid crystal display technology. Privacy is achieved when an electric current through the film is turned off, thereby rendering the glass doors opaque.

In attracting people, flagship buildings also draw other businesses to an area, and influence property values. This catalytic functioning is well known in the case of culture centres such as the Pompidou Centre in Paris, the Guggenheim Museum in Bilbao (Worpole 2000), and even Waitrose supermarkets in UK suburbs. Of course flagships also serve as inhibitors to sociability and activity. The Prada flagship store is designed to draw customers with a certain fashion sensibility, and wallet, and to discourage others who do not conform to some profile or other. Digital networks are complicit in the systems of communication, the means of dissemination and the economies by which these effects are propagated (Williams and Edge 1996). In so far as the effects of digital networks pervade markets and media, they are also complicit in the transformative function of the flagship. Flagships appear as a response by business to diffused and placeless virtuality, and the effectiveness of the flagship is in turn abetted by the apparatus of digital communications media.

So we emphasize the social functioning of the flagship, but within the context of new media sociality as well as physical presence. Spectacle gains its meanings in the context of the crowd (Debord 1983; Crary 1999). In this chapter we will exercise and test the flagship concept with examples drawn from experiments using digital sociable media, such as mobile phones and online meeting environments. We will also draw on the concept of brand to link flagships to digital media.

Brand

Brand (Sherry 1987) is integral to the flagship concept. The flagship in a naval flotilla carries the insignia of the fleet admiral. A flagship building may parade its insignia conspicuously as brand. IKEA, B&Q and other 'decorated sheds' (Venturi *et al.* 1993) provide obvious examples. Digital networks and their components are branded (Orange, AT&T, Bluetooth) and they carry brands as vectored or pixelated images and picture files: static, dynamic, interactive and sometimes with sound. Though it starts with the pictorial, a brand goes beyond the visual image. A brand is a package of desirable and recognizable attributes of an enterprise or product: service, sound, style, product range, production, delivery process, and building stock. Brand recognition generally starts with the concept of the image as picture, and other associations follow. Brands as pictures and their entailments are designed, copyrighted, and managed. The flagship store fits within a company's overall brand economy, along with product labels, signage, and mass media advertising. The flagship provides an environment in which brand is under strict control. The consumer leaves the *ad hoc* variegated brandscape of the street and indulges the corporate fetish of Topshop, Gap, Sainsbury's or Disney. The flagship introduces a highly specific, hierarchized and rarefied brand experience.

The opportunities to interact with brands are changing as media channels and usages open up. Increasingly, brand images and attributes are delivered to consumers through mobile phones, dynamic displays and other ubiquitous digital technologies. The portability of the brand image or trademark resonates with the increasing ubiquity and portability of digital devices and systems. Brand pervades and contaminates digital sociable media in many ways.

The ubiquitous presence of banner ads on websites is evidence of the close coupling between digital media and brand. The famous www.milliondollar homepage.com site displays a mosaic of brand marks linked to web pages. The advertisements cost one US dollar per pixel to mount. It seems that the entrepreneurial narrative and publicity surrounding this brand fetish lures both advertisers and viewers. A simple click leads to a branded corporate or product website, with videos and flash animations. Brand managers adopting strategies of relationship marketing, and concepts of brand communities (Kozinets 1999; Muniz and O'Guinn 2001) have attempted to create virtual gathering places for user communities. This strategy seems to work for businesses whose primary business is online, and whose customers' activities are focused websites, such as Amazon. com. The Amazon.com website is the virtual flagship of an organization that includes physical and organizational infrastructure, but no physical retail outlet. The sociable aspect of such sites is apparent as we consider their deployment of consumer reviews, voting, and personalized, targeted advertising. The 'virtual flagship' emerges as a type to be conjectured, designed, and problematized.

There are productive links between the flagship concept in digital media other than websites. We will examine brands and buildings, and look at emerging trends in digital branding and sociable media use. The flagship concept represents a meeting of brand and building. Though the flagship originates on the shifting seas, early recorded uses of the flagship metaphor pertain to land transport, the mass media (newspapers) and buildings (according to the Oxford English Dictionary). In retail, the flagship concept commonly deals with the tangible media of bricks and mortar, and spaces, either actual or represented. As a naval headquarters or *Dreadnought* the flagship conjures up ideas of power, solidity, scale, authority, expense, luxury and spectacle. The flagship is one of a kind, though others may follow. But in all this the flagship is a sociable space, in so far as flags serve to locate, to mark territory, to indicate status, and as rallying points. In what follows we will exploit this social functioning of the flag as brand in our investigation into the relationships between virtual flagships and digital media.

So the concept of the virtual flagship brings certain spatial and social relationships into sharp relief. The flagship suggests a place, a locus of interactions; the concept of brand starts with a picture, a portable mark to be inscribed on objects and spaces. In providing pervasive communications channels, digital networks constitute media for the channelling of brand images. Of course, a flagship is more than a building, a brand is more than a picture, and they are interlinked in complex ways, but they each bring certain metaphors into prominence. The flagship suggests a fixed and prominent place, whereas a brand draws on the ephemera of simplified, abstracted, reproducible and highly portable pictures. Digital networks provide media to support both. Physical flagships can be coded as three-dimensional computer models. Brands as pictures can be transmitted through digital networks. In so far as flagships are sociable spaces, they are in the company of digital networks that also provide a means for people to communicate and sustain social interactions. Overtly sociable media systems such as FaceBook and MySpace are pervaded by corporate branding that also spills into the way people present themselves. Individuals create personal profiles and a series of pictorial representations that carry the hallmarks of branding, albeit in ways that seem to be personal and idiosyncratic.

Social signs

The flagship is not the only vessel in the fleet. There are the work-a-day port paraphernalia, the barges, barques, tugs, and barnacle scrapers that bear the scars and insignias of their trades. Attention to sociable media draws attention to the commonplace aspects of brand. Brands may belong to corporations. They also belong to guilds, trades, local businesses, families and anyone who wishes to leave a mark. Sociable media, such as the communicative systems of the Internet (Castells 2001), amplify this relationship between brand and the polis.

Flags and insignias after all fit within the overall economy of signs. According to Saussure and the semiotic tradition (Saussure 1983), signs are socially and subtly negotiated, and as such are implicated in the play of power (Barthes 1973). Companies not only project brands onto consumers, but are in negotiation, or at least competition, with one another. Brands feature in our rich and variegated experience of the urban environment and the 'semiosphere' (Chmielewska 2005). Brand does not only belong to Apple, Amazon, Prada and Waitrose. Nor do brands belong only to the companies that create them. Naomi Klein's influential book *No Logo* captures this sense of shared investment in brands, their subversion through 'culture jamming,' appropriation, and the strength of feeling they engender (Holt 2002; Ahonen and Moore 2005; Klein 2005). Brands have a social aspect, aided and abetted by the possibilities of digital social networks.

What is everyday branding, and how does it relate to the flagship concept? Let us assume that society confers on its citizens the power to appropriate brand for everyday use, by controlling, claiming and re-claiming brand. We will examine some of the technologies that work together with branding to facilitate social interactions of various kinds. So there is the possibility of expanding brand from a concern with mass consumption and the promotion of elite products to everyday concerns with identity and human encounter. Brand features in meetings between friends and intimates, and small group meetings between clients and service providers, mentors and pupils, buyers and sellers, protagonists and mediators. In so far as a brand is a mark, it is a trade mark, with currency in the whole apparatus of social negotiation.

For the purposes of this investigation we join the chorus of those who protest in favour of the re-assignment of brand to quotidian human relations. But to explore the sociability of brand is not to return to some ideal pre-modern condition. Its legacy is in marks, signatures, cartouches, seals and heraldry, but brand is a modern, post industrial phenomenon, relying on mass production, commerce, marketing, corporate management strategies and mass media. The appropriation of brand can benefit from insights into digital sociable media, which in turn inform concepts of the flagship.

Branded meeting places

How are brands implicated in social interaction? The concept of the branded meeting place provides one mode of encounter. It seems that business people, clients, customers, and service providers often prefer to meet outside the office, shop or service centre to discuss, exchange ideas and transact business. They target some places above others for these encounters. It is not just convenience that draws us to certain places, but places lure us with meanings, and, increasingly, the layers of meaning in a place are indicated by branding. Brands as icons, images and symbols invoke a mood, ambience, and a sense of loyalty to a product, service or place. Consumers identify with brands and sometimes let the brand do the work of colouring the meaning and authority of the activities that take place. The Royal Yacht Britannia is now a flagship for hire, and a meeting there tells us this is an important occasion. A meeting in the foyer of the city museum perhaps invokes values associated with learning, exploration and family.

People occasionally visit flagships for informal business meetings. On 28 February 2005 we held an academic workshop in the B&Q flagship store at Fort Kinneard, a retail park on the outskirts of Edinburgh. By prior arrangement we occupied the public lecture area set aside for demonstrations of power tools and compost preparation. Our theme was commercial places and non-places (Augé 1995; Coyne 2006; Coyne and Stewart 2007). So it made sense to treat the store as a giant visual aid, to gather items in shopping trolleys for discussion, and to deploy real-time observations in our deliberations of how people used the space. Admittedly the environment already loomed large in the subject matter. But the experience demonstrated something of the capacity of all spaces to inform a subject, and to enhance the sociability of the group. Even the practical resistances afforded by a space (noise, distraction, lack of privacy) can enhance and inform the meeting function.

The social function of branding is also apparent as we reflect on how people identify with brands, develop trust and brand loyalty, and deploy brand as a shortcut to service expectation. Groups of people identify with particular branded spaces and congregate there. It is not only youths who 'hang out' in branded spaces such as shopping malls (Fiske 1989). So branded meeting places invoke meaning-rich, symbolic, alluring qualities of a place that supports people's desire to be there, and provides a performance setting, sometimes independently of the tangible, material or informational resources that the place provides.

The ubiquity of brand in human sociability is further amplified by the portability of brand, a phenomenon that carries through into the customization of wearables from sets of design elements to be mixed and matched. So not only do clothes display brand, but the casings of mobile phones, screens and ring tones are accessorized, mixed and matched according to brand templates (Ito *et al.* 2006; Castells *et al.* 2007).

In the same way that flagships can inhibit, brands also serve as barriers. They both attract and repel. Brand is deployed as a means of marking out a space of encounter. So people outside the target demographic of a brand may be less inclined to enter the space. Someone branded with Prada is less likely to find themselves willingly in the company of someone who brands themselves under the mark of Spineshank (the name of a 'nu' heavy metal band).

Both the brand and the flagship are complicit in contemporary forms of sociability. Brand is the portable, distributed and dynamic aspect of the flagship concept. Brand is a kind of currency, to be acquired, banked, managed and exchanged. To stretch a metaphor, the flagship is the fixed capital of the brand economy. In this cultural economy the flagship is not just a showcase, but a meeting place. People gather in such places to meet friends, to interact with other enthusiasts, to be seen, and to participate in actual and vicarious sociability. This potential is brought into sharp relief when expanded to a consideration of sociable digital networks and play.

Flagships and play

Communications channels are served by digital networks. Research into the social aspects of telephone use, email, and online forums such as Internet chat and collaborative work environments attest to the social power of these media (Turkle 1995; Rheingold 2002). Social networking sites such as Facebook, Bebo and Myspace, are growing to be the dominant branded social spaces of our time, with millions of participants. These are places to see and be seen, to meet, interact and watch others in a highly designed, controlled and branded environment. Sociable media afford text, voice-based and video communications, and spaces for collective expression, memory and observation.

Online computer game environments also present a particularly interesting aspect of sociable media relevant to the flagship concept: they present communications in activity contexts that are highly graphical, interactive, and spatial. Computer game environments also resonate with the ludic, experiential, forward looking and novel aspects of the flagship concept. The Toys-R-Us flagship store on Broadway, New York City, features a Ferris wheel as its centrepiece. The Tiso outdoor shop in Glasgow, Scotland, claims: 'Adventure starts here at the Glasgow Outdoor Experience! It's Europe's most exciting outdoor equipment and clothing store where you can browse, buy, eat, climb and learn … all in one spectacular setting.

Perfect for all the family' (www.tiso.com). Even at sites less overtly ludic, the emphasis on theme, narrative and spectacle speaks of play. Atria, conspicuous people movers, and other prominent architectural devices, as deployed in John Portman's futuristic hotels of the 1960s and 1970s (Portman and Riani 1990), highlight the role of novel and ludic experience, harking back to the role of the arcade, the vitrine (shop window), and consumption as experience (Nesbit 1992; Benjamin 2000). Though computer games constitute a different mode of interactivity, they appeal to similar commercial instincts, and for critics such as Stallabras, computer game environments mirror and reinforce the imperatives of consumption (Stallabras 1996).

Computer game genres include MMORPGs, a clumsy acronym for 'massively multiplayer online role playing games,' that present three-dimensional game environments shared by large numbers of people working from individual computers (Oliver 2002). World of Warcraft and EverQuest are such popular game environments steeped in quasi-Medievalist fantasy role play (Eco 1986; Coyne 1999). Players see one another on their computer screens as avatars, or animated mannequins, within a persistent three-dimensional environment. Players can design and customize their avatars to look like themselves or any other creature. Much as people customize mobile phones, the avatar can be customized and branded from standard templates. Players communicate with one another as in an online chat system, typically by typing at the keyboard, or by voice. Communication channels between players are opened up when they, or at least their avatars, are close to each in the Cartesian space of the game world. Names, groups, status, inventories, and permissions are important in determining what you can do in the three-dimensional space: where you can go, what actions you can perform, what others can do to you, what you can acquire and the general well-being of one's game identity.

It is not only in MMORPGs that we see the use of these 3D social environments. Other systems strip away the game narratives, and make the technology available for sociable economic, artistic and work activities. Virtual online social environments have existed in parallel with their game cousins for a long time. The Digitale Staat started in Amsterdam in the early 1990s introduced the idea of building a house in an imaginary land. Active Worlds, Etropia Universe and Second Life add further sophistications. In SL (Second Life), players (referred to as 'residents') build their own environments within the larger landscape of the game world, known as the 'metaverse' or 'grid' (Rymaszewski *et al.* 2007). Players can also program objects in three-dimensional space to have properties, such as being able to move of their own volition, and respond to touch (being clicked on). Objects can be worn, ridden and traded, and they can channel information into and out of the game world via the Internet. Objects can also impart behaviours to the avatars that touch them, enabling avatars to follow dance moves, perform gymnastics or join in group performances. The capability to populate the world with one's own operational creations is important in sustaining the putative sociability of these environments. You are aware of former occupation even though you may not meet many people as you travel across the virtual landscape. Amongst other lessons, these environments teach us that sociability involves more than being shaped like a human being, moving in Cartesian space, and being able to dispatch text messages to the person next to you. In many respects what persists with luminous clarity through this diminished sociability and shadowy spatial experience is the propensity amongst 'residents' to claim land, to replicate luxury, and in many cases to follow the line of least technical, creative and intellectual resistance.

What do 3D online social environments have to do with flagships? These are sociable media and amplify the flagship concept in several respects. Systems such as SL are flagships *in extremis*. They amplify aspects of the flagship concept (and suppress others). Not least they amplify issues of control, commerce, and the role of pictorial material. Our research into virtual flagships has led us to a study of the SL environment in which we are both observers and participants, an ethnographic study in which we have procured land, built, negotiated with fellow residents, and kept records and logs of activity over several months. Our studies led us to identify five major points of contact between the flagship concept and 3D online social environments.

The first major similarity is that both flagships and 3D online social environments have an obvious basis in commerce. World of Warcraft requires players to compete, overcome obstacles, and slay enemies in order to win gold, which can then be used to buy virtual objects and privileges. In so far as SL has any form of gaming goal, making money becomes the objective. The usual game quest of advancing through levels and achieving status is replaced by the challenge, or the potential at least, of managing and making money in real trading. You can do other things there, but most of the activity and the impetus for developments in SL are predicated on the actual or imagined capacity of getting others to pay for what you provide. So people can make 'real' money through their activities in SL. There are celebrated cases of SL millionaires who speculate on virtual land (Olson 2006). Digital goods include information, land, clothes and accessories for one's avatar, object models, buildings, and programmed body gestures. The SL world is populated by many points of sale set up by companies and individuals.

The second point of contact between SL and the flagship concept is that SL virtual retail outlets are invariably represented as buildings, over-scaled and vying for attention in excess of the scale of their products. Other web-based points of sale (on the web outside SL) such as hotel booking services or book sales draw on the metaphor of the trade catalogue, but retail in SL typically interfaces with the customer though a representation of a three-dimensional structure or building. You have to go to the place, walk, fly or 'teleport', in order to see or sample representations of the goods and to effect a transaction. The necessity to be constantly on the move, while window shopping, searching, and navigating, contributes to the spatiality of the game environment. SL is populated by buildings, or their three-dimensional surrogates. Surprisingly, many of the points of sale resemble flat screens with only pictures of the goods for sale. The virtual building as flagship serves to lure the consumer to the environment that houses the commodity, its catalogues, and its download functions.

Third, at the time of writing, interest in SL is such that organizations are employing skilled designers to create spectacular and distinctive building models that will attract interest and act as a showcase of some kind. One SL designer known to us received a commission that specified 'an outstanding office building with high-class interior decoration and communication devices included.' SL is an environment for showing off and for some a means of corporate branding. Whether for corporate showcase or science park, SL supports the flagship as showcase function. With low numbers of users and high attention in the mass media, these SL edifices are a global version of physical flagships. The existence of these virtual flagships contributes to the formation of a wider brand image as much as the commercial and social events that are supposed to happen within them.

Fourth, is the prominence of two-dimensional graphical images. Three-dimensional computer game environments are made up of large numbers of surfaces. As indicated above, one of the challenges of three-dimensional design work is to keep the number of surfaces to a minimum so that the screen display can be refreshed quickly in real time. To keep the number of surfaces rendered to a minimum, three-dimensional game environments such as SL rely for their richness on texture maps, which are flat images projected onto surfaces. Objects in game environments often have abrupt edges, but subtly and richly textured surfaces. Applying textures to surfaces is relatively economical. It is as simple to paste a logo onto a surface as it is to paste a wallpaper pattern. So brand is everywhere in SL, and without the statutory limitations demanded of advertising in our usual every-day inhabited spaces. In SL, brand marks can be changed at will by the residents who install them, or under the control of automated programs. SL encourages a fetish for brand, for branding, and is heavily populated with flickering brands and their ostentatious flagships.

Fifth, is the social aspect of the virtual flagship of SL. The SL environment is inevitably sparsely populated by avatars, who drift in and out of one's patch, unless one organizes a meeting. In fact for most desktop computers, the game environment becomes more sluggish the greater the number of avatars in view. Of course the sociability of virtual environments extends beyond the meeting places they purport to provide online. The deployment of digital sociable media is often multimodal, highly reflexive and there is a ready commerce in meta-discourses. So for us the apparent sparseness of residency and the lack of crowds do not negate SL as a sociable medium. We take its role as a simulacrum of urban existence as secondary. It is a sociable medium with characteristics different and supplementary to everyday life.

Systems such as SL apparently succeed due to their means of organizing the chat function, facilitating forms of socializing, their activity base, and the seductions of the spatial metaphor. SL has also reached a level of acceptance sufficient to bring other adopters on board. Like a flagship, it serves a catalytic function for sociability and activity. Of course Second Life is a brand in its own right that both attracts and repels, includes and excludes. Some consumers are suspicious of private companies that purport to oversee a world 'built by its residents.' SL is in the company of privately owned multi-purpose megastructures and gated communities presenting as 'cities' with their own security services (Graham and Marvin 2001). To function in SL you have to have an avatar, which is like requiring every business person to carry a Barbie or Ken doll in their briefcase. The three-dimensional environment bears a large overhead, and is inevitably distracting for some. In all, 3D online social environments are not to everyone's taste. They carry the risk inherent in all brands and flagships. People may be prepared to accept the product, were it not for the packaging.

Virtual reality and tangible media

In contrast to the idiosyncratic deployment of MMORPGs, 3D online social environments and virtual worlds, mobile phones are often discussed as at the vanguard of a category of sociable media that are grounded and ubiquitous, with demonstrable social impacts across a spectrum of human activities. Ubiquitous personal information and communication technologies (pICTs) such as personal stereos, portable gaming, cameras, location devices, wearables, tagging devices, streamed media and PDAs (personal digital assistants) are converging in various combinations, and the mobile phone currently leads as the demonstrator ubiquitous technology.

Weiser was an early advocate of augmented reality and ubiquitous digital media, of which telephony provides just a part. He drew the battle lines between ubiquitous media and virtual reality 'which attempts to make a world inside the computer,' particularly immersive virtual reality as conjectured to require special eye goggles and body suits, the next generation of MMORPGs. Were full virtual reality (VR) as commonly envisaged (Heim 1998; Murray 1999) a possibility it would require an infinite regress of computational sophistication in delivering three-dimensional modelling of extraordinary complexity and detail, as well as accommodation of the characteristics of vision (e.g. stereoscopy, variable focal depth) and full sensory excitation (Coyne 1995). But according to the advocates of ubiquitous and tangible media VR is unnecessary and perhaps undesirable in any case, drawing us away from the world as encountered. So interaction designers now commonly emphasize augmentation ahead of simulation, highlighting the need to augment, enhance or complement the reality with which we have to deal on a daily basis (Winograd (ed.) 1995; Rogers *et al.* 2007).

'Augmented reality' suggests the embedding of digital interaction inside everyday tangible objects. These emergent technologies give us the potential to negotiate between the spatial and the social, the two elementary dimensions of the flagship, and to conjecture an evolutionary trajectory to the flagship. The Flagship concept can be reinterpreted and appropriated anew. Perhaps we can posit new instantiations of the flagship concept and overlay them on the everyday urban fabric.

In so far as the flagship presents a rarefied, purified brand experience, it is in the company of virtual reality. It takes the consumer out of the day-to-day world to entertain a series of fantasies, which always carry the possibility of failing to deliver the promised excitement. But this is also a function of the fairground.

Participants of VR, MMORPGs, and flagships have to suspend their disbelief and enter into the game. VR is also a game in the way that language is a game (Wittgenstein 1953). We have to learn the perceptual rules of any visual encounter (Turbayne 1970). Initial exposure to the visual aspects of MMORPGs often presents a kaleidoscope of flickering coloured patches on a computer screen, but which we rapidly turn into buildings, trees and people by our capacity to imagine and interpret. We acquire the means to interpret whatever is put before us. So we can be as immersed in a text-based chat room as much as we might be immersed in a three-dimensional simulation of a meeting place in an MMORPG. To stretch an analogy, the flagship is to virtual reality as brand is to ubiquitous technologies. Brand is the portable, distributed, sensorially unassuming, stripped down manifestation of the flagship concept that demands most from our capacity to interpret and to imagine.

Mobile phones and branding

Mobile phones constitute a lead personal ICT, that brings not only personal communication but access to commercial information and brand messages. Mobile telephony has interesting and subtle spatial implications that nuance those posed by the presence of a building. The fact that you can be speaking with someone by mobile telephone from almost anywhere poses a challenge to what it means to be in a place (Meyrowitz 1985; Laurier 2001; Meyrowitz 2005), and mobile phones can be said to subvert the reach of branded places. Mobile phones also deliver flagship functions in that they are used to attract attention for advertising and telesales. Mobile phone users gather and 'swarm,' making up sociable places on the fly, without prior appointment. The formation of 'smart mobs' has become emblematic of the complicity of ubiquitous devices in creating place (Rheingold 2002). People can communicate by mobile phone to descend on a place, even a flagship, and in protest. In this light mobile telephony has the potential to diffuse, democratize, subvert and 'jam' the flagship concept.

Mobile phones also purvey brand, as in their capability to carry logos and ringtones as identity markers: logos of TV shows, video games, pictures of celebrities, musical promotions, film scores and catch phrases. As well as supporting the consumption of branded media, the arrival of the phone camera has introduced new visual practices into social behaviour, and has instigated a new commerce in visual signs. Though the size of display on small devices is unspectacular, images can be of high resolution, and can be ported to other media, such as blogs, TV and into print. Mobile phones also challenge the ownership and control of branded spaces. Many stores forbid photography of branded marketing support and products, and the brand owners of events and venues regard the widespread use and sharing of images and sounds as a breach of copyright. Mobile phones are the quintessential sociable medium, and in this role appear to be transformative, introducing new and controversial spatial and visual practices.

Portable branding

Mobile phones and their networks are part of the global communications milieu that fosters the flagship concept. But in many respects mobile telephony works against the need for the grand gesture of the flagship. Here we present four themes, backed up by design experiments, that reveal something of the potential and character of mobile phones in the context of the flagship.

Both the flagship and brand depend on the pictorial image. How can the image be deployed operationally, to enhance, challenge or bring into relief aspects of the flagship concept? Our studies draw on the abilities of a software and infrastructure system known as Spellbinder (Mobile Acuity Ltd). The system uses a server and database of images and content, and sophisticated image recognition algorithms to match captured images to data records. A mobile phone user photographs an image of a designated object (poster, label, sign) using their camera phone and sends the image to the server. The content associated with that image is returned as text, graphics, web content or a voice message. The software deploys a highly reliable smart image matching algorithm that accounts for different angles of view, light conditions and noisy data. The user can also store content associated with that site, available for someone else to collect when they too visit the site and take a picture of the object. The commercial application of Spellbinder is for brands, logos or any graphical image, either extant or planted in the environment by advertisers, to be deployed to trigger communication flows between consumers and providers.

In this investigation we deploy a research-by-design methodology (Argyris and Schön 1989; Frayling 1993; Coyne and Triggs 2007), involving teams of designers, whose activities were monitored and recorded. We presented the mobile phone image matching technology to teams of designers to see what uses they could invent for the technology in a social context. They were supported by a researcher who was able to implement software changes to help them develop their projects. The projects did not begin with detailed specifications, but involved rapid prototyping and iteration. We did not steer the inception of the applications, but wanted to see what emerged. The marketability of the final outcome of each project was of less interest to us than what the outcomes reveal about flagships and branding, and the potential each opened up for further investigation. The design projects and other interactions have inspired four research themes that expand the flagship concept.

Culture jamming

Culture jamming involves the overt or covert subversion of a brand message (Klein 2005). To put it more positively, culture jamming involves the appropriation of brand for one's own use, often political. 'Jamming' here suggests blocking, but also play, in the way that musicians might improvise around a theme, pass the theme to each other, and make the theme their own. In an odd twist, some brand managers have re-appropriated the culture jamming concept as a means of marketing. Assuming a brief that suggested the ability to leave digital graffiti on public surfaces, one of our design teams developed and implemented an 'Invisible Art' exhibition, where a phone user visits designated spots around the city and photographs particular wall surfaces. The viewer then receives pre-prepared images via their phone of the same surface with a 'hidden' graphic revealed on it.

How does this safe, digitally mediated culture jamming relate to the flagship concept? Needless to say, the play of such imagery has the character of graffiti. Here it was deployed to demonstrate the potential of subverting the sanctioned surfaces of significant buildings. In one case the designers targeted the Edinburgh John Lewis flagship department store, and daubed one of its walls with their own virtual art. We developed this idea and superimposed images of chicken carcasses over the local storefront of a popular fast food chain, and the logo of Gamblers Anonymous on a local bookmakers. Of course the system could also be deployed to enhance brand imagery, unlocking brand messages and artefacts around the city, or enhancing existing brand support. The system can provide users with links to websites with follow-up content, or messages and information about others who have visited the same location.

Brand play

Consumers can play around with brands, mixing, matching, and distorting them in a manner similar to how story-tellers create their own versions of other writers' plots and characters. Penley provides a compelling argument about the subversive aspects of certain consumption practices in the context of popular television programmes (Penley 1991), for example where individuals publish their own unofficial and salacious versions of Star Trek stories. While brand and copyright owners have initially objected to these activities, it is now recognized as a key motivator for their most loyal fans and customers (Kozinets 1999).

Brand play is ubiquitous. Conventional game play frequently involves the manipulation of tokens with which one identifies, as in the use of plastic symbols that are moved around the Monopoly board, or the character profiles and their imagery adopted by players in the game of Cluedo (Colonel Mustard, Mrs Peacock, etc.). MMORPGs are sociable game media involving similar identification with an avatar. Mobile phones also support games that can be played as representations on their small screens, and these can be multi-user games. There are also games that deploy mobile phones as portable devices. One design team produced such a game based on the game of tag, which also bears similarities to the 'paint ball' game and 'capture the flag' and could take place in any urban or rural setting.

There is commercial potential here as the players can be wearing brand marks from any source, tapping into a long tradition of branded clothing from sport or fashion. The game is yet another experience of the kind that one could see in a flagship environment. On the other hand the game diffuses the flagship concept further by amplifying the sociability of play outside the context of a specific building. Any environment can be turned into a site of play. Any transitory site can be the standard bearer of brand. The game further highlights the possibility of setting the flagship adrift. It also highlights the role of the image. Flagships and celebrities are there to be photographed. Why not demonstrate the society of the spectacle for what it is: a play of images!

Social network sites and physical network sites

Digital networks further emphasize mobility and nomadic existence (Careri 2001). Certain sectors of society now rely on informal contact via mobile phones in order to decide where to meet up, relying on techniques for alerting one another of where they are. Some of the major social venues now are online. Think of the computer user at home or at work, whose presence is registered through messaging systems that signal availability, and provide a log and commentary on everyday activities. Social network systems such as Facebook, Plazes or Twitter provide even more information through a user's network, including their current activities, location and moods. This capability seems to mirror aspects of everyday sociability and spatiality as we enter and meet in different physical places, or pass in the corridor or street.

In our experimentation with and discussion of such a system it is interesting how readily we veered towards metaphors of projecting physical spaces into digital spaces, or enlivening physical spaces through the logic of social network sites. The contrary can also be envisaged. Their visitors to online equivalent spaces are signalled on screens or otherwise in the physical space, through icons, images and messages. Such a capability also provides opportunities for linking peripheral and less celebrated venues to the flagship concept. The specialness of a place can be amplified through this kind of access to social networks. Social networking sites can be repositories of memories of the way a place is used, its events and visitors: not only celebrity events, but the ordinary and everyday. These records might be important in constructing the meaning and value of a place for groups and individuals, and in providing a showcase for past events. Everywhere can become a flagship for some activity or other.

These experiments amplified the notion of covert branding, play and access, and prompted further synthesis and experimentation. To explore some of these ideas further we connected these functionalities to Second Life, which supports similar operations in a three-dimensional, ludic world context.

Cross mapping sociable media

Our fourth experiment developed as a hybrid of these approaches, deploying the SL environment, image matching and location identification. It is possible to port messages in and out of SL via mobile phone SMS (the mobile phone small messaging service) and text fields on websites. This opens up the channels of communication to include visual images, including those produced while on the move, outside the office and about town. As the images are projected onto the walls of the SL room they also have the effect of evoking an atmosphere. This is not to replicate a real world environment, but provides a series of images that are suggestive of the location of a meeting.

The second innovation was to introduce a simple capability for identifying locations. We created a series of locational 'brand markers' and positioned them on the floor of eight different real life rooms. The marker indicates roughly where you should position a mobile phone camera to take a photograph that would identify the room. When you enter the room you would take a photograph as indicated, dispatch it to the server, and the image matcher would compare that image in its database to determine where you are. That locational trigger would then signal a change in the SL environment. The system provides a means of identifying at which of the eight locations the meeting participant is positioned. These location triggers are date stamped and the history of movement kept as a record for later inspection. For this test we considered only the location of a single peripatetic participant, but the system is expandable to multiple participants.

Detailed findings of this study are reported elsewhere, and pertain to the necessity or otherwise of physical representation in online meeting environments, and the value of hybrid and multi-channel meeting facilities. It seems that it is not necessary for virtual environments to take place in persistent environments. SL and similar environments present a unified world view that is the same for everyone. SL as meeting environment is a further manifestation of a highly technologized, instrumental, and mathematized one-world view targeted by phenomenologists such as Martin Heidegger (1977). Users of communication environments do not need to subscribe to totalizing Cartesian grids, other-worldliness, and other physical representation of a physical space in order to conduct online meetings. There is no inevitably strong relationship between three-dimensional practice and the narratives people develop in meetings. According to Graham and Marvin, in the world of communications 'there is no single, unified "cyberspace"' (Graham and Marvin 2001). 3D online social networks attempt individually to homogenize the communicative experience, were it not that there are many such environments, and they are competing with other modes of communication.

The flagship concept emerged in our studies in a direct way. Flagships, virtual or otherwise serve a 'demonstrator function'. The major advantage of conducting such studies in the SL environment is as a means of inviting people to demonstrations. SL is populated by curious researchers interested in new ideas. SL is widely accessible. People can be encouraged to attend (virtually) informal demonstrations and provide feedback. This is certainly possible in other shared environments, but in this case the common access, novelty, theatricality and spatial references of SL work in favour of the promotion and progression of a research project. Our virtual flagship research project bears the traces of previous visitors to the demonstration. Persistence works in favour of the study as the experimental environment is accessible to all users of SL, and it persists even when the researchers are not present.

These experiments highlight ways in which the flagship concept can be extended and developed in a new media age, where communications technologies fragment the barriers of place to invite participation, but at the same time have the potential to enhance the importance of place through these new media.

Conclusion

The flagship takes many forms. One client for a SL design project we know about, required that the building resemble the company logo when viewed from above, as it invariably appears on SL maps, and residents after all encounter much of this artificial world while in free flight (i.e. avatars can fly). The functionality of the buildings is minimal in terms of habitation and security. So SL buildings function as advertising beacons, an architecture that is just a sign, a flagship without crew or passengers. Such treatments are also evident in the everyday lifeworld, with surface textures in the Nevada desert formed into the KFC logo to be seen from space or aerial photographs (coined an 'astrovertisement'), and the vast luxurious residential landforms known as 'Palm Island' and 'the World' in the Persian Gulf in Abu Dhabi to be seen from outer space. The consumerist spectacles of real life copy Second Life, or at least the representation becomes the reality (Baudrillard 2001).

So 3D online social environments, virtual reality and SL reflect back on day-to-day environments. After a while you begin to think of people you see in the street as avatars and are disappointed that you cannot produce objects out of thin air by a mere gesture, or fly or teleport to your next meeting, a sense that soon fades as you begin to appreciate the intricacies of the everyday life world. According to one designer who is immersed in SL practices, 'I always have the option to logout and remember the material world which has so much to give.' Flagships as fantasy worlds deliver a similar function. We are after all grateful that the life world is not entirely a stage setting for idealized spectacles of consumption.

As we have demonstrated, the function of the flagship is a social one. Spectacle gains its meanings in the context of the crowd. We tested the flagship concept through examples using digital sociable media, and drew on the concept of brand to link flagships to sociable digital media. Furthermore we introduced concept of virtual reality and 3D online social environments. The flagship is to virtual reality as brand is to ubiquitous technologies. Brand is the portable, distributed, sensorially unassuming, stripped down manifestation of the flagship concept. Our investigation has drawn attention to the sociable aspects of flagships. The flagship is primarily a meeting place, a landmark around which people and activities gather. Attention to this function provides opportunities for design, integration with digital networks and devices, and enhancement of the flagship concept.

We treated the flagship as the fixed capital of the brand economy. The flagship is not just a showcase, but a meeting place. People gather in such places to meet friends, to interact with other enthusiasts, to be seen, and to participate in actual and vicarious sociability. So our study has sought to expand the flagship concept to embrace media other than brick, steel and concrete. We have also indicated the diffusion of the flagship concept into the world of technologies that augment everyday communications and sociability.

Glossary

Barbie and Ken: iconic dress-up dolls produced by Mattel Inc

Bebo: a web-based communication system for managing social contacts

Culture jamming: sometimes violent activities that involve the desecration of brand signs

Entropia Universe: a three-dimensional persistent game with very large numbers of users

Flickr: a sociable web-based system for storing, accessing and sharing pictures

Google Maps: a web-based map and aerial photograph display system with a search engine for finding locations and travel routes anywhere in the world

ICT: information and communications technology

MMORPG: massively multiplayer online role playing games, or 3D online social game environments

MySpace: a web-based communication system for managing social contacts

PDA: personal digital assistant or hand-held electronic diary

pICT: personal information and communications technology

Plazes: an online social network system

Resident: a user of Second Life

RFID: radio-frequency identification, the use of small tagging transmitters to locate people and goods

Skype: a free telephone and videophone system that runs on the Internet

SL: Second Life, a commerce-based MMORPG without the obvious fantasy narrative

SMS: small message service for communicating by text on mobile phones

Teleport: A means in Second Life of jumping from one location to another without walking, running or flying

Twitter: a web-based communication system for letting people know where you are

VR: virtual reality, three-dimensional visual and other sensory simulations that give the viewer the impression that they are physically immersed in the simulation

Acknowledgements

This work is supported by the Arts and Humanities Research Council. We are grateful to Penny Travlou for her participation in this project and her insights into culture jamming, and John Lee and Christopher Fincken for introducing Second Life into the discussion. Designer participants include: Nicholas Hansen, Tian Yuan, Tao Zhang, Chen Xia, Hong Xu, Michael Solo, Isaac Mpagi, Ying-Jyun Lin, and Xiaohui Xu.

5   The flagship store

The luxury fashion retailing perspective

Christopher M. Moore and
Anne Marie Doherty

A review of the tourist marketing activities of any major European city typically includes some reference to the nature of that city's retailing offer and specifically the flagship stores that are operated there by the leading international fashion companies. As such, flagship stores have emerged as an essential ingredient of the consumption landscape. For example, the Louis Vuitton flagship store in the Champs Elysées in Paris has been identified as one of the top tourist attractions. Tourists and locals alike are pulled by the allure of this great testament to the glamour, status, fantasy and prestige of arguably the world's most successful luxury brand.

But the function of the flagship store extends much further than that of a tourist attraction or a venue for the adoration activity of followers of the brand. Instead, the flagship store has served as a critical and central dimension of the trading activities of fashion retailers for many years. Typically an investment made by luxury goods retailers, the opening of a flagship store is no longer the sole domain of upmarket fashion companies. For example, the announcement in October 2007 by Sir Philip Green that his Arcadia chain would at last open its first stand-alone outlet in the USA also identified the importance of the flagship to fashion brands with a mid-market positioning. Rather than declaring an intention to open a chain of Topshop stores across the USA, Green's strategy is instead 'better off with a flagship mentality. Opening stores of 20–40,000 square feet stores is a better strategy, to get that theatrical "on stage" atmosphere' (*Sunday Telegraph* 2007: 5).

While acknowledging then that the flagship has as much a role to play in the business strategy of the mass-market fashion retailer, the focus of this chapter will be to consider the role and function of the flagship store in luxury fashion companies. Moore and Doherty (2006) define luxury fashion retailers as 'those firms that distribute clothing, accessories and other lifestyle products which are:

- exclusively designed and/or manufactured by/or for the retailer;
- exclusively branded with recognized insignia, design handwriting or some other identifying device;
- perceived to be of a superior design, quality and craftsmanship;
- priced significantly higher than the market norm;
- sold within prestigious retail settings.

Though not claiming to be an exhaustive list, retailers that conform to this categorization include Prada, Gucci, Dior, Louis Vuitton, Chanel, Giorgio Armani, Versace, Hermes, Burberry and Mulberry.

Researcher consideration of the luxury fashion sector has tended to focus specifically upon consumer behaviour towards luxury goods, issues relevant to luxury brand creation, development and protection and the issues associated with the development of luxury within emerging markets. While the role of flagship stores within the market positioning and distribution strategies of luxury fashion retailers has been noted in this literature, an understanding of their importance and role has been, hitherto, somewhat neglected. A generic definition of flagship stores was provided by Kozinets *et al.* (2002), who identified three characteristics as follows:

- They carry only a single brand of product.
- They are company owned.
- They operate with the intention of building brand image rather than solely to generate profit for the company.

Within the context of luxury fashion retailing, these dimensions have some application, but these do not necessarily have a universal application. For example, the Armani flagship store in Milan sells a variety of brands from the Armani Group portfolio – as well as other brands, such as Sony products within the electronics department in the store. Furthermore, while many of the Armani flagships are owned by the company, others, such as the London flagship are operated by a joint venture partner. What appears to be common to all flagship stores within the luxury fashion sector is their role in building and developing an image, profile and attraction for the luxury fashion brand. Evidence that these stores are unprofitable is difficult to obtain – it is unlikely that any fashion company would be prepared to publicly declare that these stores make little or no profit contribution. However, given the significant property and operating cost that is typically associated with these stores, it is reasonable to assume that in many cases, the contribution that is possible from these stores is at best limited.

In the context of luxury fashion retailing in London and New York, Fernie *et al.* (1998) acknowledge that luxury fashion brands firms restrict their representation to one 'flagship' store and distribute products via in-store concessions and wholesale agreements. Their work also provides interesting findings on the location of these flagships noting that in London, Bond Street and Sloane Street account for 85 per cent of the total designer stores in the city, with Madison Avenue and Fifth Avenue housing the majority of New York's luxury retailers. Fernie *et al.* (1997) comment on the loss making nature of many of these stores making them a particularly fascinating method of entry. They claim that 'flagship stores are maintained to act as publicity vehicles for the ranges and are not required to show a typical return on investment' (p. 373).

Moore *et al.*'s (2000) study on the internationalization process of luxury retailers places the opening of flagship stores at the centre of the process. While these firms may enter markets via wholesaling initially, their presence in a market is normally marked by the opening of flagship stores in central locations such as those noted above.

Thus, while Fernie *et al.* (1998) and Moore *et al.* (2000) have introduced the concept of the flagship store in the context of broader studies on the internationalization of luxury brand retailers, much remains to be learned with respect to the value and purpose of the flagship store within the context of luxury fashion retailing. Given the prevalence of luxury fashion retailers on the global stage, and the centrality of flagship stores to their internationalization strategy, further investigation of these entities is both worthwhile and significant.

A variety of themes can be used in the analysis of the luxury flagship store. This chapter will focus upon three critical dimensions of the luxury flagship store as follows: first their geography at the macro and micro levels; their design and branding characteristics; and finally their strategic business purpose and value.

The geography of the luxury fashion flagship store

Consideration of the geography of the luxury fashion flagship provides a useful insight into their purpose and value. At the macro level, in terms of the cities within which these stores are located, it is clear the choice of location and venue plays an important role in the development of an identity and purpose for the flagship.

Hollander (1970) noted that the international expansion strategies of the premium/luxury companies was to focus upon world centres which provide access to large numbers of the world's most affluent consumers. Termed the 'New York, London, Paris' syndrome, Hollander's analysis recognized that the establishment of stores within these important locations played a critical role in the establishment of their credentials as businesses of global significance and importance. Hollander's observations could easily be applied to the flagship locations of the international luxury retailers. Usually, the luxury fashion flagship is situated within the major cities of the company's most significant markets in terms of sales generated.

Some cities are particularly important as centres for luxury fashion flagships. Predominant among these is Tokyo. The proliferation of flagships within the city is perhaps explained by the fact that Japan accounts for one third of all luxury goods sales. Milan is another important flagship venue. Serving as it does as the centre for European luxury manufacturing, the importance of Milan as a centre for global fashion marketing communications activity has meant that those fashion retailers seeking to establish and maintain an international brand identity have, by necessity, been required to open a Milan flagship. Presence in Milan helps to secure media coverage, provides access to international fashion buyers and consumers and offers an opportunity for the internationalizing fashion retailer to claim that it has the credibility and allure to sustain the high operating costs associated with a presence in the leading luxury fashion boulevards.

New locations of importance have emerged in the past decade. Previously cities such as Moscow and Shanghai were ignored by the leading international luxury firms. However, with the emergence of a large number of high net worth individuals, the demand for luxury goods has outpaced demand within the traditional centres for luxury consumption. In response to these trends, the leading luxury companies have established flagship stores in recognition of the new demand and also as a means of cultivating that demand within foreign markets.

While distinct patterns can be identified at the macro level with respect to the location of flagship stores at city-level, it is also possible to identify common characteristics within these cities. At the micro level, flagships are concentrated within specific streets or closely knit districts that are geographically and socially proximate and accessible to 'high net worth individuals', fashion-aware consumers and international visitors/tourists. The flagships typically cluster together to create luxury enclaves that are recognized as such by the wider community. These streets, such as Bond Street in London, Madison Avenue in New York and Via Montenapoleone in Milan, provide a prestigious address which supports the luxury credentials of the retailers located there. The high concentration of luxury flagships within these specific locations serves to augment and enhance the exclusivity and allure of the luxury brands. Perhaps, more importantly, this concentration assures these areas as important shopping destinations for local and visiting consumers.

The concentration of flagship stores within these areas means that the demand for space within these locations is fierce. Given that the majority are historical locations, with finite space availability, the demand for space far outstrips the supply. Consequently, smaller fashion companies – with more limited resources – are marginalized to peripheral areas. There is also evidence to suggest that fashion companies have been bought out of locations by larger, more financially powerful conglomerates in order that these may establish new and/or bigger flagship stores.

Invariably, flagship stores are located within areas that are proximate to tourist areas and as such, these areas are often promoted as being an important element of the visitor experience as has been previously identified.

Design of the luxury fashion flagship store

The way in which a flagship store is designed and subsequently looks is inextricably linked to the luxury retailer's positioning strategy. The brand's identity, image and status clearly and definitively influence and shape the design of the flagship store. For example, in order to reflect the purity of the Giorgio Armani label, the brand's architect, Claudio Silvestrin has utilized purist materials, in the form of cream stone, plate glass and ebony shelving in the company's flagship stores. These materials clearly delineate the status and standing of the Armani brand values. These core values are replicated throughout all of the Armani flagships worldwide. This approach provides for continuity in the presentation of the values, standards and ideals of the brand. As well as providing the benefits associated with scale economies, the development of a flagship store template enables the speedy and effective roll-out of the design template across the Armani real estate.

As well as through the direction of the flagship's architect, the allure of the luxury flagship is further enhanced by the status and heritage of the building that it occupies. For example, the Giorgio Armani store in Shanghai is located in an early 1900s neo-classical building; while Louis Vuitton's Manhattan flagship is built in the New York Trust Company building. The decision to establish new flagships within landmark buildings has a practical benefit in that it helps to locate the premises for locals and visitors. But perhaps most importantly, the acquisition of imposing residencies such as the Rhinelander Mansion in New York by Ralph Lauren, or former bank buildings such as the former Royal Bank of Scotland Building by Jil Sander at Burlington Gardens, London, help to create, support and reinforce the premium positioning of the luxury brand. For example, the connotations of the Rhinelander Mansion support Lauren's brand proposition with its aristocratic associations, while the austerity of the Sander flagship reflect the clinical purity of that brand.

This strategy allows the brand to be associated and acquire the benefits of the history associated with the building, which, in turn, allows for a brand positioning based upon heritage, strength and credibility. This enhanced positioning provides the brand with the capability to charge a premium price and to claim a prestige identity.

By way of delineating the *physical differences* which characterize flagship stores, the luxury fashion flagship is typically significantly larger in scale than any other format operated by the retailers – either domestically or internationally. These flagships are between five to eight times larger than the typical retail store footprint and they extend, on average, to four sales floors, as opposed to the norm of no more than two floors. Two explanations can justify their larger size. The first is that their larger scale enhances the status of the brand – in that a large flagship gives the impression of a large brand that is significant and imposing. The second is that a large scale premises, with an abundance of space for 'product display and customer flow and movement', serves as an essential element of the luxury brand experience.

Access to these prestigious locations comes at a high cost. Fernie *et al.* (1998) noted a significant variance in the rental and operating charges of the luxury flagship districts in London and New York compared to other comparable commercial districts. Other studies have noted that premium occupancy costs for luxury districts are a feature of other world centres. Tracking the retail rental charges of 229 shopping districts in 45 countries, Cushman *et al.* (2004) reported the dominant position of streets with a high proportion of luxury brand tenants. New York's Fifth Avenue, with its high proportion of luxury fashion brands, was found to be the world's most expensive street with rents at £5,680 per square metre in 2004. Bond Street, which has a concentration of luxury fashion brands, was found to be the third most expensive street in Europe with an average rental charge of £3,036 per square metre in 2004.

Consequently, luxury analysts and other commentators have proposed that only a minority of these flagships are profitable. For example and as mentioned previously, Ermenegildo Zegna operates a flagship in London, alongside a small store in the City and a concession in Harrods. In 2003 these cumulatively generated sales of £8.7 million, but made a loss before tax of £111,000 (Foster 2004). The high occupancy and operating costs and the low levels of profitability may explain why the international retailers and not franchise partners directly own most flagship stores (Moore *et al.* 2000).

Yet, despite the high occupancy and operating costs, tenant turnover in these districts is typically low and the retailer mix tends to remain constant. This consistency in luxury tenant profile is as a result of strict landlord tenant controls and prohibitively high occupancy costs. But for whatever reason, it is also clear that access to these areas is not available to the smaller or fledgling luxury firms. Their lack of resources means that they are denied access to these prestige locations and the rich customers that these attract.

A further characteristic of the luxury fashion flagship is that these are created by the leading international architects of the day. In many resects, luxury fashion brands have emerged as the new patrons of civic architecture in the key world centres. The involvement of a leading architect provides three key benefits. First, their involvement creates a positive impact upon the image and standing of the brand. Second, the creative involvement of the leading architects affords access to new ideas, techniques and skills. Third, their involvement helps to secure media interest and coverage, which further advances the credibility and standing of the luxury fashion retailer.

While the tendency with international fashion marketing has been to standardize the retail store format, the involvement of these celebrated designers has been the generation of distinct, often unique designs, which reflect local characteristics, as well as the identity of the luxury brand. For example, Peter Marino's design for the Christian Dior flagship store in Avenue Montaigne in Paris developed in 2007 a store that had the feeling of a lush private apartment. The store is furnished with products created by Marino himself, as well as other leading furniture designers to give a sense of intimacy, privacy and interest. Further the artificial light used in the store changes from dawn to dusk to reflect the passing of the day. As such, it seeks to emulate and reflect the passing of the day as experienced within any chic Parisian apartment.

In a similar vein, Ballantyne, the luxury cashmere company have opened two flagship stores: one in London and the other in Milan. These stores have the feel of a private members club through the use of cashmere curtains, pinstripe carpets and Berger chairs. The brand's heritage diamond motif has been replicated throughout the interior of the store with the soft furnishings and the in-store mirrors. For their flagship in Osaka Japan, the French luxury retailer, Hermes has opened a store, which draws upon the heritage of the company. The store, designed by Rena Dumas, features lights that were first designed for the company for their Paris store in 1925, while the exterior of the store seeks to demonstrate the vitality of the brand through the use of a glass façade that is screen-printed with glass dots. Rooms within the store are divided by a suspended shelving system as well as glass screens. This approach provides for a flexible selling system – and also offers a retail space that is fresh, open and attractive.

Reflecting their avant-garde style, the Japanese brand, Comme des Garçons opened a new flagship store in 2007, in the important market of Hong Kong. Austere and architectural like the collections that it displays, the flagship is a windowless building that has an all-white interior. Emphasizing the link between the 'Comme des Garçons' art ethic, the store also features space for art installations of the world's leading designers and artists. These installations are displayed alongside the product and as such, serve to provide a challenging, if unique, consumption experience for the Comme des Garçons customer.

Working on a similar theme, American luxury department store retailer Barneys opened, again in 2007, a new flagship store in Dallas. The third flagship store within the chain, the opening of the store is a dominating, red cantilevered slab of steel that serves as the entrance. Throughout the store, artwork is presented in an integrated fashion with the merchandise with a view to providing a stimulating and enjoyable shopping experience. The use of glass light boxes for the display of merchandise further underlines the connection between art and the goods that are available for sale.

As well as serving as spaces for the presentation of art and other types of installation, many flagship stores within the luxury sector also incorporate restaurants, bars and food service areas. For example, Dolce and Gabbana for their menswear flagship store in Milan, have included a 1950s inspired Martini bar as a critical element of the offer. With its chic red and black interiors and its model-like sales staff, the Martini bar plays an important role in positioning the flagship store as a place for recreation and enjoyment. Dolce and Gabbana's Martini Bar – as well as providing an additional source of revenue for the business – serves as an attraction in itself and attracts customers to the flagship on a regular basis. As well as increasing dwell time within the store, the bar – and others like it – provides a useful context for customers to experience the values of the brand, as well as the opportunity to 'check out' other customers who shop at the store!

As well as their Martini Bar, Dolce and Gabbana has extended the reach of the flagship by including a Beauty Farm within the same Milan flagship store. Providing hairdressing and other beauty services, the Farm serves to underline the aspirations and values of the Dolce and Gabbana brand. In effect, these luxury flagship stores have in many instances taken over the role of the department store to provide a one-stop shop for the needs of affluent, time poor, cash rich customers.

As a result of their non-standardized, architect design, the majority of flagships have very high set-up costs. These costs, coupled with high operating costs, mean that most luxury fashion retailers can sustain only a handful of flagship stores. Consequently, it is important to note that in some circumstances the term 'flagship store' is used liberally and often inappropriately, especially within an international context. It is therefore erroneous to state that all foreign stores – company-owned or otherwise – can be reasonably classified as flagships. Instead, 'true and authentic' flagships, which serve as clear and defined expressions of the retailer's luxury positioning, are developed sparingly. Indeed, it could be argued that the idea of a flagship within every market would serve to undermine the flagship principle. By their very nature, these need to be exclusive, not only in terms of their character, but also their number. An over-availability of flagships within a luxury fashion retailer's portfolio would dilute their significance and undermine the standing of the luxury brand.

While most luxury fashion brands rely upon third parties (such as department stores and quality independent stores) to operate stores and sell their brand under wholesale arrangements within foreign markets, the majority elect to retain *full ownership and control* over their domestic and international flagship stores. There are two main reasons for this approach. The first is financial since the associated costs are excessive for a partner company to consider, far less sustain. The second relates to their desire to retain full and absolute control over every aspect of how the flagship looks and is operated since its main purpose is to accurately reflect the brand's positioning plan in the key operating markets. In all cases, the opening of a flagship store marks the first direct investment within a foreign market by luxury fashion retailers. Furthermore, it is usual that the opening of a flagship store marks the first development a retail store portfolio within their most important foreign markets. Consequently, it is usual for luxury fashion companies to view their flagships, and their locations, as essential components of the DNA of their respective brands.

Strategic purpose and value of the luxury flagship store

In their broadest sense, the flagship store plays a critical role in the formation and development of the luxury retailers' fashion brand. Recognizing that the flagship store is the central ingredient of the machinery of the luxury brand, Moore and Doherty (2006) noted that the establishment of a chain of luxury flagship stores is often a critical investment for luxury fashion companies that seek to re-establish a luxury brand position. For example, Moore and Birtwistle (2004) in their review of the revitalization activities of the British luxury brand, Burberry, noted that the company swiftly adopted a flagship investment strategy as a means of re-creating a new, clearer and more convincing luxury brand positioning. Starting with the renovation and development of the company's flagship store on Bond Street, a network was soon established within the foreign markets that were important to the company. These strategic openings, in Italy, Spain, Japan and the USA, all served to communicate the aspirations of Burberry as a luxury brand of credibility that was also supported by a clear and precisely managed growth strategy.

The significance of the flagship store to the development of a luxury brand positioning is clearly evidenced in the strategy adopted by the Gucci Group in order to revive, develop and advance both the Gucci and the YSL brands. Moore and Birtwistle (2005) identified that the Gucci Group, through investment in larger and more prestigious flagship stores, sought to signal to customers their development of a new brand identity. Developed under the design direction of the

Gucci Group's Creative Director, Tom Ford, the company was able to incorporate their flagships into their luxury brand system. As such, all of the visual and design elements of the store were consistent with the identity of the Gucci and YSL brands in terms of tone of voice, brand values and communication/identity devices. As such, Ford was able to create retail spaces which came to epitomize and represent the very essence of the Gucci and YSL brand identities. In this way, the Gucci Group were able to bring their brands to life – allowing customers to come to the flagship stores and 'live' the Gucci and YSL brand experiences.

With their glamorous store interiors and extravagant merchandising techniques and apparatus, the Gucci Group created (and continues to underline) their identity and positioning as an important, global luxury brand. Furthermore, by opening flagship stores within new territories – such as in Russia and China – as they emerged, the company was able to clearly demonstrate their international credentials as a truly luxury global brand.

A variety of other luxury brands have used the flagship store as a powerful means of demonstrating their change in strategic direction and their desire to obtain a luxury brand positioning. For example, brands, such as Dunhill, Daks and Aquascutum have all used the opening of a flagship store in London as a powerful means of communicating a change in their business strategy. As well as providing a strong signal to customers of a change in aspiration and direction, these companies also use it as an important internal communications device to indicate to investors and strategic partners a new strategy in a way that is tangible, direct and assessable.

Within this context, the remainder of this section will consider the strategic significance and purpose of the flagship store in this sector. It is important to recognize that flagship stores, while often an expensive enterprise, also serve as the first form of direct investment within a foreign market. For example, within markets, such as China and Russia, luxury fashion retailers have opened flagship stores in order to signal their long-term commitment to emerging markets, and these stores serve as a first stage in the development of wholesale distribution and retail networks within new foreign markets. These stores serve to indicate to current and future wholesale stockists the brand's commitment to a long-term participation within that market and serve as a powerful indication of their expectations with respect to market viability and development potential.

Remaining in this context, flagship stores also serve as an important mediator in the creation and maintenance of strong partner relationships between the luxury fashion brand retailer and their stockists in a foreign market. The majority of luxury fashion brands rely upon third party stockists for the majority of their income within foreign markets. As such, given the financial importance of wholesale partners, the internationalizing luxury retailer deploys a variety of devices in order to nurture and support these relationships.

Consequently, flagship stores play an important role in partner relationship formation. As already noted, a flagship indicates a commitment to the foreign market by the internationalizing retailer and raises the profile of the brand in the mind of local consumers. Furthermore, this marker also attracts stockists and franchise partners to the brand since the flagship indicates internal resource capability on the part of the internationalizing retailer and suggests the availability of some form of market development strategy. It could also be suggested that the opening of a flagship store is an important indicator of a commitment to a particular market and a sign of the brand's confidence in their long-term future within a territory. With their controlled operating standards and merchandising methods, these stores provide a tangible guide and direction to stockists in terms of brand presentation. Typically, flagships hold the complete brand offer in terms of the various sub-brands and total product options. By encouraging partners to make flagship visits, the luxury fashion retailer is able to communicate and inculcate the positioning and values of their brand.

The luxury flagship store serves as a clear expression of the image, value and aspirations of the luxury brand within a market. As the comments identified earlier by Philip Green attest, the flagship is a dramatic representation of the brand and provides a useful location for bringing the brand together with target customer groups. But in the majority of cases, the role of the flagship is to serve as a showcase for the brand, which in turn, serves as a mechanism to promote and support sales within third party stockists' stores.

Flagship stores also provide an important place for the luxury brand to be promoted to luxury fashion opinion formers. The importance of celebrity endorsements and close associations has long been recognized by luxury fashion companies (Breward 2003), and the flagship store provides the opportunity for celebrities to be fêted and then photographed as they leave the flagship with their possibly free products. Other than providing a space to host celebrity events, the flagship store also provides the opportunity for the company to showcase their entire collections to the fashion press, especially at the launch of a new season.

Positive relationships between the media and luxury retailer brand are critical for the success of the luxury fashion brand. And while it is certainly the case that editorial coverage within the leading monthly fashion magazines is determined by the brand's level of advertising spend with that publication, newspaper coverage is more at the discretion of the fashion editors and writers. In an effort to influence these fashion reporters, many luxury fashion companies will establish and staff a local Press Office. The purpose of this office is to represent the brand to the local media through the provision of corporate photography (that can be used for publication), corporate and product information, as well as press samples of their 'must have' products of the season which can be used for photo shots. Working in conjunction with the Press Office, the flagship store because of its placement within the primary fashion districts ensures that the brand remains in the memory of local fashion reporters. It should not be forgotten that the flagship store plays an important role in creating and maintaining customer loyalty. Through such initiatives as exclusive fashion shows, private shopping evenings and public relations events, such as book launches, the flagship serves as a place where the relationship between the brand and the key customer is established and enhanced.

The luxury flagship also serves as a retail formula for other stores operated either directly or indirectly by the company. For example, at the Armani Group, the world flagship is located in Milan on Via Sant' Andrea. Designed by the internationally acclaimed architect, Claudio Silvestrin, this flagship has served as the prototype for the other Giorgio Armani flagship stores the Group has opened in Paris, Moscow, Vienna, Dubai, Hong Kong and Barcelona. The influence of the world flagship upon the other flagship stores is acknowledged by the Group as providing an invaluable direction for the design and development of the international retail network.

Concluding comments

Long established as a defining element of the luxury fashion retailer's market positioning approach, it is clear that the flagship store makes a significant contribution to the trading activity of the international luxury fashion brand. While costly to create and support and complex to manage, it is clear that these stores are an important means by which luxury fashion retailers secure the support of important parties, such as the media, wholesale distributors and end consumers. The investments of the leading luxury fashion houses have meant that these stores are much more than large-scale retail outlets. Instead, these function as powerful instruments, which communicate the values and pedigree of the luxury fashion brand.

6   Flagship shopping centres

Charles Dennis

Introduction

Retail forms the heart of towns and cities in the UK and many other countries –
and the health of cities is critical to that of their regions (e.g. Birch 2002; BURA
2002; Lowe and Wrigley 2000). However, modern developments challenge the
role of downtowns as community hubs. In many countries, wealthier people and
their associated retail facilities have moved away. Many downtown areas suffer
physical, economic and social decline (e.g. Ford 1994 (US); Guy and Ducket
2003 (UK); Hankins, 2002 (US); O'Callaghan and O'Riordan 2003 (Ireland)). In
the UK, the number of independent retail stores has declined by 40 per cent in a
decade (Lang and Rayner 2001). Various strategies such as government subsidies
for industry or housing, or commercial retail development have been suggested
and tried to regenerate areas (Gopal 2003). For example, Staeheli and Mitchell
(2006) reported on the DestiNY mall at Syracuse in upstate New York, which they
found has become a *de facto* urban centre in an otherwise deprived area. In this
context, the word 'flagship' is used in its sense of a leader for others to follow. This
chapter investigates the role of the planned shopping mall as a flagship destination
that can help in regenerating downtowns or act as magnets for growth in out-
of-town locations. The introductory section briefly considers the background to
shopping centres followed by what makes shopping malls attractive. The next
section considers the retail landscape and hierarchy using Central Place Theory
– or rather, a pragmatic and practical application of the principles. Evidence for
the flagship or magnet effect of shopping malls is presented using this framework.
Finally, a section on flagship shopping malls and regeneration speculates on the
ability of shopping malls to contribute towards attracting other businesses, tourists
and residents.

The background to shopping centres

The origins of shopping centres can be traced back directly to at least the ancient
agora or forum. In the UK, the Romans formalized the already-existing market
system. For example at what is now Leadenhall Street in London, there was a
large square 200 meters across with traders around the periphery and an area

in the centre for public leisure and socializing (Forshaw and Bergstrom 1983). Medieval times saw the growth of markets in England and Wales with nearly 3000 markets franchised in the thirteenth, fourteenth and fifteenth centuries, effectively putting a shopping location within a day's walk of anywhere in southern and central England (Gosling and Maitland 1976).

Shopping malls focusing on fashion and pleasure can be traced back to the sixteenth century in the UK when financial trader Thomas Gresham built what became the Royal Exchange with an atrium and a shopping gallery in the City (financial district) of London in 1568. Covent Garden later became London's most fashionable area, centred on Inigo Jones's piazza, a two-level gallery of small shops which opened in 1631 (Adburgham 1979; Forshaw and Bergstrom 1983). Covent Garden and the shopping galleries that appeared in European capitals set the scene for stylish early modern shopping (Walsh 2003). The development of planned shopping centres focusing on the shopping experience has progressed continuously in the UK ever since via nineteenth-century arcades such as the Burlington Arcade in London, opened in 1818 (MacKeith 1985).

With the growth of motor transport in the twentieth century came a desire for the increased pleasure of shopping traffic-free, both in pedestrianized streets (starting with Norwich in 1965) (Brambilla and Longo 1977) and covered shopping centres (for example the Bull Ring in Birmingham in 1964) (Davies and Bennison 1979).

Although the terminology is confusing, we consider a planned shopping centre or shopping mall to be 'an enclosed and managed shopping area – either in-town or otherwise – having a gross retail area of at least 5,000m^2' (based on Guy 1994). In recent decades, a number of regional (larger than 50,000m^2) and super-regional (larger than 100,000m^2) planned shopping malls have opened (Dennis 2004). Experience and leisure attractions are central to these, with, for example, Braehead Park's (Glasgow) 'three ice rinks, a maritime heritage centre, a hotel and ten restaurants' and Cribbs Causeway's (Bristol) 'ten screen cinema, bowling alley, a night-club [and] four restaurants' (Field 1997). The UK's largest and (according to Allegra 2002) 'most admired' super-regional shopping centre to date is Bluewater (Greenhithe, Kent) with almost 150,000m^2 gross lettable area (GLA). Leisure and lifestyle features include over 50 eating places, a boating lake, climbing wall, cycles and tandems, golf putting, discovery trail, Land Rover adventure zone, cinemas and spas, set in 20 hectares (50 acres) of landscaped parkland with seven lakes.

Planned shopping centres are an important topic for study, not least because they represent a substantial slice of the UK economy (7 per cent of Gross Domestic Product), jobs (over three-quarters of a million) and pension funds (Dennis 2004). In addition, this chapter presents evidence that planned shopping malls are half as attractive again to shoppers compared to unplanned shopping areas, offering increased potential for the flagship effect. In all there are approximately 280 planned shopping malls in the UK that comply with our definition – including more in-town ones than any other country (Allegra 2002; Howard 1997; Warnaby *et al.* 2005). Shoppers emphatically prefer to shop in a planned shopping centre when they have the chance. A survey of 4,760 shoppers indicated that 61 per cent preferred shopping centres compared to other locations such as retail parks and high streets (Allegra 2002). The main reasons stated for this preference concern one-stop comparison-shopping and protection from the weather. Planned shopping malls therefore have the potential to act as flagships for urban regeneration, as we will argue later in this chapter.

What makes shopping malls attractive?

In the 'retail landscape' section below, we cite evidence demonstrating that a shopping centre that includes popular retail stores will act as a magnet to draw in shoppers. But shops are not the only important aspect of attractiveness; rather, shops are a proxy measure of attractiveness. The effect occurs partly because shoppers are attracted to popular shops but also because top retailers and other service and entertainment providers prefer attractive shopping centres as locations for their stores. Dennis and Newman reported three studies for which they surveyed literature on the aspects of shopping locations most associated with shopper spending and verified these attributes in town and shopping mall questionnaire surveys (n = 865 total) (Dennis and Newman 2005; Dennis *et al*. 2006, 2007). The list of attributes that those authors consider to be most critical in making shopping malls attractive to shoppers (in approximate order of their degree of association with shopper spending) is reproduced in Table 6.1. Service and leisure aspects such as security, toilets, eating and drinking are represented alongside the shopping attributes like stores and products.

The retail landscape

In establishing a theory framework for geographic retail patterns, we turn first to Central Place Theory, based on the work of the German geographer, Christaller (1933) and economist, Losch (1940). The theory attempts to explain the hierarchy of varying retail provisions of places using classical (but unsustainable) economic assumptions such as that consumers will always shop at the nearest place selling the particular products that they want. On the other hand, we will argue that consumers shop at the locations that they find most attractive and that the most attractive shopping centres tend to draw in residential and business provision to the area – the flagship effect. This is the modification to the theory that we call 'Central Place Practice'.

Central Place Theory was once 'widely accepted by the planning profession as a model of retail organization' (O'Brien and Harris 1991) and has been described as an 'elegant and ... much maligned conceptualization (Brown 1992: 40). Classical Central Place Theory is useful to the study of flagship shopping malls as it aims to provide an explanation for the Retail hierarchy:

> We always find great numbers of central places of ... lesser importance and smaller size [selling a smaller range of frequently-purchased, lower value

Table 6.1 Attractiveness attributes of town and shopping centers most associated with shopper spending

Attribute	Source
Safety and security from crime and anti-social behavior	McGoldrick[1]
Wide selection of products	Finn[2]; Severin[3]
Quality of stores	Dennis; Finn; Severin
Helpfulness of staff	Dennis[4]; McGoldrick
Cleanliness of streets	Dennis
Shopper information/TV/video screens	Dennis and Newman[5]
Friendly, welcoming atmosphere	Dennis; McGoldrick; Severin
Availability of good toilets	Dennis; McGoldrick
Eating and drinking facilities	Dennis
Nice place to spend time	Dennis; McGoldrick
Indoor shopping	Dennis; McGoldrick
Other shoppers to be nice people	Dennis
General layout	Dennis; Severin
An 'In-place' to go (stylish)	McGoldrick
Availability of public seating	Dennis

1 McGoldrick and Thompson (1992); 2 Finn and Louvière (1996); 3 Severin *et al.* (2001); 4 Dennis *et al.* (2002); 5 Dennis and Newman (2005); Dennis *et al.* (2006).

consumer goods]... . The greater a town is [selling a greater range of higher value comparison goods], the smaller is the number ... in its respective category.

(Christaller 1933: 58)

Whilst claiming to define levels of the hierarchy according to the goods on offer, Christaller actually based his hierarchical system on population numbers (analogous to Reilly's (1931) approach to measuring attractiveness). Nevertheless, in southern Germany, 'especially for the plains ... where there are no natural barriers', the theory 'often determines with astonishing exactness, the locations of [towns of specific sizes]' (pages 190–1). Other authors have reported confirmatory evidence. Clark (1982) reported the applicability to market centres in southwest Iowa (USA); once again, an area where the map can be studied relatively free of the confusing effect of natural barriers. On the other hand, Dennis and associates (2002) questioned whether the static basis of Central Place Theory explains why, for example, (i) the biggest shopping mall in the world is located in a sparsely populated province of a sparsely populated country (West Edmonton Mall, Alberta, Canada – Finn and Louvière, 1996); or (ii) the shopping mall with the world's highest number of visitors – over 40 million – being located in a state of only 5 million inhabitants (Mall of America (MOA), Minnesota, USA – Feinberg *et al*, 2000). These are flagship malls and a practical modification to the theory is required to account for them.

Applying the original version of Central Place Theory has become more difficult and fallen into disuse on account of the growing complexity of retailing (Dawson 1979). In addition, classical Central Place Theory modelling is static, and cannot account for today's fast-changing retail landscape. Nevertheless, in a paper entitled 'Central Place Practice', Dennis and colleagues (2002) argued that the principles can be made dynamic and more relevant by the simple correction of including the attractiveness of the retail offer as a basic measure rather than the population number. The key to an understanding of the locations of central places is dynamic. For example, if entrepreneurs build shopping malls of sufficient attractiveness (which Finn and Feinberg have found to underlie the successes of the West Edmonton and MOA respectively), shoppers will come despite travelling long distances, making these the greatest flagship shopping malls in the world.

Guy (1998) criticizes Central Place Theory as relying on the notion that consumers would tend to buy the goods required at the nearest available location as 'clearly incorrect … since other determinants … are also important, … such as variety and price of goods; cleanliness, spaciousness and security of the centre; and quality and quantity of car parking', i.e. the attributes that researchers have found make shopping areas attractive. Rather than defining hierarchies based on nominal measures such as population or type of goods, a more rigorous approach is based on attractiveness. For example, Guy (1994) describes the retail hierarchy of Cardiff, UK, based on the use of m^2 selling area as a proxy measure of attractiveness. From the town centre core the hierarchy radiates progressively further out with greater numbers of district centres, neighbourhood centres and finally local centres. Cardiff comprises the basis of a long-term investigation into retail change. Guy (1999: 458) observed that 'the development of a few large new food stores coincided with the closure of several smaller … shops'. Guy describes these changes as 'the outcome of a general process of concentration', disproving any static nature of the retail hierarchy. This point is further illustrated in a report of the impact of the opening of the Merry Hill regional shopping mall (UK) on the adjacent town of Dudley. On completion of this flagship shopping mall in 1989, a number of major retailers closed their stores and 'in effect moved them to Merry Hill'. Many other shops closed and the premises were reoccupied by low quality and discount stores (Guy 1999). It is a key proposition of this chapter that towns such as Dudley that have suffered decline could have new life injected by improving the retail offer once again. The effect can be seen in near-by Birmingham city centre where the high-status refurbishment of the Bullring shopping mall is bringing in new shoppers from a huge catchment area of central England, acting as a flagship to spearhead the revitalization of the city.

Some data for the classification of shopping location attractiveness is available from the 'Goad score', a system used to classify the retail hierarchy of towns and shopping malls in the UK. Shopping locations are scored by the total numbers of specific non-food multiple retailers – those judged to be most attractive to shoppers (Reynolds and Schiller 1992 – the results are mapped in GoadPlans/ OXIRM 1991). Reynolds and Schiller examined the cumulative frequency of scores of UK shopping locations, fitting the divisions in the hierarchy to the gaps between size clusters where possible. The hierarchy classifications illustrate the increases in numbers of centres at the lower levels, broadly in line with the principles of Central Place Theory (whilst nevertheless, not strictly following Christaller's geometric progression but rather having a bias towards more of the larger centres than would be predicted by the theory). There were at that time seven National and Metropolitan cities plus six out-of-town shopping malls at a similar ranking in the hierarchy, all opened in 1990. Since that time, three more major out-of-town shopping malls have opened that are flagships in their own right (e.g. Bluewater in Kent), challenging the supremacy of the cities in retail attractiveness.

Mintel (1997) used a similar attractiveness measurement scale for shopping malls and towns based on numbers of retail outlets, scoring multiples higher than others and certain specific named retailers (those particularly attractive as magnets for shoppers) higher still. In the light of the many considerations that are known to inform shoppers' choices of shopping destinations, measuring shopping mall attractiveness in the manner of the Goad and Mintel scales initially appears trivial. Nevertheless, evidence in support can be inferred from at least two independent sources. First, Finn and Louvière (1996) investigated all 17 regional and community shopping centres in Edmonton, Canada. The fit of their models was 'highly significant, with [most] image item variance accounted for by the store tenant variables' such as the presence of particular major and discount department stores. Other characteristics have some significant effects, but the additional effect on image is 'generally rather small'. Specific anchor stores have a substantial impact on consumers' images of shopping malls, accounting for 'most of the variation in centre patronage'. Second, Feinberg and associates (2000) investigated the prediction of (US) mall patronage from attraction scales. In every case, the most significant variable was the rating of specific stores that most attract customers. Findings such as these are understandable when it is considered that the most attractive shopping malls will be expected to attract the most successful and popular retailers.

It therefore appears that the retail attractiveness hierarchy can be defined in terms of counts of retailers (particularly those most wanted by shoppers). The conclusion is that nothing influences the flagship status of a shopping mall more than the numbers and brands of shops that they contain. Therefore, these counts can be used to study the extent to which towns and malls act as flagships or magnets to draw in shoppers. Dennis and colleagues (2002) developed a measure of attractiveness based on questionnaire surveys of shoppers' views of the importance of various attributes, their ratings of a range of shopping malls and towns on these attributes and correlations with shopper spending at the locations. Interestingly, those authors found that, with the proviso that stores in malls are half as attractive again as the same stores in high streets, the measured attractiveness values correlate well with systems based on counts of the retail stores. Demonstrating the relationship, the regression between the measured attractiveness (the 'Brunel index') and the shops count ('Mintel' score) is illustrated in Figure 6.1. The attractiveness measure is significantly associated with shopping mall sales turnover and rental income. In sum, attractiveness is strongly linked to the presence of the most popular retailers and planned malls work much better as flagships than do unplanned shopping areas. The larger they are, the stronger the flagship effect. A summary of Dennis and colleagues' evidence for the effects on catchment areas follows.

Following from their version of 'central place practice' based on attractiveness as measured by the retail offer, Dennis and colleagues (2002) proposed:

> P1   Population and retail provision tend to cluster around central places defined on a matrix and
> P2   Catchments and the retail hierarchy follow the attractiveness of shopping and town centres.

Proposition P1 represents Christaller's 'classical' approach, whereas P2 follows from the more recent classification systems of (e.g.) Guy and Reynolds and Schiller. P1 and P2 are not necessarily mutually exclusive, but if P2 is accepted, a trend towards the redistribution of population around attractive shopping destinations can be predicted. P2 is therefore the 'flagship' proposition.

The distribution of towns in central England supports proposition P1. This is illustrated in Martin's (1982) study of shopping patterns around the market town of Northampton (UK). Martin demonstrated that Reilly's (1931) law can be used to define a notional catchment area boundary, by calculating (and joining) multiple break points of catchment areas between towns, based on their population (those with the highest populations having the wider catchment). Martin compared the calculated break points around Northampton and surrounding towns with a survey data contour (from 1,350 shoppers in the town's Grosvenor shopping mall) enclosing the area from which 90 per cent of Northampton's shoppers travel.

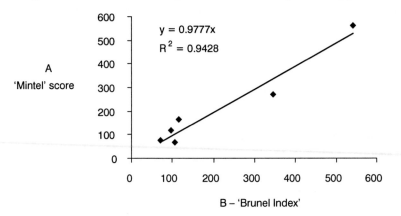

Figure 6.1   'Mintel' scores (A) of shopping centres (based on shops counts) vs. the Brunel measured attractiveness index (B) of the centres (based on questionnaire surveys – rescaled to the equivalent units of Mintel). The graph illustrates the close agreement between shoppers' assessments of the attractiveness of shopping destinations and the provision of retail stores (Source: Dennis *et al.* 2002)

As illustrated in Figure 6.2, Martin's calculated break points for Northampton produced a catchment boundary (dotted line) in reasonable agreement with survey results (dashed line). This is a quick method of estimating the catchment area, albeit with the disadvantage that there is only a single measure of attractiveness – population. Population must be an inappropriate measure for the attractiveness of the new town shopping mall of Milton Keynes, UK, which acts in effect in a similar way to an out-of-town flagship shopping mall for a large geographical catchment. Dennis and colleagues (2002) re-work the break point calculations for Northampton using the Goad attractiveness scores based on retailer counts (together with a revision of distance exponents which define the rate of decay of attractiveness with increasing distance) – the solid line in Figure 6.2. This fits the survey data well (index of fit = 0.82 – equivalent to the R^2 value – Hoel and Jesson 1982), indicating that in this case the retailer count method is at least as effective as the population method in predicting the catchment area of a town.

In line with P1, in the Northampton example, population appears to be clustered around central places defined on a matrix (classical Central Place Theory), with

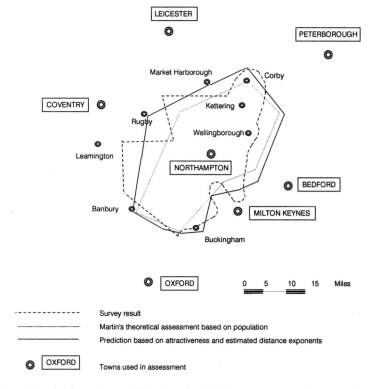

Figure 6.2 Catchment area of Northampton (UK), comparing the theoretical assessment from the Reilly/Converse 'law' vs. the survey result, with a plot based on Brunel index superimposed by the author (based on drive times and predicted distance exponents) (Sources: Dennis *et al.* (2002) and adapted from Martin (1982: 71))

catchment break points being defined by: (i) population (Reilly 1931); or (ii) retailer counts (Dennis *et al*. 2002). The population method is, however, completely useless in predicting the catchment of an out-of-town shopping mall. Accordingly, Dennis and colleagues (2002) demonstrated an alternative scenario. In line with the 'flagship' proposition P2, catchment areas and the retail hierarchy follow the attractiveness of shopping and town centres, which in turn are closely related to the provision of shops that shoppers consider to be attractive. This proposition holds not only for traditional towns and shopping, but also for new out-of-town shopping malls – thus extrapolating beyond the scope of P1.

Figure 6.3 is an example of catchment data for the Meadowhall out-of-town shopping mall, near Sheffield, UK, analyzed by Dennis and colleagues (2002) using survey data from Howard (1993). In directions other than Manchester (a major city west of Sheffield), the competing effect of the small towns is irrelevant and the predictions used population (Census 1991), drive time (Routemaster 1998) and estimated distance exponents. Figure 6.3 illustrates the catchment boundary calculated on this basis (for directions other than Manchester) compared with the boundary enclosing 90 per cent of respondents (estimated by the author from Howard's respondent 'spots').

In the direction of Manchester, however, the catchment area boundary is calculated from the break point using retailer counts as the measure of

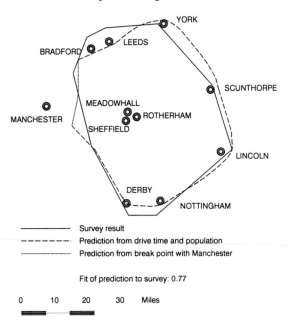

Figure 6.3   Catchment area of Meadowhall (UK), comparing the theoretical assessment predicted from distance exponents plus the 'break points' with Manchester based on retailer counts vs. the survey result (Sources: Dennis *et al.* (2002) using data from Howard (1993), Census of Population (1991) and Routemaster (1998))

attractiveness – and the fit is considerably closer to the survey result than is the standard calculation based on population. Illustrating the benefit of using retail counts as the basis of catchment predictions, we can also compare with drive time isochrones (which practitioners tend to favour for estimating catchment areas). The break point method based on retailer counts predicts the catchment boundary in the direction of Manchester more closely than does either the standard population calculation or the 50-minute isochrone (which encloses 90 per cent of the residences of the Meadowhall shoppers). The predictions using the break point method again fit the survey result well (Hoel and Jesson index of fit = 0.77). The Meadowhall results support the 'flagship' proposition P2 over P1: catchment areas and the retail hierarchy follow the provision of attractive shops, particularly in planned shopping centres.

The dynamic nature of shopping behaviour following the provision of shops can be further illustrated by comparing the famous, traditional English university cities of Oxford and Cambridge. These are of similar population size (and socio-demographic profile), but Cambridge's consumer non-food spending is estimated at 27 per cent more than that of Oxford. Reynolds and Schiller (1992) suggested that this is due to Cambridge's flagship effect of the Grafton Centre mall.

The evidence above demonstrates that shopping centre attractiveness is dynamic and that shoppers will tend to follow the development of flagship shopping centres. We also contend that residential and business development tends to follow the shoppers. In support of this principle, Des Rosiers and associates (1996, Canada) reported a positive correlation between house prices and proximity to shopping malls, illustrating the tendency of shopping malls to act as magnets or flagships for population residences. It is forecast that movements of population towards the new 'central places' will follow developments of flagship shopping malls. This effect is observed in the USA from as long ago as the 1970s (Gosling and Maitland 1976; Lion 1976). Young (1985) documented the US trend for residential and office development around 'suburban growth poles' centred on regional, out-of-town, flagship shopping malls, sometimes growing to 'minicities' of 300,000 to 500,000 residents (for example Brae, California). In these 'edge cities', flagship 'malls usually function as the village squares' (Garreau 1991).

The author contends that classical Central Place Theory can, in practice, be modified in the light of the 'flagship' proposition P2. Catchments and the retail hierarchy follow the attractiveness of shopping and town centres. And residential and business developments tend to follow the shoppers. This is a valuable finding as the provision of retail offerings can be modified by planners and developers, providing opportunities for regeneration, which we will turn to in the 'flagship shopping malls and regeneration' section below.

Shopping area image and environment

The section above set out the case for the attractiveness of shopping malls determining their influence as flagships. This section presents a theory framework, based on store and shopping centre atmosphere, image, emotion and environmental psychology. First, we briefly draw attention to literature on the atmosphere of the retail environment. Next, we review selected research on store and shopping mall image. The addition of emotion completes the framework.

The atmosphere of the retail environment: Turley has drawn attention to a number of studies indicating an association between store atmosphere, image and consumer purchasing behaviours (e.g. share of household spending, Hildebrandt 1998; store loyalty, Sirgy and Cocksun 1989) (Turley and Chebat 2002), concluding that the link between atmosphere and sales is 'very strong and robust' (Turley and Milliman 2000). Spies and co-workers (1997) reported a quasi-experiment, a comparison of two stores differing in atmosphere, but otherwise very similar. That study measured shoppers' moods before, during and after shopping. The authors concluded that pleasant atmosphere and better store image were associated with enhanced mood, goal attainment and higher spending on unplanned purchases.

For decades, retailers and researchers have been aware that shopping is not just a matter of obtaining tangible products but also about experience and enjoyment (see Martineau 1958). For example, Dennis *et al.* (2002) found that service and experience attributes were more associated with shoppers' choices of malls than were shops and merchandise. Enjoyment and entertainment have been demonstrated to be important benefits of shopping (e.g. Babin *et al.* 1994; Sit *et al.* 2003; Yoo *et al.* 1998), valued by consumers, and reflected in their spending (e.g. Donovan *et al.* 1994; Jones 1999; Machleit and Mantel 2001; Sherman and Smith 1987; Smith and Sherman 1993). There is considerable evidence to support the influence of atmosphere on shopper spending. Nevertheless, the intangible notion of atmosphere is notoriously difficult to measure. In the subsection below we consider the more concrete and measurable notion of the image of shopping malls.

Shopping mall image attributes: in our context, image is a concept used to mean an overall evaluation or rating of something used in such a way as to guide actions (Boulding 1956). Boulding used the example of a temperature controller. The sensor measures an 'image' of (e.g.) a furnace temperature. The controller uses that 'image' to guide an appropriate action such as the opening or closing of a fuel valve. Similarly, it is postulated that the shopper has an image of a mall that is used to guide the 'action' that is the main focus of the study, i.e. spending. Image includes both functional qualities and the 'aura of psychological attributes' (Martineau 1958: 47). For example, shoppers are more likely to buy from a store that is considered to have a positive image on considerations such as price, customer service or atmosphere. This is an approach that has been demonstrated to work in store image research over many years (e.g. Berry 1969; Lindquist 1974). Image measurements have demonstrated that a positive image of a mall is associated with greater patronage behaviour as malls with strong images have higher sales turnover, catchment area and rental income than those with poorer images (e.g. Dennis *et al.* 2002, Finn and Louvière 1996, Severin *et al.* 2001).

Although it may be a circular argument, our measure of mall image predominantly includes aspects that are related to spending. For example, 'general layout' is included as Dennis and colleagues (2002) found this to be the image attribute most correlated with spending at malls. The overall list of mall image attributes, in approximate ranked order of influence on spending, is reported in Table 6.1, above (based on Dennis and Newman (2005); Dennis *et al.* (2006; 2007); Finn and Louvière 1996; and Severin *et al.* 2001). As mentioned in the 'What makes shopping malls attractive' section above, these are the image attributes most associated with spending.

Emotion: Customers' pleasure, emotional responses, and as a result, impulse purchasing can increase in a store or mall with a pleasant atmosphere compared to an unpleasant one (Ang *et al.* 1997; Chebat and Michon 2003; Spies *et al.* 1997). The Chebat and Michon study is notable as one of very few concerning a shopping mall (in Canada) rather than stores. The effects of emotional aspects such as pleasure have been found to be additional to the cognitive image variables such as price, variety and quality of the merchandise (Donovan *et al.* 1994; Sherman and Smith 1987). Sherman and Smith (1987) conducted an investigation into shoppers' *actual* behaviour (rather than the more usual but less concrete behavioural intentions) and found shoppers' moods to be positively related to spending and number of items bought. Importantly, shoppers' moods can influence behaviour *after* the decision to shop has been made, and therefore extra spending may depend on *marketer-driven stimuli* (such as décor, music or aroma) (Sherman and Smith 1987). There is thus a weight of evidence that manipulable cues can influence mood and lead shoppers to spend more than intended.

Previous research on the links between emotion and shopping behaviour has been based on the stimulus-organism-response (SOR) framework of Mehrabian and Russell (1974). Their model holds that responses to an environment can be described by approach or avoidance behaviours, mediated by emotional states such as pleasure and arousal. In most studies, pleasure has clearly predicted response-shopping outcomes, but the influence of arousal has not been as clear-cut (e.g. Chebat and Michon 2003; Donovan *et al.* 1994). Pleasant atmospheres generate greater levels of arousal leading to greater approach behaviours such as spending. We expect that arousal influences approach behaviours through pleasure rather than directly (Huang 2004).

The concepts above of atmosphere, image and emotion all overlap but nevertheless provide a mainly consistent picture. A pleasant atmosphere, positive image and pleasure emotion positively influence shopping behaviour. Dennis and Newman have carried out a number of studies to develop an environmental psychology framework based on SOR, illustrated schematically in Figure 6.4 (Dennis and Newman 2005; Dennis *et al.* 2006; 2007). Their results are in line with previous findings such as Chebat and Michon (2003) that the cognitive construct of image mediates the effects of stimulus-emotion links. The results demonstrated that mall manager-controlled stimuli such as plasma TV/video screen captive audience networks (Dennis and Newman 2005; Dennis *et al.* 2006, 2007) and aroma (Chebat and Michon 2003) may positively influence shoppers' perceptions of store and product brand images not only directly but also through improving the image of the mall environment. Other researchers have found similar effects for (e.g.) music (Dubé and Morin 2001); colour (Belizzi *et al.*

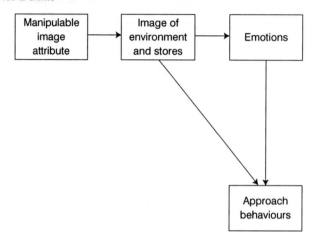

Figure 6.4 Schematic illustration of environmental psychology framework (Source: adapted from Dennis *et al.* 2007)

1983); lighting (Golden and Zimmerman 1986); and design (Baker *et al.* 2002). The potential effects of marketer-manipulated atmospheric stimuli may thus be effectively modelled, demonstrating the likely effectiveness of changes.

An atmospheric stimulus may increase shoppers' approach behaviours towards a mall. Dennis and colleagues (2002) reported that this can be a flagship or magnet effect that improves the attractiveness of the surrounding town of an in-town mall. The effect of the stimulus image variable is not direct but mediated by the image that shoppers hold of the mall or town environment. The effect of the stimulus on the image of stores and products acts through the image of the mall or town environment. Shoppers' images of the stores and products influence their approach behaviours such as spending directly but the strongest effect of image on approach behaviours is not direct; rather it is mediated by emotions, particularly pleasure. The stimulus can enhance shoppers' evaluations of other environment image variables and environment image can enhance evaluations of stores and products.

Results of environmental psychology studies such as those mentioned above have typically found that service, leisure and pleasure (alongside shops and products) are major variables in modelling shopping behaviour. Successful shopping malls generate an arousing and pleasant atmosphere that is key to shoppers enjoying the experience and shopping more. The previous section demonstrated that developers and planners can create flagship shopping centres that attract shoppers and investment. This section demonstrates that marketer-driven stimuli can increase the flagship effect. In-town shopping malls can increase the attractiveness of the town and increase shoppers' approach behaviours such as spending not only in the mall but also in the rest of the town shopping areas as well – part of the flagship effect. The following section considers the potential of shopping malls in urban regeneration.

Flagship shopping malls and regeneration

Planned shopping malls can leverage their attractiveness to act as flagships bringing people, pleasure and prosperity to an area – and not just to town centres. For example, West Edmonton Mall in Canada, mentioned earlier (arguably, the world's largest shopping mall, located outside a relatively small town), conjures up an image of a safe and happy environment with many shops and entertainment facilities (Gopal 2003). In the UK, some of the best-known out-of-town shopping malls (The Metro Centre near Gateshead and Lakeside near Thurrock (Mintel 1997); and Braehead near Glasgow (Lowe 2000)) have attempted to be reclassified for planning regulation purposes as 'in-town', on the grounds that residential development and other business such as retail parks have been attracted to the area. According to Lowe (2000), UK shopping malls are becoming 'the new high streets' in a trend even more marked than in the US.

The positive effects of malls are just as marked downtown as out-of-town. In many towns and cities, there is no organization to promote common interests like maintenance, security and parking. The planned shopping mall can bring those benefits; add entertainment and the shopping experience; and thus act as a magnet for business and residential development. For example, the refurbishment of the Wood Green Shopping City (UK) mall is a 'first step in urban regeneration' and 'a focus for the north London community and improve[s] the surrounding area' (*Retail Week*, 9 June, 2000). Reviewing nine case studies of attempts to revitalize rundown downtown areas, Gopal (2003) found that the three that are most successful (Times Square, New York, US; Bloor-Yorkville, Toronto, Canada; and Manchester City Centre, UK) followed a retail-led strategy. And, as mentioned above, the magnet effect of a planned shopping mall is half as much again as that of traditional high street retail (Dennis *et al.* 2002). Shopping malls deter vandalism and crime, making areas even more attractive to shoppers and attracting non-retail employment to an area (BDP 1992). Shopping malls can therefore act as flagships or magnets for regeneration, as part of a dynamic process in which planners and developers can take the initiative, leading to changes in population, expenditure, residence patterns and indeed bringing new life into run-down areas. Flagship shopping mall projects can function as 'a marketing tool ... to change ... downtown from images of dereliction, emptiness and crime to those of quality, entertainment and festivity' (Fitzsimmons 1995). The approach is formalized in the 'festival marketplace' concept, aiming to attract both local and out-of-town shoppers into downtown areas previously perceived as dirty and dangerous. For example, Maronick (2007) carried out a longitudinal study of Harbor Place festival market in Baltimore, USA. Harbor Place is designed to appeal to shopping tourists but it also attracts local residents for convenience shopping, dining and entertainment. In line with Dennis's and Newman's environmental psychology findings concerning the role of pleasure and arousal in choices of shopping destinations, festival marketplaces tend to offer not just shopping but also a wide choice of eating, drinking, music and live entertainment. As a second example, the Boston (US) Faneuil Marketplace opened in the late 1970s and drew in nearly 2 000,000m² of additional office space over a couple of decades (Gopal 2003). The approach is replicated in the UK, for example in Manchester's re-built Arndale Centre (Gopal 2003) and the Gunwharf Quays redevelopment at Portsmouth, which bring not only jobs, housing and shoppers but also tourists to the formerly-deprived inner city area (Cook 2004). Gunwharf Quays comprises approximately 40 per cent retail; 40 per cent leisure including cinema, bowling alley, comedy club, bars and restaurants; and 20 per cent offices, totalling 50,000 m². The waterside view and architecture are designed to communicate that the centre is a place to visit and relax, not just shop (Howard 2007).

Coverage in the popular press (e.g. *Daily Mail*, 15 July 1996: 'Shops Turn Corner In War On Malls'), anecdotal evidence from both sides of the Atlantic together with limited research findings (e.g. Dennis *et al*. 2006), indicates that many consumers love small traditional town centres with character. Researchers such as Hallsworth (e.g. 2000) have reported the attraction of such (UK) towns and their fight-back from decline. Despite the appeal of the traditional small towns, though, many of us tend to shop for preference at (planned) shopping centres. Easton Town Center, Columbus, Ohio, was one the first of a new breed of 'Lifestyle centre' focusing on leisure and entertainment combining the 'traditional' town centre with shopping centre and 'edge-of-town'. The sales area is approximately one-third shopping, one-third leisure and one-third eating and drinking. It is designed to look like a classic American main street, with public spaces, fountains, a street grid, and metered storefront parking. Easton comprises over 150,000m² of retail space built within a larger 5 km² development. From a visual perspective it appears to be a conventional-looking town with streets and a town square – but this is entirely a planned and managed shopping centre. There is even the 'edge-of-town' Wal-Mart and Home Depot (hardware shed) on the perimeter. Such shopping centres are adding pleasure to the experience of shopping and enhancing their flagship effect. By 2007 there were over 130 lifestyle centres in North America (up from only 30 in 2002), representing a luxury growth market at a time when more conventional malls were contracting. A CNN article (12 January 2005) captured the essence of the appeal: 'You'll see leather lounge chairs in place of hard plastic benches, and natural sunshine instead of fluorescent tube lighting. Rather than a maze of escalators, you'll find tree-lined streets and beautifully designed stress-relieving fountains'. Lifestyle centres in the US can act as flagships with, e.g. the Ridge Hill Village Center in Yonkers, NY, having not just retail stores but also a cinema, office space, hotel and conference centre, plus 800 units of rental housing. There is a Town Square at the centre, a 'public' space modelled on Gramercy Park (a small but famous, fenced-in private park in Manhattan, New York) (Blum 2005).

UK and European shopping centres are tending to move towards a greater emphasis on leisure and experience. For example, Bluewater in Kent, as mentioned earlier, and Xscape in Milton Keynes, which is more leisure than retail. Xscape has a snow slope, health club, multiplex cinema, bowling alley, bars, restaurants and 'urban sports and lifestyle' retail outlets over a total of just under 40,000m² (Howard 1997). Nevertheless, the UK has yet to embrace the concept on the same scale as in the US. One rare UK example of a lifestyle centre, Dickens Heath Village Centre, is a purpose built so-called Village Centre in Solihull, West Midlands (not to be confused with the term 'shopping village', which refers to discount-based 'factory' outlet centres in the UK). Dickens Heath Village Centre is an unusual (for the UK) mixed use development, described as: 'Live, shop, meet, dine and be inspired with conveniently located community amenities including a library, village hall, medical centre, village green and children's play area, perfectly complemented by a stylish shopping, leisure and residential environment' (Dickens Heath Village Centre, 2007). One reason why the US-style lifestyle centres are yet to take off as flagship shopping destinations in the UK, may be that many UK, in contrast to US, town centres already provide safe, attractive shopping and leisure facilities.

Before closing, it needs to be acknowledged that the flagship effects of shopping malls are not always universally welcomed, with some authors maintaining that they benefit the 'haves' at the expense of the 'have nots'. For example, Gunwharf Quays (Portsmouth, UK) is said to have brought the 'wrong sort' of jobs (described as 'McJobs'), housing (outside the affordable range for locals) and shoppers (prices too high for locals) (Cook 2004). Staeheli and Mitchell (2006) argued that DestiNY (upstate New York, US) has created a private community that diminishes the democratic public one in as much as only some kinds of people, behaviour and tenants are acceptable. The list of forbidden activities of one lifestyle centre (Desert Ridge in the US), for example, includes: 'non-commercial expressive activity' and 'excessive staring' (Blum 2005).

Whilst empirical cost/benefit evidence to resolve this issue is lacking, retail intervention may benefit low socio-economic status local residents even when they are not the target customers of the development, e.g. by providing access to more nutritious food (Wrigley *et al.* 2003) or the provision of community rooms for meetings and events (Staeheli and Mitchell 2006).

Concluding remarks

In the US and the UK, flagship shopping centres have predominantly taken the form of out-of-town malls, with prominent recent examples including DestiNY New York in the US and Bluewater, Kent, UK. Examples have been presented above, documenting the potential for flagship shopping centres to bring in residential and business developments over the medium to long term (e.g. Brae in the US and Lakeside in the UK). UK development of out-of-town malls is now severely restricted by legislation and planning guidance aimed at protecting the vitality and viability of town centres. This strategy appears to be working when carried out in conjunction with flagship shopping malls, as illustrated by the success of the refurbished Bull Ring in Birmingham in contributing to the regeneration of the area. The Bullring is a 110,000m² redevelopment comprising 150 shops, two department stores and 18 cafes and restaurants, serving a catchment of 4.3 million people. The redevelopment has been a flagship for the revitalization of the city centre. The overall £800 million partnership investment by the Birmingham

Alliance was the largest ever city centre regeneration in Europe, covering over 40 acres in the city centre and creating over 8,000 jobs (Virtual Brum, 2003).

Similarly, the Oracle centre in Reading has 65,000 m² including a significant proportion of leisure facilities with a multiplex cinema plus 20 bars and restaurants, along the riverside and the traditional high street in Reading town centre. This development has achieved the 'revitalization of a long neglected and derelict part of the city centre' (Howard 2007).

At the same time, the refurbishment of smaller in-town malls is contributing more modestly to the regeneration of smaller towns, with, for example, Uxbridge in West London having a new mall (The Chimes) completed early in this century plus a late twentieth century one (now known as the Mall Pavilions), refurbished in 2007. The owners of these two malls, together with major landlords, the police and local authority, Uxbridge College and Brunel University, as well as a number of community organizations in the town, contribute to Uxbridge Initiative, which aims to improve the town centre for everyone that uses it. Spearheaded by a Town Centre Manager, these joint efforts help to ensure that the town is an accessible, clean, safe, and welcoming place, a flagship town for the surrounding area, overwhelmingly preferred by local shoppers in preference to other shopping destinations in the area (Dennis *et al.* 2006).

The contribution of leisure facilities to the flagship status of UK shopping centres appears to be mixed. It has been claimed, for example, that health and fitness clubs 'are often included for planning reasons ... or to fill an otherwise awkward space, rather than through any perceived synergy' (Mitchell 2002). According to Howard (2007), the leisure revolution is really the food revolution, with bars and restaurants simply filling a gap left by declining retail. On the other hand, people who combine a meal with a shopping trip tend to spend more time and money in shops (Howard 1993). According to Howard (2007), this adds real synergy to the shopping centre offer, as opposed to 'retailtainment', which is of relatively marginal size in the UK. According to Howard (2007), leisure-led (in the tourism sense) flagship shopping centres such as Gunwharf Quays are very much the exception in the UK. This, perhaps, opens up the possibility of future UK developments along the lines of the US lifestyle centres.

In conclusion, the modified, dynamic version of Central Place practice combined with environmental psychology together explain the flagship effects of those shopping malls that provide attractive shopping, entertainment and dining. Whether for a town, city, suburb or green field, the planned shopping mall with leisure and especially food and drink provision can act as a flagship and a magnet for the development and renewal of jobs, homes and community activities wanted by people.

7 'From dome to dome'

Exploring cultural flagships and their contribution to achieving regeneration goals

Debi Hayes

Introduction

This chapter examines the role of cultural flagships in relation to regeneration and discusses to what extent they create a legacy with the urban landscape and its communities. It demonstrates the necessity of having a clear vision and policy from the outset and the importance of stable support from stakeholders who align with the vision. The development of a successful cultural flagship also highlights the need to manage media relationships since their coverage of the project is influential in shaping public perceptions of the project's legacy.

The case studies of the Eden Project and Millennium Dome illustrate two contrasting approaches. The visionary focus of the founder of the Eden Project was instrumental to its success, whereas the lack of vision, constantly changing rationale and shifting stakeholder constituencies contributed to the perceived failure of the Millennium Dome. A vision of the future gives a purpose to the development and to ensure effective implementation it must be shared by key stakeholders. The relative fortunes of the Eden Project and the Millennium Dome exemplify the need for active support and high level of involvement over and above mere acceptance. In addition, this chapter demonstrates the extent to which education, learning and entertainment contribute to realization of these two contrasting projects.

Types and dimensions of cultural flagships

A flagship development is a 'development in its own right, which may or may not be self-sustaining; a marshalling point for further investment; a marketing tool for an area or city' (Smyth 1994: 4–5). This broadly commercial perspective alone raises a number of strategic issues. The flagship will have a physical presence but it will also have some symbolic function. Its geographical scope extends from a local influence to an entire metropolitan area or city. Its position as an element of a conscious marketing strategy may be to communicate urban regeneration through formal promotional planning, to advertise the city as a place for others to invest or spend. It can create demand for inward investment, should deliver the required benefits to attract investment and consumption and may be a fundamental tool to stimulate the local economy. Flagship projects are 'significant, high profile developments that play an influential and catalytic role in urban regeneration, which can be justified if they attract other investment' (Bianchini *et al*. 1992).

Cultural flagship is a term used to define buildings, structures, specific areas and neighbourhoods in a city, often referred to as Cultural Quarters, which are at heart, cultural entities, and which house visual art, design, music, film, dance and drama industries. Of intrinsic cultural value themselves, they very often have a significant value as a visitor attraction for a whole area or city, becoming honeypots for tourism and providing facilities to stimulate or enhance the potential of cultural tourism (Richards 1999). In some cases they act as a magnet for creative leaders to work or live in a locality (Hospers and Van Dalm 2005) and at the very least, flagship buildings give an area an appealing sense of quality (Miles 2005).

Commercial and cultural flagships

Commercial flagships are concerned with consumption of products, leisure, images and spaces and the main beneficiaries are their owners. Cultural flagships on the other hand, are expected to have a broad range of stakeholder constituencies, including the local community who may have competing vested interests in the project's long-term success. These developments should relate to their stakeholders' cultural priorities, inspire and stimulate cultural pride and participation as well as provide a sense of identity for an area. When they fail to do so it is often the consequence of the need to compromise between the multiplicity of interests.

Cultural flagships must connect with the region, through either its history, or values. The cultural flagship can be typified by its 'celebratory' purpose, providing a focal point which connects a person or activity with a place or possibly a moment in time. These flagships could have developed organically as a place with meaning for a community that, over time, achieves an iconic status. Theatres may perform such a role in celebrating ideological and creative aspirations. Joan Littlewood's Theatre Royal in Stratford, London, and the Theatre in the Round at Stoke on Trent, consciously locate place with their founding lights, Joan Littlewood and Peter Cheeseman. The Citizen's Theatre in Glasgow deliberately identifies itself with the community. The flagship can have a less participative function, and still form an important focus for the community. The Cutty Sark is a distinctive presence in Greenwich that defines the place in contrast with the nearby Maritime museum. Celebration of a life or event can symbolize the identity and aspirations of a region. The Lowry Centre performs such a role for Salford. Communities need not just be local communities but communities of practitioners or professionals, exemplified by St Ives's community of artists, or the Bloomsbury Group at Charleston. Further, a gallery or exhibition space or festival could be a flagship for an artistic movement or style, or individual influential artists.

The cultural flagship's emphasis on historical connections (Zukin 1995) raises issues of authenticity and contested space. The Globe Theatre is a successful manifestation of Sam Wanamaker's vision to reconstruct this theatrical space to encourage public celebration of Shakespeare. The Globe is a showpiece, a place of homage to Shakespeare; the *Cutty Sark* ship is similarly evocative of the maritime history, and neither need to be authentic. These flagships are socially constructed and through their symbolic capital, they provide a focal point for commemorating and celebrating the past. Moreover the celebration of the past through its location, can relate to people whose activities are scarcely known. The heritage industry uses Stonehenge as a cultural flagship to showcase the achievements of pre-historic ancestors; the pyramids visually define Egyptian civilization. Cultural flagships can have a specific temporal dimension (Wynne 1992; Pratt 1997; Deffner 2000). Time and culture are not constraints but are viewed as a resource in this context. Celebrating the consciousness of a moment in time, the Crystal Palace, the Eiffel Tower, or the London Eye, relate to mega-events, and their associated hopes and aspirations.

The function of city marketing and branding, what Evans (2003) describes as the 'hard branding' of the cultural city, reduces the distinction between cultural and commercial flagships (Landry 2000). The development of a cultural flagship may be built to symbolize the brand values or core message that the city wishes to communicate, including 'intelligent', 'educated', 'green' or 'creative'. However, while commercial flagship objectives are fairly coherent and ultimately concerned with strengthening brand image and identity particularly in the mind of the target audience, cultural flagships are expected to deliver a host of social, economic benefits in addition to branding place and space. Increasingly proponents of a cultural flagship would be expected to produce a complete business case that embraces projected visitor numbers, and economic and social impacts, using a range of social indicators.

Finally, the role of government policy should be recognized in the deliberate creation and support of prestigious national showcases for culture and the Arts. The Louvre is a national institution, and the Royal Opera House represents a flagship of artistic excellence supported by state funding. The National Theatre in London was the result of government planning for the South Bank as a showcase for the arts, and a perceived need for a 'state' theatre. The intervention of planners and politicans in regeneration projects often increases their complexity, since this introduces an ideological dimension and it is necessary to mediate the interests of the various stakeholder groups.

Cultural flagships and urban regeneration

As cities have grown over the ages, it has become increasingly difficult to find free space to construct large, impressive, cultural buildings unless on the edge of the city, on the site of an existing building, or in a redevelopment area. Culturally significant buildings need space but also funding. The visual sense too is important, since the main contribution of cultural policies to urban regeneration is in the construction of urban images able to attract visitors. Cultural flagship projects like the Burrell Collection, and the Antigone district in Marseilles have become powerful physical symbols of urban renaissance

(Bianchini 1995). A cultural capital will be inspired by a vision of the city as a place where art, culture and design are omnipresent (Zukin 1995). Therefore it is not surprising that today's cultural flagship is often a vital part of a larger vision, which encompasses regeneration.

'Regeneration' itself has been defined as transformation of a residential, commercial or open space that has displayed the symptoms of environmental, social and cultural decline (Evans 2004). Evans relates culture to regeneration at three levels of integration: first, cultural-led regeneration where culture is used as the catalyst and engine, typically through flagship projects. Second, cultural regeneration describes a situation where culture is planned and integrated into an area strategy along with environmental, social and other activities. The third scenario fails to integrate culture and regeneration into the master planning stage or strategy; the two are kept separate. The first of these describes urban policy during the 1990s, as it turned towards 'rebuilding the city' through large and iconic buildings. These projects emanated from the belief that new urban developments could greatly improve a city's outlook. Large-scale projects and place marketing arose from the planners' belief that they would help future growth and attract investment, and since urban development contributes to local government finance, it is not surprising to find that the state has played a very important role in significant projects (Swyngedouw *et al.* 2002). In this way the Scottish Development Agency and the Glasgow District Council worked together to transform Glasgow into a successful post industrial city, using place marketing and cultural projects in order to attract external funding (Mooney 2004).

Carriere and Demaziere (2003) writing about Lisbon's EXPO 98, refer to a 'recipe' followed by most large flagship projects, 'the reliance on a mega project' (p. 78) in order to market the site internationally, the attempted restructuring of a large urban area which was previously rundown and the involvement of significant private investment. The United States saw much of this type of urban flagship development, where powerful physical symbols could be spectacular too. A leader in urban regeneration policies from the development of Baltimore in1970, by the end of the century entertainment-led themes led to a 'fantasy city' style of development (Hannigan 2004). Public private partnerships contributed to the development of 'big box' projects that blended commerce, arts and entertainment. Such partnerships are not exclusively North American as evidenced by the Rhonda Pop factory success in the UK (Aitcheson and Evans 2003).

However, regeneration may blend prestigious buildings with smaller scale projects. Barcelona is cited as a model for the design, planning and regeneration of urban spaces, where urban projects are combined with small-scale improvements of squares and streets' (Bianchini, 1995). Grand flagship projects can be planned and co-exist with small local improvements so that tourists and the local community both benefit. The city could undoubtedly be used as a model for the renewal and redevelopment of its nuclei, even if it cannot so easily be transferred to the more dispersed form of urban planning practised by North American and some European cities (Monclus 2003).

Creativity provides a second perspective on the role of cultural flagships in urban regeneration. Landry discusses how the 'creative milieu' of a city can be triggered through the four activities of place marketing, a statement of intent, branded concepts and hallmark events (Landry 2000; Deffner and Labrianidis 2005). Cities can invest in cultural flagship projects in order to attract the most creatively talented people, who seek out places that are in tune with them. However, as Florida (2002) demonstrates, creative people tend to be less interested in conventional flagship projects and their synthetic and commercialized environments. Creatives do not want finished places but rather 'authentic places that aren't finished yet, places where you can add something of your own' (Hospers and Dalm 2005:10). A cultural incubator approach to regeneration typified by cultural clustering, and the creation of cultural districts or quarters to stimulate the local community engagement and economic development can foster more authentic engagement with cultural activities (Hannigan 2004).

Nevertheless the creative process of regeneration is at its most visible in iconic buildings and locations, and their integration into cultural urban regeneration has attracted considerable attention. Bilbao is a pre-eminent example of a city where signature architecture is used as the focus for an urban redevelopment. Evans (2003) believes that the Guggenheim museum, the centrepiece of the city's post-industrial development, is the first iconic building that 're-imaged an entire city' (p. 432). Many flagship buildings are designed in the context of a waterfront regeneration project, so that they can be seen from both within and from outside the city, acting as a beacon in each case, and evident in UK projects on the Tyne at Gateshead, the Tate Modern on the South Bank in London, and the Cardiff Bay area. However the transferability of an iconic building's approach between regenerational strategies requires careful evaluation. Simply because a successful policy works in one city does not mean that this can be replicated in another city or in another country (Miles 2005).

The success of the building, and indeed the regenerated area is often seen in its capacity to increase tourist visits and expenditure. The Guggenheim's significant positive impact on Bilbao as a mass cultural tourism attraction, has been observed almost since its inception (Plaza 2000; Evans 2003). However, it also raises concerns about its long term attractiveness, 'over-emphasis on the architectural aspects of the project' (Carrière and Demazière 2003: 71) and for the lack of communication with the local community. While the iconic building may indeed act as a magnet for visitors and tourists it is often questionable whether it improves the quality of life for existing residents (Dicks 2003; Miles 2005). Evans (2005) highlights the problem of towns and cities that believe they can achieve cultural city status by constructing their own iconic projects not because they wish to improve a particular area or provide specified community benefits but more from a desire to keep up with their peers.

Many grand schemes involving the construction of an iconic building attract a proportion of funding from the public sector in the knowledge that the publicity about the proposed structure is likely to entice private sector finance too. It is crucially important that the cultural flagship is supported from the earliest planning stage right through to its ongoing role in the area and with the local community. This will require a vision for the project so as to provide a focus and sense of purpose. Nevertheless, such visible and high stake projects can attract a great deal of political debate and conflicting pressures on the direction of the project. The Vienna 'Museumsquartier' was initially envisioned as an urban regeneration project but then, recognizing the challenges from other cities in Europe, turned to a more ambitious cultural flagship strategy (see chapter 8). Ultimately the inauguration of the project 'was accompanied by a professional image campaign, embracing the internet, print media, urban events and political speeches' (De Frantz 2005: 53). Conflicting pressures in the regeneration of the Bristol waterfront project combined inadequate design concept, weak leadership, and voluble opposition that resulted in a failed solution (Bassett *et al.* 2002). In both cases there is an evident tendency to evaluate the cultural flagship through images of what Evans (2005) describes as a 'blue sky background to a person-free building' which concentrates on the aesthetics of the building rather than any regeneration effects or outcomes. In both cases too, image formulation and image communication play a crucial role in the city marketing mix (Kavaratzis 2004).

Sustainability

In examining the sustainability of flagship cultural projects, Evans (2005) highlights the need to ensure that developers and project managers learn best practice from successful schemes, which have managed to achieve the necessary integration of the buildings with the community and the locale. Unrealistic expectations often accompany new cultural regeneration schemes, and the combination of a number of funding opportunities, lottery, European grants and local government, has led to a possible over-supply of cultural attractions.

The debate continues to grow over whether the benefits of cultural-led regeneration are actually real in terms of being measurable. Miles and Paddison (2005) question the long-lasting impact of cultural-led regeneration. Evans believes that culture-led regeneration schemes are often conceived without due regard for evidence as to whether they will work and the evidence is hard to find. The impact of commercial forces and private sector investment in sustaining cultural regeneration, was acknowledged by the DCMS (Aitcheson and Evans 2003). Competition between cultural icons can be an important stimulus to sustainability. The global impact of major cultural initiatives can be measured by the reaction of cultural competitors (Evans, 2003), the result being seen in the refurbishment of MoMA in New York after the very successful opening of the Tate Modern in London and in Glasgow's 2004 city marketing programme.

However, cities and cultural organizations requiring substantial funding are increasingly being asked for evidence that cultural regeneration works to improve poor neighbourhoods. Miles (2005) believes that it is people's sense of belonging that is crucial to success or otherwise of flagship iconic projects along with help for the community to make the most of the opportunities afforded by the project.

The Glasgow 'renaissance' arguably masks the continuing problems of poverty and unemployment in the city (Mooney 2004). Subsequent DCMS consultation (2007) records a general feeling that too much emphasis was put on buildings and more focus was required on smaller scale community based schemes.

Evans (2005) points to a number of developments that have either not included the local community in the planning phase or have met with resistance from the community and have not been seen to deliver sustained benefits. Evans (2005) comments that 'some communities in self-styled cultural cities tend to remain' outside because they think the newly created buildings or areas are not for them. Too often regeneration projects do not take into account the local arts and cultural groups due to the differing perspectives of those involved in the regeneration. There is often a tension between the local community and developers concerning 'improvement' strategy. Developers usually opt for new-build solutions, whereas communities often have attachment to existing landmarks and structures, therefore 'revitalization' or 'refurbishment' strategies are their preferred approach. In this respect the global nature of the leading architectural practices and arts organizations can actually contribute towards dividing rather than integrating communities.

Criteria for evaluating cultural flagships

These perspectives frame the problems facing the effective evaluation of flagship cultural projects. The DCMS in measuring the benefits, defined them as the added value that culture brings to delivering key social policy objectives, and noted that it is 'very difficult to measure hard outcomes and collect quantitative evidence for culture's benefits'. Their proposals included changes in land values, economic stability of an area, reduction in anti-social behaviour; and outcomes of resident surveys. Evans (2005) summarizes the need for both hard and soft evidence, and recommends a number of methods including advocacy and promotion, and project assessment and project evaluation, programme evaluation, performance indicators, impact assessment and longitudinal studies.

The value of the cultural flagship can be highly contested depending on the perspective of the stakeholder and judgements about the contribution to cultural or regeneration goals. They are also subject to a temporal dimension, as early judgements about the project's value can change over time. This raises issues about the selection of value systems, evaluation criteria, and the acquisition of evidence – approaches suggested in the literature are summarized in Table 7.1.

In an early review of cultural flagship developments, Smyth provided important criteria from a planning perspective which examines stakeholder responsibilities and identifies key project dimensions (column 1). Subsequent evaluative guidelines or successful cultural intervention in regeneration and renewal projects placed more emphasis on local community engagement (DCMS 1999: 8; Aitcheson and Evans 2003) and these are shown in column 2. As cultural regeneration has gained momentum, the assessment of a wider range of projects has been possible, and four further dimensions have been identified. The first is the vision behind the project and which for its future success must be evident at the outset of scheme.

Table 7.1 Cultural flagship evaluation criteria

The planning perspective, Smyth 1994	Community-led cultural regeneration projects, Aitcheson and Evans 2003	Design rationale, Hayes
• An overt strategy • Strategy and management may be project, area or city based • Success is not contingent on public versus private engagement • All organisations must take responsibility for the impact of their development • Management of policy formulation, and the implementation and evaluation process • Marketing concerns bringing together supply and demand factors • Design and management should arise from social relations in the affected areas and those envisaged for the area • Political legitimacy and economic necessity will demand participation of local residents and other interests	• Valuing diversity • Embedding local control • Supporting local commitment • Promoting equitable partnerships • Defining common objectives in relation to actual needs • Pursuing quality across the spectrum • Connecting with the mainstream of art and sporting activities • Recognising the importance of commercial-led investment • Balancing flagship projects with smaller initiatives • Working to develop existing skills bases and/or cultural interests	• Vision needs to be articulated at outset • The design is critical for visibility, promotion and to create a distinctive identity • Audiences need to be defined in terms of visitors and local communities • Fit with history, traditions and geo-demographics of the area

The design of the building will increase the project's visibility in the widest sense, and have a promotional function as a distinctive place to showcase one or more aspects of culture. The flagship will have increased the visitor and tourism capacity of the area, with the aim of existing with and supporting visitors from outside the immediate community. Finally, the project will have a good fit with its location arising from geo-demographic assessment of the area.

In order to test out the value of these criteria two projects have been compared. While being very different entities in some ways, they also share similarities (see Table 7.2). They also make a significant contribution to the debate concerning the educational function of museums and their relationship with the leisure industry. While the advantages of a closer involvement with the heritage industry are obvious in terms of being placed on the tourist map, the disadvantages are more subtle involving a balance between providing a sustainable return on investment, but also retaining the integrity of purpose evident at their inception.

The Eden Project

The original concept for Eden emerged in 1994, when former record producer Tim Smit was inspired by the complete absence of any aesthetic or cultural vision left by the earlier Ebbw Vale garden festival. The lesson from this and other garden festivals, was that they were too transitory and that local communities needed the legacy of a permanent infrastructure (Smit 2001).The Eden Project therefore, aimed to capture visitors' imagination, and to provide as much information and stimulation as people wanted, while avoiding stuffy and over-scientific language. Eden would be fun and brave in facing up to global environmental problems. It would have a core message pervading the whole organization, and aim to produce a 'total experience' for the visitor already familiar with the 'superstar museum' (Frey 1998).

The project's success began with the vision and enthusiasm of its leader, Smit, who 'chased his dream' and the choice of title, Eden Project, was very well accepted. Initially he worked with a small knowledgeable team, which although it expanded during the project development, remained both focused and tightly knit. Smit used words like 'mission' and 'adventure' to move the project forward, and dismissed the idea of an exit strategy.

Table 7.2 Millennium Dome and Eden Project: shared features

• Conceived as cultural flagships acting as an attraction for their local area	• Designed as semi-permanent domes, with plastic panelled structures
• Announced and constructed in a similar timeframe, starting in 1994	• Constructed on brownfield sites on the edge of established areas of tourism
• Serving immediate communities that were socially and economically disadvantaged	• Continue to fulfil dual roles as educational and recreational attractions

It benefited from good judgement of the funding risks and perseverance in the early stages to keep the project moving forward. The project was particularly fortunate to persuade a signature architect, Nicholas Grimshaw, and the rest of the development team, including consulting engineers, Ove Arup, to initially work on the project for nothing. These factors enabled the team to put together a submission for Millennium Commission funding. The legacy of this commitment was manifested in 2007 by its selection as the best UK building of the past twenty years by the British Construction Industry.

The stakeholders included influential friends and supporters but also local support, which proved to be crucial. Expert environmentalists and conservationists were engaged at an early stage. Many funding bodies too, were won over. In order to generate interest in the Eden Project, the public and potential funding partners were able to view it as it took shape and the marketing staff deliberately tried to create a sense of wonder and drama about the landscape and the scale of the development (Blewitt 2004), and the whole team engaged with the media throughout.

The project was financed through a Trust to secure Millennium funding from the recently established Millennium Commission (MC). Initially the project team applied for a maximum grant of £50 million leaving £100 million to be found from sponsors. Implicit in this was the need to take leaps of faith while waiting for funding decisions. The project's backers realized they needed to obtain secure commercial backing and embed local control (Aitcheson and Evans 2003).

The location was identified as very important at a very early stage in the planning process. The team wanted to create a landscape that gave the impression of a civilization newly discovered, so the first step should be to identify a site, and the second to work on the design. However to start with, the designers had to work using the 'wrong' site, until the team's contacts found the 'right' site, and subsequently created a completely new feature from a redundant space, a former clay pit. From the beginning, the project established wide environmental and educational aims and objectives. In this, it was assisted by its timing, as awareness of sustainability and climate change issues were beginning to establish themselves in the public consciousness. Moreover the project was allowed to evolve, from an initial concept of exhibiting plants from around the world, into grand displays relating the plant world to human life. Blewitt subsequently described it as 'both a major tourist attraction and striking learning environment' (2004: 175). As neither a theme park, nor open air museum, nor botanical garden, it was 'unique'.

Eden offers multiple perspectives that are on the whole complementary citing tourism, commercialism, environmental management, consumerism, enterprise, regeneration, globalization, conservation, entertainment sustainability, public relations and education. This multi-layered effect of the project, in providing a little information and a lot of entertainment for some and a large amount of in-depth information and less entertainment for the more serious visitor is one of the project's great strengths (Blewitt 2004). However, problems arose from the discrepancies between the projected image and the reality. The vision, architecture and scale of the development were praised but the follow-through for some critics was questioned. Kingsnorth (2001) described it as containing 'very big greenhouses full of occasionally interesting plants pretending to be something far more'. Russell (2002) found that the project 'lacked a clear educational vision' and provided 'cutesy edutainment'. In other words, for some critics, the project lacked intellectual gravitas.

Nevertheless it had created a completely new feature from a redundant, ugly space. From the beginning it established wide environmental and educational aims and objectives. In this, it was assisted by its timing, as awareness of sustainability and climate change issues were beginning to establish themselves in the public consciousness. Moreover the project was allowed to evolve, from an initial concept of exhibiting plants from around the world, into grand displays relating the plant world to human life. Its balance between husbandry and stewardship made it an enduring symbol of regeneration, ecological awareness and sustainable development (Smith 2007).

The Millennium Dome

In the same year as the Eden Project was conceived, Lord Brooke, a government minister, proposed the idea of a millennium festival with a large exhibition. The concept would be comparable to the 1851 Great Exhibition and the Festival of Britain 1951. It was to provide a centrepiece for the nation's Millennium celebrations by opening on New Year's Eve and running through the year 2000 (NAO 2000), and reference was made to the purpose and design of another great dome, in St Paul's cathedral (House of Lords debates 29 November 2000). Decisions about the Millennium Dome were taken at Cabinet level and the site was chosen in February 1996 (House of Lords 2000). It would occupy a 130-acre site on former industrial land on the Greenwich peninsula, and was designed to be the largest domed structure in the world, centred around performance spaces, exhibitions and twelve time zones.

The vision for the new Dome was less evident (see Table 7.3). It firmly looked to the future, from its forward-looking design, to its use of the latest technologies in the futuristic exhibitions (Philips 2004). Planning permission was requested for exhibition use, but there was clearly a view of a longer term legacy. However, McGuigan and Gilmore (2002) believe the lack of clear direction and the varied nature of the attraction 'part trade fair, part theme park, part museum' tended to confuse visitors as to the Dome's purpose. Urry (2002) held it up as a good example of 'edu-tainment', but while many enjoyed it, it was difficult to define its function. Even in a mass of facts and figures and design and build information from the early planning days, there was no mention of the purpose of the dome other than it would be 'the highest profile event in the UK in the year 2000'(Green 2000). The design was undertaken by a leading architectural practice under the direction of Richard Rogers. Even so, its necessary compartmentalization detracted from the fundamental features of a traditional dome: the circle and its meaning, and the unifying purpose of the structure and the location of the site on which it was built, were missing (Markus 1999).

The stakeholders were led by the government, and from the outset the idea was driven by politicians, rather than commercial or cultural interests. The New Millennium Experience Company (NMEC) was established as a limited company wholly owned by the Government, to build, fit out and run the Dome. Although it was originally intended that the private sector would deliver the project, in 1996 it became clear that they wouldn't accept the risk and the project continued to be funded by the public sector (House of Commons 2000). In October 1998 the auditors drew attention to the inherent uncertainty of the company's ability to achieve the project within current financial projections and MPs were determined that the project should not receive more funding than the agreed £449 million (White 1999).

Its longer term failure can be found in the diversity of stakeholders' interests and lack of clarity about its direction. As a prestigious government project, it subsequently became the subject of considerable interference in its direction and organization. Complex organizational arrangements were put in place, with three distinct bodies, three accounting officers and two ministers (exercising three distinct roles), a chairman, a chief executive, a board of directors, and nine millennium commissioners (House of Lords debate, 29 November 2000). Not surprisingly David James, the executive chairman from September 2000, attributed the problems to 'confused priorities, lack of a clear plan for the contents, weak financial controls and the wrong management structure.'

The project was seen to be an early example of the public – private partnership sought by the Labour government (Philips 2004). It was planned to be funded from three sources: the National Lottery, visitors, and commercial sponsors (NAO 2000). However, the company lacked sufficient operational expertise. There were inadequacies in the financial systems which were manifest in the inability to produce reliable forecasts to track contractual commitments, and to quantify the extent of liabilities (NAO 2000). Political euphoria overturned sound analysis of projected visitor numbers; 12 million visitors had been forecast, well beyond any other comparable attraction, and eventually the site achieved 5 million. It was thought that it would be promoted but there would be significant word of mouth and free marketing because the public would be fascinated by the idea of the Dome and its exhibitions. This led to a low marketing budget. In the end, 1 million schoolchildren were given free access to the Dome, leading to estimated revenue losses of some £7 million.

Moreover, sponsorship income did not achieve the expected levels. Managers had failed to draw up any contingency plans to cover the shortfall in income (Bourn 2001). The major sponsors were closely linked to thematic zones, for example Boots with the Body Zone, and Tesco with the Learning Zone. Since they were able to make their sponsorship payments in cash, in kind or in 'enhancement', it was very difficult to estimate accurately total sponsorship. Eventually it produced £150 million.of the total expenditure of around £800 million (House of Commons 2000; McGuigan and Gilmore 2002). Nevertheless McGuigan and Gilmore (2002) believed that the dominance of corporate sponsorship was a significant factor in the perceived failure of the Dome and that, ultimately, the role of sponsorship was more important to the government ideologically than financially (BBC News 2001).

The Dome was beset, too, by the weak implementation of its communications strategy. Even the launch event was mismanaged, as the House of Lords commented, '... on 31st December it was not a good idea to keep newspaper editors, with their guests, standing in the drizzle at an Underground station so that they missed the Dome's opening party. After that debacle the press never gave the Dome a chance' (House of Lords 2000).

By November 2000 it was noted that the Dome project had been the subject of sustained and detailed parliamentary scrutiny throughout its life, comprising 1,200 parliamentary questions, eight debates, five select committee inquiries, a National Audit Office (NAO) report and a Parliamentary Accounts Committee inquiry. Although acknowledging all that the Dome had achieved, Lord Falconer stated that 'in truth the Dome has not lived up to the expectations of those who supported and initiated it' (see Table 7.3). He believed this was as a result of the extra lottery funding over budget that had to be made available (£179 million). He cited the conclusion of the NAO report: 'The main cause of the financial difficulties is the failure to achieve the visitor numbers and the income required' (House of Lords 2000). In terms of stakeholder support it was noted that there had been insufficient public consultation in advance about the project generally and specifically about the content of the Dome (House of Lords 2000).

Nevertheless the Dome recorded a number of achievements. It opened on time and received a very large number of visitors, with some 99,453 people visiting it in the first week of opening (National Audit Office 2000). The majority of visitors to the Dome enjoyed their experience, with satisfaction ratings of 84 per cent in April to 90 per cent in October, towards the end of the attraction's life (McGuigan and Gilmore 2002). Contrasting it with the Festival of Britain which lauded the country's postwar achievements with the Millennium Dome, Philips (2004) believed it had honoured commerce and 'validated private rather than public enterprise'.

Conclusion

One of the main themes to emerge from the analysis of the two projects is the necessity of a holistic view of the impact of the proposed creations in terms of the

Table 7.3 Shortcomings of the Millennium Dome

• Link between flagship and creative industries	• Property-led regeneration at the cost of artists' workplaces
• Regenerative trickle-down claims are over exaggerated	• Often built at the expense of local/ regional cultural services
• Compelling proposition	• Failure to capture public imagination
• Failure to attract key constituencies of support	• Media and communications (poor mediation)

Table 7.4 Evaluation of the Millennium Dome and Eden Project

Evaluation criteria	Millennium Dome	Eden Project
Vision	• Confused and lacking clarity • Building-led • No planning for long term sustainablity • Government sponsors from both major parties • Individuals changed during planning phase • No real continuity or champion • Critics by contrast were vocal and maintained momentum • Eroded media support	• Coherent vision • Distinctive • Content-led • Sustainability a key priority • Individually driven by the visionary champion • Supported by strong and committed team • Expert stakeholders supported project • Built media support through careful and sustained management
Design	• Iconic • Signature architect – Richard Rogers • Designers and cultural commentators – critical • Dome concept has little obvious residual use	• Iconic • Signature architect – Nicholas Grimshaw • Almost universally acclaimed • Dome has a good fit with an 'eco-bubble' concept
Visitor attractiveness	• Uncertainty about purpose, education and entertainment function • 5 million visitors compared to target of 12 million	• Clear focus on sustainability theme • Generally blends education and entertainment • Project has evolved to achieve ambitious but achievable objectives
Location and community fit	• Greenwich, South East London • Close to Docklands redevelopment, potential beneficiary from London's tourism • Polluted riverside location • Socially disadvantaged urban borough • Not integrated with local community • Employment opportunities shortlived • Well connected with transport systems	• Cornwall • Holiday destination • Disused china clay quarry • Rural location • Socially and economically disadvantaged community benefiting from direct and indirect employment opportunities • Good local support and engagement • Car/coach parking

balance between attracting tourists and delivering benefits for the local community, and thereby providing the necessary cultural infrastructure. Eden succeeded excellently and while the building of the Dome enabled nearby neighbourhoods to be redeveloped there was insignificant connection made between its creation and the wider opportunities for regeneration.

The evaluation of the two sites (see Table 7.4) demonstrates how the four new criteria can assist in determining the sustainability of the cultural flagship regeneration projects.

The Eden Project was led by a visionary founder with a clear purpose. It continues to develop, probably beyond its founder's original aims and objectives. Like the very plants it showcases it has a central core, which is permanently growing and flowering throughout each year, due to the very firm initial foundations.

By contrast, the Dome was planned with a limited and short-term vision, guided by the temporary exhibitions of the previous centuries, but uncertainly reconciling commercial and cultural interests, education and entertainment. It was haphazardly put together, and managed by a committee of ever-changing personnel. No one owned the project sufficiently and its purpose after the year 2000 remained unclear. Consequently Eden flourished while the Dome stood empty for nearly six years.

Both projects were designed by signature architects on industrial wasteland. However the marketing of the two projects was very different. Eden took its potential public, funders, and the local community with it on its journey from disused quarry to fabulous biospheres, building up trust and feelgood factors, and thereby empowering the small dedicated workforce to believe in its evolving creation. The Dome by contrast was built by constructors to a tight immovable deadline, always over budget with the interior put together in a piecemeal fashion by its zone sponsors. While the Eden Project shared visions of amazing plants and visually stunning architecture, the Dome was beset with stories of gloom and doom which fed the media interest.

In evaluating the visitor attractiveness of the projects, the Eden Project benefited from its position in Cornwall as a holiday destination and took advantage of public interest in ecology, sustainability and climate change. Appealing to plant lovers, it created a cultural agenda beyond the garden festival that combined education and entertainment. The Dome was a further attraction for London's visitors, and the Millennium itself provided a blank canvas to create interesting and exciting content. In the end, these opportunities were wasted and the project remained a temporary attraction, of interest to visitors from within the UK, but always subject to the vagaries of the media and word of mouth recommendation

The final point of evaluation concerns location. The Dome had a clear initial advantage. It enjoyed proximity to central London through a new underground line, was positioned close to large local communities and was the focus for support from government and businesses. However, its position at the tip of the Greenwich peninsula, surrounded by large areas of development land meant that it was deprived of an immediate neighbourhood – a situation exacerbated by central government control and limited local engagement. Unusually the Eden Project is a cultural flagship in a largely rural area with high unemployment and few long-term economic prospects. But it made good use of its former quarry site, and enjoyed local government and popular support as a regeneration project for Cornwall. As it has flourished, it has created a capacity to connect with mainstream cultural interests and to develop local cultural interests through smaller initiatives and activities.

In the end, neither project is truly a cultural flagship. The Dome because it came and went so quickly without really leaving a footprint on the nation's consciousness except as a ready measure of how not to carry out a project. And Eden is really too alive and too fertile to be merely called a flagship, with its connotations of solid buildings and urban landscapes; rather, it is a unique living, growing entity.

8   A cultural quarter flagship

The MuseumsQuartier, Vienna

Simon Roodhouse

Introduction

This chapter focuses on an important Austrian cultural quarter international flagship development, which, on closer examination, enables consideration to be given to a number of developmental perspectives.[1] At a policy level these include Austrian government cultural sector policy, practice and funding attitudes. The management and marketing of the MuseumsQuartier addresses the nature of the structures, organization, stakeholders, and legal relationships. These give rise to tensions between the individual autonomy of institutions and a state-imposed umbrella organization, the characteristics of creativity in comparison with the requirements for conformity, and the compatibility of facility and programming management. However, it is important to place these perspectives in a context of cultural quarter principles and practice derived from modelling largely undertaken in the United Kingdom.

Defining cultural quarters

A useful definitional framework of a cultural quarter, which creates the parameters for the Vienna model is:

> that it is a geographical area of a large town or city which acts as a focus for cultural and artistic activities through the presence of a group of buildings devoted to housing a range of such activities, and purpose designed or adapted spaces to create a sense of identity, providing an environment to facilitate and encourage the provision of cultural and artistic services and activities.
>
> (Montgomery 2003)

A distinction can be made between a cultural quarter and a cultural industries quarter. The latter is dedicated to cultural business development, e.g. the Sheffield cultural industries quarter, and the former is an identification of a geographical area in which cultural activity is encouraged to locate, a physically defined focal point for cultural activity, for example the Wolverhampton Cultural Quarter. A cultural quarter represents the coherence and convergence of the arts and heritage in culture, and culture as a manifestation of society. Cultural quarters provide a context for the use of planning and development powers to preserve and encourage cultural production and consumption.

Up to the present time, cultural quarters have invariably developed from an existing embryonic cultural presence, as a result of a public sector initiative. Cultural quarters are often part of a larger strategy integrating cultural and economic development, usually linked to the regeneration of a selected urban area. They are characterised by a complex cluster of activities and networks embedded in a particular place.

A further distinction needs to be made at this stage between cultural quarters, creative industry quarters and cultural iconographic regeneration, which includes examples such as the new Royal Armouries in Leeds, the Tate Modern, Cornwall, or the Baltic Contemporary Visual Arts Centre, Newcastle upon Tyne. Although these singular projects often provide a focus for regenerative activity, the distinction lies in their designation as a spatial area for a particular form of development.

The success of a cultural or cultural industries quarter as an urban space can be measured in three dimensions: first, activity defined by economic, cultural and social elements; second, form as the relationship between buildings and spaces; and third, meaning, in terms of the historical and cultural sense of place (Canter 1977). Brooks and Kushner (2003) share a similar definitional framework when quantifying the North American version of cultural quarters, cultural districts. They adopt a classificatory approach to cultural district strategies to facilitate analysis, which is:

- Administration (delivery structure): how does the institutional landscape change as a result of creating a cultural district?
- Degree of public involvement (funding and regulatory structures): how is the government involved in the district?
- Degree of change in the cultural district (spatial relationships refurbishment and new build): how much physical change is evident in the district as a result of cultural designation?
- Programming (cultural activity): what is the content, centralized or decentralized programming of cultural activity?

From this it is apparent that the ingredients for a successful quarter are similar to those in North America, which include spatial and build issues, cultural activity, and delivery structures. However little reference is made in this model to the meaning of a quarter; that is a sense of place, the people's history and culture.

Criticisms of cultural quarters

Critics of the cultural quarter approach to regeneration focus on the artificial planning and building development-led approach, suggesting that this has little to do with communities, their needs, or creative activity. This debate is often typified as a top-down versus bottom-up, or directed as opposed to collaborative, with the engagement of communities, their needs and creative activity being the collaborative bottom-up means of developing cultural quarters rather than the building-centred-directed profit oriented mechanism.

The Sheffield Creative Industries Quarter regeneration example commenced with creative individuals taking over a redundant building associated with the old cutlery industry in a derelict city centre area near the railway station and university, to provide a venue for popular music. As this became more successful, recording studios were established and more people moved into the area, including artists. The primary motivating factor for those involved in the early stages was to meet their needs for a live and cheap venue for their kind of music. As happens in many cases, including the Manchester cultural quarter development, local authorities and other public agencies progressively take over control, with the result that gentrification creeps in and the creative individuals move out to another 'poor' area because they cannot afford the rents or purchase-price of accommodation. Sometimes, it is also concerned with a generation or cohort of creatives who enjoy being associated with each other, who want to locate and interact with each other, who eventually begin to fragment and follow their own personal and professional interests. This driving away of the creative core is cited as a weakness of the structured approach to cultural quarter development.

The Custard Factory in Birmingham is a regeneration project that relied less on individual artists and more on a creative entrepreneur with vision and determination to succeed, despite the odds, to provide high quality facilities at competitive prices for creative businesses. However, the individual entrepreneur model does not fit comfortably into a planned public-sector-led system with the associated regulatory requirements, procedures and collective decision-making processes.

Finding cheap places to live and work provided the driver for the artist-led Newcastle studio development, and triggered in the 1970s and 1980s artist-owned studio cooperatives such as SPACE and ACME. ACME, a London based charity established in 1972, is the largest artist support agency in the UK with over 380 studios, 25 units of living accommodation, and 4,000 artists. Yorkshire Arts Space Society, part of the Sheffield creative industries quarter, performs a similar function.

The ingredients for a successful cultural quarter

Montgomery (2003) points out that cultural quarters are not new, with examples of the Left Bank in Paris, the Lower East Side in New York and Soho in London. Similarly, Brown *et al.* (2000) suggest that the models we consider are derived from the North American experience of the urban village and the British industrial district model based on pre-Fordist economies of small and medium-sized enterprises clustering around complementary skills and services, both competing and collaborating at the same time. Science and business parks are a typical example of this approach, and proved popular in the 1980s. It is suggested that quarters are networks of activity and exchange integrated in a place, which acquires a series of associations, which can be both iconic and social.

Montgomery describes cultural quarters from an urban planning perspective as:

> The use of planning and development powers to both preserve and encourage both cultural production and consumption. Moreover, cultural quarters are often seen as part of a larger strategy integrating cultural and economic development. This is usually linked to the redevelopment or regeneration of an urban area, in which mixed use urban development is to be encouraged, and the public realm is to be reconfigured. In other words cultural quarters tend to combine strategies for greater consumption of the arts and culture with cultural production and urban place making.
>
> (Montgomery 2003: 294)

He goes on to suggest that it is possible within this framework to establish indicators that can be used to assess the relative success of cultural quarters (see Table 8.1).

The Vienna model: Austrian cultural policy influences

This Vienna cultural quarter is located in a particular geographical area of the city which acts as a focus for cultural and artistic activities through the presence of a group of buildings devoted to housing a range of such activities. The quarter has purpose-designed or adapted spaces to create a sense of identity, providing

Table 8.1 Place characteristics of Cultural Quarters (Montgomery 2003)

Activity	
Diversity of primary and secondary	Variety and adaptability of building stock and uses
	Permeability of streetscape
Extent and variety of cultural venues and events	Legibility
	Amount and quality of public space
Presence of an evening economy, including cafe culture	Active frontages
	Meaning
Strength of small firm economy, including creative businesses	Important meeting and gathering spaces
	Sense of history and progress
Access to education providers	Area identity and imagery
Built form	Knowledgeability
Fine grain urban morphology	Design appreciation and style

an environment to facilitate and encourage the provision of cultural and artistic services and activities.

The project is a dynamic international scheme that sets out to raise the profile of the city as an international cultural tourism centre; in fact the city and state wanted to establish themselves as the seventh most important centre in the world. Although Vienna has a substantial international reputation for music, it has not been able to promote other cultural dimensions, including museums and contemporary arts and design. This is what makes the MuseumsQuartier so interesting. It is visionary, dynamic, exciting and at the same time resolves a range of local cultural re-housing issues.

The Austrian government, then in office in February 2000, emphasized from the margins the need for new economic structures for culture, the arts, education, science and even social affairs. Severe cuts of public subsidies resulted from this policy and have impacted on cultural institutions in Vienna institutions. However the political intention to build and maintain this quarter, mainly out of public funds, remained.

The claim that 'creativity should more and more become part of economics' by Franz Morak, Austrian Secretary of State for the Arts, introduced a radical break with traditional Austrian cultural policy and posed serious problems for artists and arts institutions in Austria. To understand this situation it is necessary to describe two main features of Austrian arts policy. First, Austria defines its national identity, to a high degree, in terms of artistic and cultural values. To other countries and foreign citizens it presents itself as a 'cultural nation'. Foreign observers are often astonished by the public attention artistic events attract, but this interest is highly superficial with the engagement centred on events such as festivals, international concerts and, of course, cultural scandals. A second characteristic of arts policy in Austria has been, until recently, the extremely close relation between politics and the arts. The arts have been almost fully financed by public means, and private sponsorship has scarcely any importance at all, hence the reason why the artists depend, to a very high degree, on the benevolence of politicians and bureaucrats.

The roots of this situation are historical. The prosperity of the Habsburg territories was an important reason for the flourishing of the arts, as well as for their dependence on state support. Well placed members of the nobility and a smaller number of upper bourgeoisie of Vienna and the nearby territories, spent liberally on their courts and mansions and provided employment for many composers and performers (Baumol and Baumol 1994:73).

Furthermore, culture and the arts have traditionally been a means to promote the political ends of the Austrian state:

> Already at the time of the monarchy cultural policy was not only patronage. Art as the highest means to build up a state, as an outstanding possibility of appropriating history, should help to ensure the unity of the diversifying national interests. The huge buildings of the 'Ringstraße' built in the second half of the 19th century (...) bear witness to these considerations.
> (Österreichisches Zentrum für Kulturdokumentation 1992)

Generous public support for the arts, as a characteristic of cultural policy, has survived the end of the monarchy; 'the state's support for culture continued in its own management the long-term practice of the royal court' (Pleschberger 1991: 63).

It would be extremely attractive to ascribe the end of this kind of cultural politics to the political changes actuated by the change of government in 2000; as a matter of fact new ways of financing the arts have been in discussion for at least a decade. The history of establishing the MuseumsQuartier can be seen to coincide with this discussion; missions for the quarter have been constantly oscillating between the idea of a 'cultural manifestation' of Austria and the striving for the largest number of visiting tourists possible. But the concept of bringing 'creative industries' into the MuseumsQuartier in order to generate at least a moderate income from rents gained momentum under the government, creating further pressure on small under-funded cultural initiatives. There is little knowledge in Austria on how to find sponsors, or on selling artistic products, and so lip service is currently paid to the creative industries, while, in reality, the big and traditional museums that are the most prominent parts of the quarter continue to be financed by substantial public subsidies.

So, up to now the new market orientation of cultural policy has not been much more than a catchword and/or a veiled menace for cultural initiatives. The above-described close relation between politics and the arts lead to a situation in which rules of accountability and measurability are never clearly defined but replaced by negotiating processes between officials and representatives of cultural institutions. For observers from outside Austria it is surprising how little information on hard facts, such as revenue and visitor numbers is available. Decision-making processes on public support for the arts are usually based exclusively on artistic judgements, often of a specialized jury. In this way, a broad room for arbitrariness is opened, as aesthetic quality is not really a category that can be measured. On the other hand, the broad room for negotiations enhances the flexibility of Austrian cultural policy that can benefit artistic innovations. The MuseumsQuartier is a typical outcome of this policy with a commitment to state funding based on the value of the arts to Austrian society as an intrinsic part of life.

A description of the MuseumsQuartier

The MuseumsQuartier is a 'brand name' for a physical, single cluster site, the Imperial Stables, which at present comprises about 40 diverse cultural organizations,[2] and culturally related activities, occupying 53,000 square meters of usable space. This includes two new museum buildings and two discrete theatres with seating capacity of 1,200. Additional exhibition space is available for hire, along with offices, workshops and ateliers. This short-term space has been grouped together under the brand name Quarter 21;[3] described as 'a structure of self-responsible, constructively competing content-entrepreneurs, a modular-action platform for independent small institutions, culture offices and temporary initiatives' (Waldner 2001). Many of the smaller cultural organizations are included here. Alternatively, it can be described as the vehicle for a cultural industry cluster with a focus on creative activity, new and multi-media technology. In addition to these institutions there are also private tenants, restaurateurs and shopkeepers, as well as those who have rented space over the years and have their homes there.

A typical smaller cultural organization found in the MuseumsQuartier is Basis Wien, a documentation centre with an online database on contemporary art in Austria that also aims at presenting and discussing contemporary art. Basis Wien relies on grants from the state government and the city of Vienna and found itself in a major financial crisis in the summer of 2002, when funding from both bodies was reduced, as well as paid out late, and a mainly EU-funded project was therefore at risk. Its precarious financial situation also places the organization in a weak negotiating position when determining its future with the MuseumsQuartier Co. However, contrary to other smaller and critical institutions such as Depot and Public Netbase that have been driven out of the MuseumsQuartier, Basis Wien could come back to its quarters within the MuseumsQuartier after having spent more than a year in an interim location.

The major institutions, such as the Leopold Museum, which perceives itself as a national museum and is funded almost entirely by the state government, forms one of the key MuseumsQuartier landmarks. The Leopold family handed over, including important works by twentieth-century Austrian artists, the museum's collection to a private foundation on condition that the state and the National Bank of Austria (a sponsor) paid them 2.2 billion schillings (Parnass 2006). In addition, the state agreed to provide premises in the MuseumsQuartier, cover the costs of the new building, supply the Foundation with an annual budget for purchases, and cover the foundation's annual operating deficit.

The influence of a building and location

The MuseumsQuartier cluster of cultural activity forms part of the historic city centre and is expected to strengthen the existing provision, primarily museums such as the Kunsthistorische Museum (Museum of the History of the Arts) and the Natural History Museum situated in the immediate neighbourhood, by adding a more active and lively contemporary dimension. At the same time, it is intended to provide a previously missing link between the Imperial Palace, with its museums, and the narrow meandering streets of an old suburb at the rear of the stables. It is easily reached by the metro and tram system and the vision is to create a major cultural focus in the historic city centre for visitors.

The Imperial Stables, a seriously decaying national heritage site, presented a significant physical and restoration challenge in the sense of marrying, in a single location, the needs of a wide variety of organizations with the severe limitations of important but decaying eighteenth-century buildings. The ornately decorated Winter Riding School, formally designed reflecting the tradition and expectations of the empire at that time, now contrasts with the comparatively austere functionalism of the adjacent Kunsthalle of the City of Vienna, Leopold

Museum, and Museum of Modern Art. The exterior of the Kunsthalle is entirely built of red brick and truncated at both ends; inserted at either end is a gleaming metallic cantilevered surface. The Kunsthalle is an independent structure that is, however, placed in close proximity to the longitudinal front of the Winter Riding School and whose brick roof overlaps the ridge of the latter. The exterior of the Leopold Museum is a white stone cube and is contrasted by the leaner dark grey stone block of the Museum of Modern Art Foundation Ludwig Vienna.

The juxtaposition of the historical and contemporary is a surprising and successful feature which epitomizes an underlying philosophical approach to the development, that of integrating the past with the present. It is, however, a characteristic of the quarter that is only visible from the inside. Externally the new structures cannot be seen; the main front of the building is the original eighteenth-century facade. This solution is the result of a long fought over compromise between those who wanted the Viennese city centre to retain its historic form and those advocating contemporary architecture.

There are at least six restaurants, cafés, and bars, with some cafés open until 4.00am. In addition there are museum bookshops in the Leopold Museum and Museum of Modern Art Ludwig Foundation Vienna, and in the Kunsthalle is a large art bookshop with an attached café in the main entrance, leased out directly by the MuseumsQuartier Development Company. The chairman of the MuseumsQuartier Development Company describes this as 'the landlord with his own shop in his own home' and does not perceive this activity as contrary to the purposes of the company such as facility management or exploitation of a unique position. In all cases these facilities are subcontracted out to private operators and it is expected that they will compete with each other for business and similar facilities in the individual museums.

It is apparent that little attempt has been made to avoid duplication and overlap in order to provide the visitor with choice and maximization of income for the operators; it seems that competition is viewed in this case as healthy and an example of diversity and autonomy at work. However these activities are an important source of revenue for the MuseumsQuartier Development Company and the museums and will ultimately rely on a substantial regular flow of visitors throughout the year if they are all to succeed. Other facilities include a general bookshop, the Infopool (an information centre), a visitor centre, toilets, seating areas, public courtyards, clear signposting and special tours for groups in German and English. The MuseumsQuartier Development and Operating Company provide all these facilities.

A state instrument: the MuseumsQuartier Company

The MuseumsQuartier Developing and Operating Company, the umbrella organization, was set up in 1990 to manage the MuseumsQuartier on behalf of the state and city governments. It is a limited company with shareholders, a board of directors and a Chief Executive. The Federal Government established the terms of reference as:

1   The objective of the enterprise is […] the planning, construction, maintenance, the administration of the real estate and the management of the MuseumsQuartier […]
2   The company is […] entitled to all businesses and measures that are necessary and useful to achieve the aim of the company. The competences of the museums […] are not affected by this entitlement.
3   Above all the following activities can be carried out by the company:
    a)   planning, management and realization of investments to create the MuseumsQuartier including the acquisition of areas necessary for the MuseumsQuartier;
    b)   to make available and keep ready rooms, equipment and services for the institutions of the Republic of Austria, above all for the collections and museums of the Republic.
    c)   the acquisition, planning, preparation, organization and carrying out of exhibitions and events as well as the organization and carrying out of related fringe events and leisure time programmes;
    d)   the letting and leasing of rooms in the MuseumsQuartier;
    e)   in connection with the MuseumsQuartier the running of cinemas, distribution and marketing of movies as well as production, showing, distribution and marketing of videos;
    f)   advertising and P.R. as well as producing publications for the MuseumsQuartier;
    g)   visitor services by arranging visits of artistic and educating events, etc., also in commission of third parties;
    h)   running of an information service.

                    (Grundsätzliche Überlegungen zur Unterricht und kulturelle
                    Angelegenheiten an den Misterrat vom 26 September 1996)

The company is wholly owned through a share distribution by the state government and the Vienna City Council, the landowners. The MuseumsQuartier Co. has extensive powers, which go well beyond that of typical facilities management functions for a particular site. It has a clearly defined creative programming role. The letting arrangements, a key remit of the MuseumsQuartier Co. as facility managers, are inevitably complex in such a large scheme. The major institutions, for example, are independent organizations with substantial funding from the government. However, the city and the state are the primary MuseumsQuartier shareholders, and the main contracts are let to them and they in turn sublet the contracts to the organizations they fund. Consequently, through this mechanism, the city and the state determine the tenants for the MuseumsQuartier. In the case of the smaller organizations the contracting takes place through the Quarter 21 administration, which is also managed by the MuseumsQuartier Co. In every case the contracts include a service charge to include keeping the site clean and tidy, which, in combination with the rents, provides a major source of revenue for the company.

Organizational simplicity, confusion and the creative dilemma

The adopted organizational structure for the MuseumsQuartier is based on a land ownership model, with a limited company, the MuseumsQuarter Co., as the umbrella organization responsible for the site and its operation including the renting of space (Gesellschaftsvertrag der MuseumsQuartier Errichtungs- und Betriebsgesellschaft mit beschränkter Haftung, 29 März 1999). The company rents space to nearly 40 cultural organizations including the Leopold Museum and the Museum of Modern Art Ludwig Foundation Vienna; these organizations are autonomous with their own boards of management and constitutions. Thus, stakeholders require all the rentable space on the site to be let, in order to minimize the annual deficit and enable the company to generate surpluses, which can be used to cross-subsidize the rent for the poorer and smaller cultural organizations.

At one level the organizational relationship is that of landowner and tenant; however, structural disjuncture occurs when the MuseumsQuartier Co. engages in cultural promotion and presentation activities, or attempts to control the autonomy of the individual organizations through the introduction of common ticketing and telephone systems, as it believes it can. The Mission Statement of the MuseumsQuartier emphasizes this by seeking '[...] as much autonomy as possible and pursuing as many common interests as necessary, the MuseumsQuartier strives for the degree of joint facilities needed for the successful operation of the complex as a whole' (Gesellschaftsvertrag der MuseumsQuartier Errichtungs- und Bertriebsgesellschaft mit beschränkter Haftung, 29 März 1999). This results in a loss of independence for tenants and increased competition between tenants and the landlord, leading to a reduction of efficiency and a predictable lack of cohesion. This general situation causes confusion and, at times, friction over roles and responsibilities, with the independent cultural organizations guarding their autonomy as much as possible and resisting stakeholder funding pressures to conform.

Complexities are amplified with the Quarter 21 concept, which is a mechanism to enable the MuseumsQuartier Co. to directly control the tenants in the smaller spaces that they own, manage and let on a short-term basis, by a selection process. Consequently, there seems to be a blurring of the MuseumsQuartier Co.'s role as facilities manager with that of cultural patron and promoter. This becomes all the more obvious if one takes into account that the implementation of Quarter 21 not only brought new institutions to the MuseumsQuartier but drove out other institutions at the same time. Public Netbase, the Institute for New Culture Technologies, and Depot Art and Discussion, both small institutions that participated in activities against the Austrian right-wing government, were not given acceptable leases in Quarter 21, although they had been active in the MuseumsQuartier during its construction.

The management structure of the MuseumsQuartier Co. has no formal constitutional relationship with the occupants of the MuseumsQuartier, which is surprising given the size and nature of the site as well as the number and diversity of tenants. For example, there are no representatives from the 20 tenants on the MuseumsQuartier Company Board of Directors, although there is a formal subcommittee, which includes all tenants and is chaired by the Director of the MuseumsQuartier Company who reports to the Board. In addition no tenants association or equivalent independent organization exists to act on the behalf of, and represent, collective interests of the tenants.

The management model for the MuseumsQuartier is hierarchical with the company controlled by the state and the city that indirectly determines the strategic policy and operational decisions. This involvement goes well beyond the conventional facilities management role, incorporating active engagement in promotion, ticket sales and programming. Although the organizations in the MuseumsQuartier are constitutionally independent the majority are directly, or indirectly, funded by the state or city. Consequently the level of autonomy to act independently of the MuseumsQuartier Co. is severely curtailed.

Individual programming of events, such as exhibitions, remains a competition between individual tenants and the MuseumsQuartier Co.; whilst there is a desire to recognize 'richness in diversity' by the MuseumsQuartier Co., the demand for cohesion and synergy seems to be the preferred policy. The difficulty with a hierarchical structure and control management system is that they restrict the creativity of tenants because creative activity is often about breaking rules, extending boundaries, and challenging conventions.

The questions then, for the MuseumsQuartier Co., are whether creativity can be fostered through the existing management structures, and whether the company can live with the consequences of the outputs that may be at times unpopular and controversial. This poses less of a problem for the MuseumsQuartier Co. in its relationship with the large state or city funded organizations such as the Leopold Museum where the creative controversy will often rest with the interpretation by the curatorial staff of the collections. However, the conceiving, making, production and presentation of the contemporary arts, promotes Austria as a world cultural centre. The civil servants see it from the city and the state perspective as a mechanism for re-positioning Austria in the modern world by celebrating the past and showcasing the contemporary. In the case of the Leopold Foundation, state nominees form half the board of governors. Although there are aspects of the Foundation structure that reflect the particularities of the Austrian legal system, it is recognizable as a model found in other parts of the world. The state trust model is a similar convention to the Foundation as used in the MuseumsQuartier by the tenants, and one used by governments as a means of exercising devolved control, for example the Sheffield Museum and Gallery Trust (Roodhouse 2001).

National museums have been established, as state trusts with a board of Trustees and are autonomous of government. However, the government approves all the appointments to the board and receives an annual revenue grant from the state. It supposedly gives the managers of the museum or cultural organization greater freedom to manage, and the Austrian government more flexibility to choose, how and at what level to fund the organization for 'agreed' purposes. Other legal structures that have been adopted are limited companies, which is the preferred model for the MuseumsQuartier Development Co. The association model is popular with smaller cultural organizations as it is relatively easy to establish at low cost and has little direct government interference, although it is possible for the state, through grants, to influence their governance. This diversity of legal structures generates additional complexities for the MuseumsQuartier Co. as the facilities manager, requiring different tenancy agreements that recognize the legal independence of each organization. The common factor, however, is that the state and/or the city of Vienna fund most, if not all, of the cultural organizations in the MuseumsQuartier directly or indirectly.

Financing the MuseumsQuartier and its inhabitants: a public sector dinosaur?

The capital cost of converting the stables into workable space, and building two new museums, is estimated to be over $200 million. The finance has been provided by the city and state governments, both as grants and as guarantors for the banks (to facilitate cash flow) who have lent the money to the MuseumsQuartier Co. Boris Marte observed that the city council in particular recognized the MuseumsQuartier Co. vehicle as the most efficient devolved mechanism available to city and state for the purposes of a major capital project, and subsequent leasing of the rentable space.

The revenue needed to operate the site and provide the facilities, as well as service the debt, is derived from the rents of the occupants. It is expected that the rental income and the service charges will, when the site is fully let, cover all the costs incurred by the company in repaying the capital debt and servicing and maintaining the site. However, the city and state governments provide the subsidized rentals for the poorer cultural organizations by allowing the company to run an annual deficit.

There is very little private sector involvement in the MuseumsQuartier and the commercial activity seems to be centred on the selling of food, drink and books. All venues sell tickets and this on average amounts to 10 per cent of the annual revenue for these organizations. Sponsorship is evident and the MuseumsQuartier Co. is actively looking for sponsors; unfortunately, a coordinated strategy with the tenants is not well developed. In addition, it is recognized by the federal government that sponsorship is difficult to attract in Austria, as there are few major international companies and the traditional source of patronage, the aristocracy, is no longer in a position to fulfil this role.

From whichever financial perspective the MuseumsQuartier is considered, the city and the state governments are the largest and most important capital and revenue funders. In reality the federal government is Austria's primary cultural patron replacing the aristocracy and supported by city councils (Ministerialrat Dr Rudolf Wran, personal communication). In general there seems to be little pressure on the managers of the MuseumsQuartier Co. to attract visitors because the bulk of the income is derived from the leases, and that is largely guaranteed by the city and, or, state governments. In its first full year of operation the MuseumsQuartier attracted 1,116 million visitors. Visitor numbers thus only slightly exceeded the conservative forecast of 1.1 million. However, national and international critical acclaim matters, and at this stage in the development of the MuseumsQuartier visitor numbers do not seem to be a critical success factor in financial or cultural terms. Consequently there is little interest in performance indicators. It does not seem that the managers in the MuseumsQuartier are under the same pressures colleagues in North America, Italy, France, the UK or Australia in attracting more and more visitors and alternative revenues. For the MuseumsQuartier cultural manager, emphasis is placed on the importance and significance of the cultural product and/or service in national and international terms. Artistic critical acclaim is seen as the primary performance indicator.

Cultural programming: a question of control?

With the number and diversity of cultural organizations involved in the MuseumsQuartier all with a direct interest in programming as the central focus of their work, it is no surprise to find limited cooperation, particularly if artistic critical acclaim is the primary performance indicator. Jealousy and mistrust between the organizations, and with the MuseumsQuartier, over programming is evident, largely as it relates to the core identity and purpose of the organizations themselves, in other words their rationale for existence. Although at an informal operational level there is evidence of information exchange, the mechanism for formal interchange and exchange of ideas, plans and future activities have noticeable limitations as a communication tool. In particular, the representatives of the institutions are only able to make recommendations for action, which can be accepted or rejected by the MuseumsQuartier board and management.

This safeguarding of the individual organizational identity through the protection of programming is unsurprising, although there is an inevitable danger in duplication, overlap and confusion. Consequently there is little in the way of formal joint exhibition and event planning as it is expected that because programming is a 'creative' activity, organizations and individuals will build up their own relationships over time, which may lead to future collaboration. At present there is no incentive to collaborate, particularly with the MuseumsQuartier. The diverse and *ad hoc* nature of the programme offerings is perceived as strength and part of the quarter's attraction to the visitor. This is underlined by the federal government which 'values the freedom of the arts', sees no need for 'artistic' co-operation, and does not wish to interfere directly in the affairs of individual cultural organizations, even though it funds them (Ministerialrat Dr Rudolf Wran, pers. comm.).

This 'richness in diversity' approach has conveniently side stepped other complications such as joint education and marketing programmes. In the case of education the large museums, the children's museums and creativity centre, as well as the Architektur Zentrum Wien, all have a direct interest in children and relationships with schools. A similar pattern can be detected for public lectures and discussions. Staff are employed on behalf of their organizations to develop and deliver education and marketing programmes with no formal interaction or channels of communication to facilitate the sharing of practice, ideas and information between the tenants and the MuseumsQuartier Co.

Marketing and branding the MuseumsQuartier: conflict or co-operation?

The one obvious area of common interest and mutual benefit for all concerned in the MuseumsQuartier is marketing, including branding, and yet confusion abounds and fragmentation exists between the individual organizations and the MuseumsQuartier Co. over roles and responsibilities. There is a general lack of internal communication between the tenants and the company, a central tenet of marketing, with no agreed marketing strategy that includes all parties and their activities. The Leopold Museum, for example, has developed its own marketing plan without reference to the Museum of Modern Art or the Kunsthalle. Similarly the Vienna Festival plans seem to have little relevance to the Architektur Zentrum Wien programme, Quarter 21 and the Children's Museum activities, let alone the museums and galleries. The company, however, accepts responsibility for marketing and branding of the quarter as a location, and that the marketing of programmes is an 'individual' matter left to the tenants themselves regardless of how confusing this may be to visitors.

The company is expecting to 'arouse the curiosity of the old and new target groups' and annually attract 1.1 million visitors with the Leopold Museum as the star attraction with around 250,000 to 300,000 visitors a year. For all this there has been limited consultation and discussion between the MuseumsQuartier Co. (location and branding marketers) and the tenants (specific brand image/ communication concept marketers) about how they want to be represented in the marketing literature produced to promote the location. This is indicative of the structural fault lines that have resulted in a lack of effective communication channels. Although there is an established logo for the MuseumsQuartier, described as 'simple, practical, effective, consciously non-artistic' it has not yet been enthusiastically adopted by the tenants and is used only partly in their literature and general marketing.

Many of the organizations generate temporary exhibitions and tour these shows nationally and internationally with related lecture programmes and education services for children, all of which need marketing. There is some evidence of working collaboratively but a lack of understanding of the benefits of supporting each other in strategic partnerships, and the MuseumsQuartier Co. is failing to promulgate these concepts. For the company to do this requires an overall strategy to be developed, agreed by all concerned, resourced and realized.

There is a general consensus that the MuseumsQuartier and its marketing activities are expected to increase visitor numbers for the tenants and that this growth is largely through international tourists. Much of the evidence and understanding of the existing audience is derived from tenant ticket sales. For example, the Kunsthalle, with around 160,000 visitors in 1999, has identified that 80 per cent of them are under 40 years old, 51 per cent come from the city and

24 per cent are overseas visitors. There are an equal number of men and women, and a high number of students. The Museum of Modern Art Ludwig Foundation Vienna attracted between 110,000 to 150,000 visitors in 1999 to its two sites in the city, and expects to at least maintain 150,000 visitors in the new premises in the MuseumsQuartier with a higher proportion of overseas tourists. The Vienna Festival is well established and with the new and expanded facilities predicts paying audiences of around 200,000. The smaller organizations are largely serving local, regional and national cultural markets often associated with practitioners, critics and curators. It is expected that the MuseumsQuartier will act as a 'honey pot' for practitioners and be a visible focal point for international collaboration. How this is to be measured remains unclear, and whether this reflects the nature of creative practice is yet to be seen. For all this, there remains deep distrust between the tenants and the company, and between tenants themselves, and consequently there is a reticence to share what is perceived as sensitive and 'commercial' information about visitors.

Conclusion: the last of the big spenders or an international exemplar?

What is perhaps the most surprising aspect of this project is the willingness of the Austrian government, at national and city level, to commit substantial levels of capital and revenue funds on cultural activity in a time of public sector constraint. This can be regarded as a bold and welcome example to the world, or the last vestiges of an old empire, just as France and the United Kingdom have been required to reinvent roles as a result of the loss of empire. The close interrelation between the state and the arts can be understood as a legacy of Joseph II, the son of Maria Theresa, who started this tradition (Marchart 1999). Whatever else is said regarding this project, the management challenges are considerable and the key to future success is how the MuseumsQuartier reinvents itself after the building works are complete, and the business of attracting visitors comes to the fore, along with the need to make the Quarter 21 work as a centre for the development of creative businesses.

Is this, however, the ultimate cultural palace? The quarter can be described as the ultimate cultural palace as far as the city and the state are concerned but the problem lies in the perception of the cultural tourist, which is yet to be seen. Although the quarter has set out to combine the business of presentation with practice epitomized by the establishment of Quarter 21 alongside the Leopold Museum, it has yet to be proved whether this combination will work. There are no formal mechanisms for genuine interchange between tenants to encourage interaction between presentation and practice. There is also a danger that the practice activity is seen as a showpiece for the public which has never worked in the past and is likely to drive creators elsewhere. What also follows from this is whether the management, and related structures, is capable of encompassing the essential anarchy of artistic practice. The indications are that the structures that have been put in place are set up to enable the state and city to exercise control, and hence aesthetic judgement, as public patrons, Public Netbase and Depot being cases in point. Is this a desirable model for the well being of cultural activity in Austria?

What is difficult to understand in the quarter is whether the original intention of saving a national heritage site, and meeting the housing needs of a number of cultural organizations, has been overtaken by a desire to engage in the new cultural agenda, the creative industries. Consequently, the need for a long term negotiated, agreed and realistic strategy has never been stronger and a shared vision has yet to materialize. Disappointingly, there is little evidence to suggest that this development will make a tangible difference to the individual practitioner in the city, except for those who are lucky enough to be chosen to occupy ateliers as artists in residence, or rent space in Quarter 21. If anything, there are emerging concerns that cultural resources from the city and the state will be jeopardized as the Quarter 21 develops.

Although this development makes best use of an important set of buildings, and answers the housing-the-arts crisis, it is doubtful if any measurable expansion of the activity in the city is likely to occur as a result. However, there is little doubt in the early stages that the quarter will be an attractive focal point for cultural activity. In a wider context the MuseumsQuartier has already changed cultural activity in Vienna as it is clearly attracting cultural initiatives to the surrounding area. Small galleries and arts mediating institutions settle down around the MuseumsQuartier, complementing in this way the small creative businesses in the area behind it.

Jobs are being created in the quarter and a set of buildings has been brought back into use along with increased creative industry activity in the immediate vicinity. There is a potential through Quarter 21 to develop creativity and businesses, as well as 'artistic endeavour', which may provide a catalyst for further expansion of creative businesses in the city if the management system is flexible enough in the future. It seems the MuseumsQuartier includes the traditional characteristics of a flagship such as that found in the retail industry, with an increasingly recognized engagement with cultural needs placed in a spatial construct, the cultural quarter, which plays into creative city and urban regeneration practices.

Sources

Structured Interviews were conducted during the period 2001–2002 with:
• Claudia Bauer, Kunsthalle Wien; Konrad Becker, Public Netbase; Thomas Hübel, Depot Susanne Jäger, Depot; Mag. Bettina Leidl, Kunsthalle Wien; Ministerialrat Dr Franz Loicht, Chairman of the Board of the MuseumsQuartier Errichtungs- und Betriebsges.m.b.H; Boris Marte, Büro des Stadtrates für Kultur der Stadt Wien; Mag. Robert Reitbauer, Museum moderner Kunst; Mag. Romana Schuler, Leopold Museum.
• Richard Schweitzer, TanzQuartier; Irene Strobl, Kindertheater; Dr Wolfgang Waldner, Director and CEO of the MuseumsQuartier Errichtungs- und Betriebsges.m.b.H.; Ministerialrat Dr Rudolf Wran, Bundesministerium für Bildung, Wissenschaft und Kultur.

Documents

Bundesgesetz vom 7. Juni 1990 zur Errichtung einer MuseumsQuartier-Errichtungs- und Betriebsgesellschaft; Gesellschaftsvertrag der MuseumsQuartier-Errichtungs- und Betriebsgesellschaft mit beschränkter Haftung. 29. März 1999; Grundsätzliche Überlegungen zur Besiedlungs- und Betriebsphilosophie des MuseumsQuartiers Wien, 1996; Grundsätzliche Überlegungen zur Unterricht und kulturelle Angelegenheiten an den Misterrat vom 26. September 1996; Vortrag der Bundesministerin für Unterricht und kulturelle Angelegenheiten an den Ministerrat vom 26. September 1996; M. Wailand/V. Weh, Strukturkonzept für das 'Quartier 21' (Q 21) im MQ Wien, Kurzfassung (Stand 14.12.2000); Mission Statement of the MuseumsQuartier.

Notes

1 This chapter is based on work originally published in Roodhouse, S. (2006) *Cultural Quarters Principles and Practice*, Bristol: Intellect.
2 Organizations involved in the MuseumsQuartier (omitting Quarter 21[3]):
   • The Architektur Zentrum Wien (a centre for exhibitions, presentations and debates);
   • The Art Cult Centre – Tabakmuseum; Basis Wien – art, information and archive;
   • The Kunsthalle Wien (an exhibition venue for international contemporary and modern art); The Leopold Museum (which includes the largest collection of works by Egon Schiele); The Museum of Modern Art Ludwig Foundation Vienna (which houses one of the largest collections of modern and contemporary art); The Tanzquartier Wien (a centre for modern dance and performance); The Theaterhaus für Kinder (a theatre for children aged 4–13 years which includes dance, musicals, puppet theatre and opera);
   • The Vienna Festival; wienXtra (a children-oriented information centre);
   • Zoom (a creativity centre and exhibition space for children engaged in art, culture, society and science).
3 An explanation of the Quarter 21 mechanism: this mechanism is intended to address the question of the small under-funded cultural organizations, and how contemporary creative activities are incorporated into the MuseumsQuartier. The elements of the Quarter 21 are: the forum for cultural theory; studios for artists; platform for cross-over activities; cultural joint office; digital media area (Internet café, independent media centre, media studios, platforms for music and film); arena, reading room; creative industries start-up offices for design, film, photography, e-music, fashion, new media/IT, literature/book stores, art publishers; commercial users (book stores, bars and cafés)
     The users are expected to take responsibility for their work, the outputs, and to pay the rent for the space in the Quarter 21. The MuseumsQuartier Co. manages the general infrastructure and space such as the visitors centre, arena, conference rooms courtyards and the square in front of the building. In addition it operates the lease contracts for the users in Quarter 21, as it does for all other parts of the site, however in this case there are three categories of lease, cultural (heavily subsidized), semi-commercial (subsidized), and commercial (no subsidy).
     The management of the MuseumsQuartier has established an advisory board, 'Network 21', which recommends to the Chief Executive which users should be offered a lease contract in the Quarter 21 and in which rental category. The Chief

Executive can either accept or reject the recommendations and reports his actions to the Board. It also has a wider remit to advise on the content and programming for the common spaces.

Users, once chosen, rent a space of the size they can afford and this is maintained on their behalf by the company as part of the lease agreement. Any alterations to the space are also the responsibility of the company and the consequent costs are incorporated in the rental charge. General technical equipment is provided and maintained by the company and users must prove they have the financial means to meet their operational costs, including all rental charges appropriate to the lease category.

9   The department store

The metropolitan flagship in national networks of fashion consumption

Bronwen Edwards

'Simpson Piccadilly' is necessary – as the keystone of Simpson's fighting policy. Imagine in the heart of London's smart West End, a vast new modern building wholly devoted to a complete range of Simpson-tailored garments. Imagine the millions who will daily pass its windows, talk of it, visit it. A men's store second to none in size and position, it will immediately invest the name of Simpson with an overwhelming first-class West End reputation.[1]

This was the rallying cry of Simpson Ltd, a successful, modern, nationally-distributing menswear manufacturer, on the brink of significant change. This family company had recently gained an enthusiastic and innovative new head, Alexander Simpson, and was about to embark on a venture into retail that would transform the company. Within a year, the company had indeed opened a shop in Piccadilly, 'in the heart of London's smart West End'. It is this shop that provides a useful case study of the role of the retail flagship within fashionable consumption networks.[2]

For 'Simpson Piccadilly' was not simply a small West End menswear showroom. It was a highly prominent, substantial, brand-new, nine-storey building. It was also explicitly presented as a department store. The chapter considers how this particular retail format enabled the site to operate in a particular way as a flagship for the company, both as an important architectural landmark and as an exemplar of a new kind of fashionable men's retailing in the metropolis. Indeed the argument is that these two things were carefully connected at Simpsons, providing insights into how architecture has been used by retailers in the promotion of their business.

The other central contention is that a retail venture like this can best be understood through uncovering the layered and intersecting networks of architecture, retailing and fashionable consumption in which the store functioned as a hub. Some of these networks were virtual, but it also becomes clear that the specifics of actual place were at the centre of 1930s shopping cultures: infusing shopping practices, retail strategies and narratives of consumption: it was no accident that Simpson Ltd had anchored its flagship department store in the core of London's West End, long associated with the nation's most high-profile and fashionable consumption. This helps us to track the continuous trajectory of the *metropolitan* retail flagship,

May 8, 1936   THE ARCHITECT & BUILDING NEWS   155

The façade to Piccadilly. The use of Portland stone was a condition imposed by the landlords.

MESSRS. SIMPSON, PICCADILLY
Architect : Joseph Emberton, F.R.I.B.A.

Figure 9.1   Simpson Piccadilly (Source: Architect and Building News, 8 May 1936: 155)

in a period more commonly associated with developments in suburban or out-of-town consumption. By looking at the store's place within the microgeographies of the West End, the chapter also considers the role of the flagship department store in subtly reconfiguring shopping maps, and permanently altering the urban landscape.

The research draws on a range of material from the store's archives: correspondence between retailer and architect, architectural drawings, minutes, promotional material. It positions these business records amongst other voices: extracts from local and national newspapers, architectural journals, and the building itself. This is a methodology which connects the real architectural fabric of the store with the narratives that surrounded it, making sense of it as a flagship for the company.

It is a historical case study, certainly, and aims to add a new geographical-architectural dimension to the wealth of existing work on the historical department store, the bulk of which has been focused on the late nineteenth century (see, for example, Bowlby 1985; Domosh 1996; Leach 1993; Miller 1981; Nava 1996; Rappaport 2000). Whilst explicitly concerned with the development of the modern city, these stories have been preoccupied with class and gender, with novelty and the spectacular, and whilst architecture figures as a marker of success, progress and zeitgeist, there has been limited attention to the actual physical fabric of the city, and the connections between architectural style and the modes of consumption of fashionable goods. By picking up the story of the department store in its 'mature' period, this story of mid-twentieth century London considers how stores worked in more developed systems of consumption, where the careful construction of routes and networks was increasingly important in a store's success or failure to thrive.

It is also argued that a historical study like this additionally provides useful perspectives on the contemporary urban environment, where the flagship department store has become a crucial component of the regeneration, and indeed rebranding, of our cities. I think here of the much-lauded Future Systems store for Selfridges of 2003, located in Birmingham's formerly notoriously run-down Bullring area, and the Brooker Flynn and HMK Harvey Nichols in Leeds of 1997 – a key element in the city's successful post-industrial reinterpretation as 'the Knightsbridge of the North'.

But the connections with the past are also material: the thoroughfares of our major cities are still littered with the striking architectural forms of the iconic department stores of the nineteenth and twentieth centuries. Some are still in business; others are now different kind of flagships. Simpsons Piccadilly was taken over by the booksellers Waterstones in the late 1990s, attracted by the building's landmark status, and geographic positioning. It is now promoted by the company as 'Europe's largest bookshop', riding the recent book-trade boom, but vulnerable to the increasing strength of virtual commerce that competes with the iconic and design, material solidity and essential 'locatedness' of a building like this.

Nine floors of store exclusively for men

Most striking about Simpsons was the scale of the enterprise: a large building which dwarfed the traditional outfitters and tailors of Jermyn Street and Savile Row, and was also substantially larger than the flourishing chain stores like Montague Burton and Austin Reed. Indeed as Simpsons' nearest competitor was the upmarket menswear chain Austin Reed, one might have expected the company to adopt a similar format. But Simpsons had significantly expanded its manufacturing base and range of goods and was committed to a shop floor of massive proportions. From the outset, the retailer planned for a remarkably extensive stock of ready-made tailoring to be on-site. In a detailed letter to his architect, Mr Simpson specified space for a minimum of 10,000 lounge suits, 1,500 to 3,000 overcoats (depending on the season), 800 raincoats, 600 dinner suits, 700 full dress suits, 120 dress overcoats, 400 morning coats and vests, 600

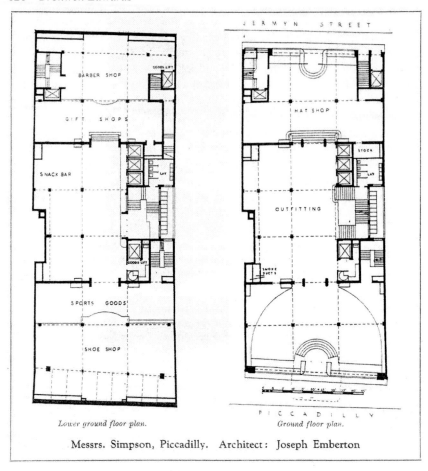

Lower ground floor plan.   Ground floor plan.

Messrs. Simpson, Piccadilly.   Architect: Joseph Emberton

Figure 9.2   Plans of Simpsons' ground and lower ground floors (Source: Architect and
Building News, 8 May 1936: 158)

black jackets and waistcoats, 1,000 striped trousers, 100 wedding vests.[3] Travel
and sports clothing were also comprehensively covered: tropical suits, plus fours,
golf suits and riding clothes, which could be tried on with the aid of a dummy
horse in the changing room.[4]

The store was furthermore specifically billed as the first *department store* for
men with a whole range of goods and services, an exemplar of a new kind of
masculine consumption. The lower ground floor alone was designed to house a
barber's shop, soda fountain, gun shop, shoe shop, chemists, florist, fishing shop,
wine and spirit shop, luggage shop, snack bar, dog shop, sports shop, cigar and
tobacconists, gift shop, saddlery shop, theatre agent, and travel agent.[5] This was
significant. By functioning as this kind of 'universal provider', Simpsons was
associating itself with the major West End department stores already dotted through
the West End: including nearby Swan and Edgar at Piccadilly Circus; Liberty and
Dickins and Jones in Regent Street; Selfridges, D. H. Evans and Marshall and

Snelgrove on Oxford Street. This was clearly a network of fashionable feminine consumption; the department store indeed credited with legitimizing women's presence in the city since Victorian and Edwardian eras (Domosh 1996; Nava 1996; Rappaport 2000).

Simpsons was also described in the *Daily Mail* as 'nine-floors of store exclusively for men, where they can revel in all the delights of shopping'.[6] The department store project by necessity entailed adopting, indeed 'showcasing', shopping cultures and practices previously labelled 'feminine': shopping for pleasure, browsing, window shopping, socializing. These practices, central to the store's spatial organization and approach to display, were necessary to secure the multiple purchases required to support a store of this size. Mr. Simpson wrote of his plans to encourage this kind of shopping,

> I rather think it is a good idea that there should be small show cases in the barber shop, displaying goods that are on sale throughout the rest of the store: a pair of shoes, box of golf balls, an article or two from the gift shop, an unusual sports shirt, a hat, etc... . I am sure it would give the customer an opportunity of discussing merchandise with the barber, and I believe we could train the barbers to interest customers generally in the store.[7]

A self-styled 'man in the street', reviewing Simpsons for *Art and Industry*, was distinctly unhappy about the manipulative effect the interior displays and layout of this department store had had on him, 'I must admit that I felt like buying lots of other things. On the other hand ... I almost feel as if I'd been fooled into looking at all the other stuff.'[8] His unease hinted at the 'unmanliness' of being manipulated in this way. So whilst the goods sold here were unmistakably masculine, the store's department store format meant it trod a dangerous line within the nervous world of inter-war gender identity, worthwhile because of the markets it opened up.

For one thing, the scale of the enterprise and range of goods certainly enabled the company to align itself with an emerging genre of men's 'lifestyle consumption' particularly effectively. This new kind of man's shop explicitly traded in identities – not in itself a novel thing in retailing, except that they offered to transform a customer *single* shopping trip, through the provision of good quality ready-to-wear tailoring, extensive ranges of outfitting, and the concentration of additional services in one place. Display expert A. Edward Hammond noted,

> In one of these modern stores a man can arrive from the uttermost parts of the world, looking like a tramp, and, after a short while, leave with the air of a well-turned-out City man. He can have had a bath, a shave, and a manicure, and can have purchased everything from shoes to full-dress clothes, while a valet has pressed and sent home his old garments.
>
> (Hammond 1930b: 91)

Austin Reed had already capitalized on the new provision of a variety of goods and services, running an advertising campaign with the slogan, '... Just a part of the Austin Reed service' during the early 1930s. It was possible to shave, bathe, buy tobacco, have suit pressed and so on at the Regent Street store. In a game of one-upmanship, with its significantly larger scale and range of departments, Simpsons was able to offer even more transformatory potential.

The company wanted to create within its store a consumer profile that on the one hand appealed to a broadly-defined middle-class, but on the other was still associated with metropolitan cultures of 'elite' fashionability. Simpsons' stock and advertising suggested the new consumer could be equipped here for the exclusive English social calendar: metropolitan soirées, days at Ascot and country weekends. He was also equipped to travel the world with his tropical suits. Whilst planning the store, Mr. Simpson wrote to his architect, 'We do know ... that in addition to the suitable tropical clothing we must also stock the type of furniture these people carry around with them.'[9]

Alongside this traditional elite outfitting ran a distinctly modern, youthful strand, as the shop cast itself as a 'sportsman's paradise': 'The sports shop at Simpsons does not merely glisten and gleam with equipment for every sport ... but is staffed by men who have been specially picked for a peculiar knowledge of their subject. Triple blues learn things here which they hardly knew before.'[10] For example, in 1938, the winter sports department was supervised by minor sporting celebrity Bill Bracken, the Olympic ski runner. Customers were invited to 'discuss with him the merits of this pair of Norwegian skis, of that Kandahar binding ...'[11] This sports department addressed a fashionable, modern and relaxed sporting culture, exemplified in the hugely successful Daks range of casual, outdoor trousers: 'when you get into Daks it's impossible not to feel you're cutting rather a good figure.'[12]

This was also an urban, West End fashionability based on the business suit; interpreted both as a formal morning suit or smart lounge suit, an image suggesting work in a city office, but leisure in the West End's streets. One of Simpsons' most long-running series of advertisements featured 'Men about Town'. Yet within this repertoire, impeccable bespoke garments rubbed shoulders with a quantity of ready-to-wear tailoring within the store, exemplifying the struggle to accommodate exclusivity and availability, tradition and modernity within the store. This was partly about maintaining the delicate balance between the cachet of the brand and the large volume of sales required: a new dilemma for this class of menswear retailing but a familiar issue for the department store. But it was more complex: Alexander Simpson publicly claimed that increasing the accessibility of 'elite' male fashionability was a personal goal, as well as a business strategy. One obituary noted, 'He dreamed of owning a store where men would be able to obtain things that are normally only sought in the most exclusive and most expensive West End establishments at competitive prices.'[13]

The company certainly built a thriving business marketing ready-to-wear tailoring to a higher class of customer, raising its status within the hierarchy of masculine dress. It employed the supposedly stigmatized terms 'ready-made', 'ready-to-wear' and 'ready-tailored' prominently in its advertisements featuring the exclusive Simpsons image. The assault on traditions was two-fold: on one hand, ready-made suits were presented as acceptable in situations where previously

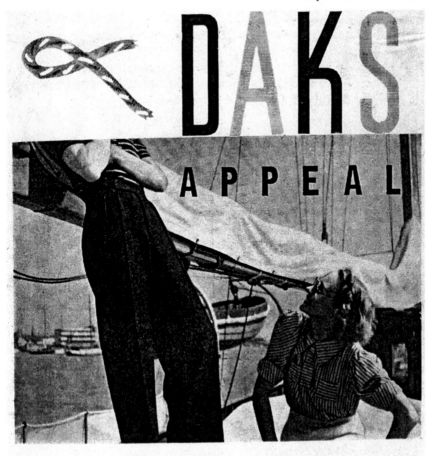

When you get into Daks it's impossible not to feel you're cutting rather a good figure. You see, Daks hang so superbly. The fit at the waist is so neat. The comfort-in-action cut gives you such an air of well-dressed freedom. Begin with a pair of Daks greys. If you're fond of boats and beaches, be sure to see the crisp Daks linens in white, Breton red, Royal, or Lincoln. Then have a look at the lovats, blues, whipcords, or the new Daks pinpoints. – 30/- a pair (shorts 21/-), from most men's shops, or write to Simpson, 202 Piccadilly, London, W.1.

Figure 9.3   Daks advertisement (Source: Punch, 11 May 1938)

only bespoke would do. On the other, they were infused with associations of the bespoke, hence providing the 'look' and cachet of elite West End tailoring for a smaller budget. *Art and Industry* summarized the success of the Simpsons image in these terms: 'It has reached young men who could scarcely afford the price which Simpsons charged for their clothes, and others who could easily afford a higher price but who preferred to buy from Simpsons.'[14]

The new department store project was a gamble for Simpsons, but it was also a crucial tool in defining new models of masculinity to which the goods were designed to appeal.

The Simpsons consumer would have a new relationship with acquiring the clothes with which his image was pieced together, and a new visibility within the West End's principal shopping thoroughfares.

The first building to state in modern terms the modern purpose of the street

Architecture and design were key strategies for Simpsons, used to create a building that operated as a modern flagship in the shopping street and within wider networks of modernity: 'flagship' architecture that would be noticed, talked about, visited, copied. This was a well-established approach for department store retailers by the 1930s, and mirrors contemporary projects.

In tandem with the positive reception in the fashion trade and popular press, claiming the store as a menswear innovator, Simpsons was successful in attracting a bubble of publicity that immediately established the building as an architectural icon. With its smooth stone skin, horizontal glazing bands and cutting-edge floodlighting and neon signage, it was stylish, eye-catching and certainly modern, recognized by *The Scotsman* as 'an expression in every way of the modern spirit.'[15] The building was designed by Britain's leading commercial modern architect, Joseph Emberton, a significant choice. His work was also already internationally recognized, featured in the influential book by F. R. Yerbury, *Modern European Buildings* of 1928 alongside that of venerated European modernists Mendelsohn, Dudok and Perret. Emberton's Royal Corinthian Yacht Club at Burnham-on-Crouch of 1931 was one of very few British buildings included in the 'International Exhibition of Modern Architecture' held at the Museum of Modern Art in New York in 1932, providing a useful international profile.

The building was loaded up with the best of modern design. The structural engineer was Felix Samuely, who had recently worked on Mendelsohn and Chermayeff's iconic De la Warr Pavilion at Bexhill. Many of the furniture and fittings were designed by Emberton himself and made by Bath Cabinet Makers, the firm of choice for fitting out British modern buildings. Leather and curved plywood armchairs and plywood tables were by Alvar Aalto, with other chairs by avant-garde manufacturer Pel. Carpets and rugs were by leading designers Marion Dorn and Duncan Miller, along with Ashley Havinden and Natasha Kroll. The store archive even includes unrealised plans to commission sculpture from Eric Gill and Henry Moore.

The shop was at the centre of the 1930s flowering of British modernism. The shop was reviewed extensively in architectural journals, singled out for attention in the *Architects' Journal*'s round-up of the best buildings of 1936. It was feted as an icon of British modernism, described by the *Architect and Building News* as 'an object lesson to future rebuilders in Piccadilly ... the first building to state in modern terms the modern purpose of the street.'[16]

It also quickly established its place within international architectural networks, within the popular as well as the professional architectural imagination, situated in a European and North American landscape of modernist shops. Significantly, Simpsons was one of the seventy-seven buildings in a seminal exhibition of 1937: 'Modern Architecture in England' at MOMA. In the context of the 1930s West End, a modernist shop like this would also have been striking and unusual, the exception rather than the rule within the street scene still littered with Georgian and Victorian architecture. Mr. Simpson planned research trips abroad to gain inspiration from the best foreign shops.[17] However, this was not just a question of influence, but of the situation of this West End shop within an international, particularly European and North American, landscape of modernist shops.[18]

This landscape was mapped out within a literature on foreign shops published in Britain. The Westwoods make reference to an extensive European literature, including Louis Parnes' *Bauten des Einzelhandels* of 1934, Adolph Schumacher's *Ladenbau* of 1934 and Roger Poulain's *Boutiques* of 1931 (Westwood and Westwood 1937). Studio publishers were responsible for a series of books on the modern arts in the 1930s aimed at a crossover professional and popular market. In this series, Herbert Hoffmann's *Modern Interiors* of 1930 had a substantial section on shops and exhibition interiors, with examples chosen from Berlin, Vienna, Amsterdam, Stockholm, Los Angeles, Cologne, Madrid, Copenhagen, Munich, Hamburg, The Hague and Zurich (Hoffmann 1930).

These international references contributed to the sense that modernist shops, and indeed modern architecture in general, were to some extent still considered 'foreign' within the British context. This was noted by *The Builder* in 1929, 'Following on the precedents of Paris and Berlin a break is being made with all tradition, and new shopfronts of what at first seem to be strangely exotic design are appearing in our best streets.'[19] This foreignness was exaggerated by the attribution of modernism to the influx of prominent émigré architects, including Mendelsohn, Gropius, Lubetkin, and Goldfinger (Benton 1995). To commission such a building, then, involved a further element of risk, but ensured it would be noticed.

The *Advertisers Weekly* commented, 'What other store owner would have gathered about him the people Alexander Simpson collected? Nobody else, probably because no other man in London is young enough, rich enough, has vision enough' (27 May 1937). Yet Simpson was not simply acting as patron: a flagship store showcasing the best of modern British design was an investment due to the way it promoted his business interests.

A reading of architecture as symbolic and representational, revealing of cultural tropes including gender and gender relationships, has been increasingly prevalent within architectural history and theory. Notable here is work by Colomina, Ward and Wigley, who have argued that this characteristic was especially highly developed in the modern architecture of the inter-war years. (Colomina 1994; Ward 2001; Wigley 1995). Retail architecture had in fact long been interpreted in contemporary comment in terms of its symbolic nature, and had been harnessed by store owners to promote their stores in particular ways. In particular, the owners of the first department stores made a direct link between the splendour of their buildings and the promotion of the luxurious nature of their goods, as famously described by Zola. His store owner, Mouret, argued the case for a new building project, 'An advertisement! An advertisement! This one will be in stone, and it'll outlast us all. Can't you see that it would increase our business tenfold!' (Zola 1998: 313).

Emberton understood this architectural function well. By the time he was given the commission for Simpsons, Emberton had an established practice in the architectures of modern leisure, from shops to pleasure grounds (Ind 1983). Indeed, he had designed for menswear chain Austin Reed, and for the shoe shops Lotus and Delta and Earl and Earl. He had close association with the advertising world, having designed the exhibition hall at London's Olympia in 1931, and acted as architectural director of several of the British Advertising Association's exhibitions from 1927, designing numerous exhibition stands.

Simpson hired the leading advertising agency, Crawfords, to do publicity, with the talented Ashley Havinden, and from 1938 Max Hoff, working on the Simpsons account. Appropriately, Crawfords' whole ethos was one of modernity. In promotional material of 1930, the company linked their aesthetic with the frenetic pace of urban life,

> Taller, simpler buildings rising every day. Faster cars and aeroplanes linking city to city. Express lifts, express meals, express news and pictures. But nothing so swift as the pace with which ideas are moving, changing! Are you trying to sell to nineteen-thirty with the voice of nineteen-ten? Crawford advertising – never a minute old in manner or inspiration – is the work of young and up-to-date people whose minds are in tune with this urgent, modern world.[20]

By engaging this firm during the developmental stage of the store, ideas about the use of architecture as advertising influenced the design and concept of Simpsons as a whole. *Art and Industry*'s review of Simpsons described how the fabric of the building was indeed essentially reduced to advertising,

> the store ceases to be architectural in conception and becomes spectacular display. This is merchandising at its best ... a store, in every respect, is an extension of the advertising idea, an idea that should permeate the whole building; façade; fittings; window; signs; and even down to the garments of the commissionaires and sales people. It should be the union of the architectural and merchandising. Taking his courage in one hand and Mr. Joseph Emberton in the other, Mr. Alec Simpson has got nearer to this association of the spectacular and the commercial as a total display, than has any other store I know of.[21]

In a particularly impressive move, the services of former Bauhaus artist László Moholy-Nagy were secured for the dedicated display department – and the shop's innovative curved-section non-reflective windows became home to an array of modern, geometric displays. Simpsons made great play of showcasing the best modern design talent available in London at this moment, and also exploited to an impressive degree the communicative register of inter-war modernism. But more than this, by housing its new masculine consumption cultures and modern fashions in this impressively authored building, the company went a long way to legitimizing precisely those cultures and fashions that might have proved problematic in business terms.

The inestimable benefits of a 'West End house'

This kind of mammoth advertisement in stone, glass and steel amounted to an enormous investment. Simpsons was built at a cost of £150,000, with a ground rent of £11,000 even before operational costs were taken into account. Simpson Ltd told its chain of agents 'This project is extremely costly. It is so costly, indeed, that Simpsons cannot hope, and are not hoping, to derive any profit whatever from its actual trading – at least for several years.'[22] Simpsons was not alone: at this time, substantial numbers of retailers were building or rebuilding their West End bases, suggesting that metropolitan retail businesses and their associated consumer cultures were sufficiently buoyant to support such projects in a period of acknowledged national, and international, economic depression, and also

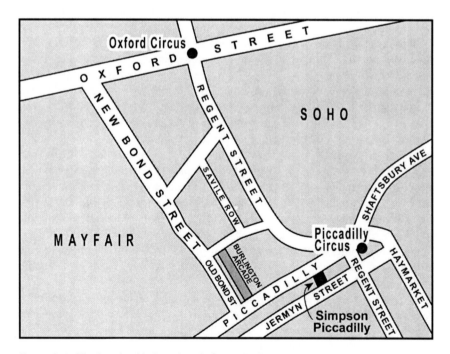

Figure 9.4   The inestimable benefits of a 'West End house'

suggesting that the positioning of a flagship store in such a costly location was felt to be worth the trouble.

New West End department stores were plentiful and high profile. For example, D. H. Evans was unveiled in Oxford Street of 1937, and in Kensington High Street there were Derry and Toms of 1933 and John Barker of 1937–8. The department store chain John Lewis had two major prestige projects: Peter Jones in Sloane Square of 1936, and John Lewis Oxford Street of 1937–9, whose rebuilding was interrupted by the outbreak of war. Only the rear block on Cavendish Square completed. These were years of investment and expansion, when the major West End thoroughfares were littered with building sites.

Also significant was the contemporaneous reemphasis on West End flagships amongst national clothing chains. The inter-war period witnessed the almost exponential growth of multiple stores, indicating the importance of other kinds of networks, linking urban, suburban and provincial high streets across the country. According to Winship ' "widened, scythed through" encapsulates the undercutting of place by market and the changing landscape of chain stores (chain cinemas, chain pubs, chain teashops) which dramatically pushed their way into British high streets in the 1930s' (Winship 2000: 18). Yet it is suggested here that the vibrant consumer culture of the 1930s was broad enough to encompass cultures associated with the suburban and provincial high street *and* those with the more affluent and fashionable West End; and furthermore that the place of the West End still had a powerful aspirational pull for those ostensibly excluded by the geography, prices, and 'exclusive' atmosphere associated with this location.

Indeed, geographical location was central to the identities of the West End store, the provincial/suburban chain store alike. In this respect, as in many others, British retailers drew directly on the new imported methods of American chains. Leading British shop design experts Bryan and Norman Westwood wrote, 'Correct siting is one of the most important factors determining the success or otherwise of shops. The conspicuously successful 'chain shop' firms of to-day owe at least part of their prosperity to their research departments, whose job it is to analyze the prospects of any proposed new shop ...' (Westwood and Westwood 1937: 13). Their preoccupation with sites, in terms of positioning the shop within the street, the relationships to side streets, parking, aspect and most importantly the colonization of the high street was representative of broader discussions within the retail trade press, and was fundamentally about place. It was also about the specificity of location: individual high streets had locally meaningful identities, which many architectural commentators and groups such as the Campaign for the Protection of Rural England were busy arguing at this time could not, or should not, be overridden by the arrival of a chain.

1930s chain store networks were often anchored in the West End with a flagship store, which was differentiated from others in the chain by its use as, or proximity to, the company's administrative headquarters. Displays around the country frequently followed the model of the West End store. These buildings were also lavished with extra resources, spent on architecture and interior design, staffing, stock and so on. For instance, Marks and Spencer's massive expansion of the 1930s included two very significant Oxford Street shops: the Marble Arch store of 1930 and the Pantheon of 1938, and it is clear from company records that both held particularly important positions within the company's portfolio.[23]

Similarly, in 1939, Austin Reed had a total of twenty-seven shops across England, two in Scotland and one in Northern Ireland.[24] National and international advertising campaigns promoted Austin Reed through distinctively metropolitan masculine identities, as well as identify the company as 'Austin Reed of Regent Street', pointing to the importance of this 1920s flagship store. Through the centralization of these networks into radials from a London base, chains in local high streets could be infused with a certain measure of West End shopping cultures. This argument about the continued importance of specific urban sites within national chains echoes Gilbert's work on the relationship between the global and the urban within late twentieth-century fashion cultures. He writes, 'While developments such as out-of-town shopping and e-commerce seem to presage the homogenization and de-urbanization of consumption, there are aspects of fashion culture which actively encourage production of active and differentiated urban spaces' (Gilbert 2000: 8).

This metropolitan magnetism was exploited by the big West End stores, using the common devices of mail order shopping and delivery systems to bring a piece of the West End to suburban and provincial locations, and to compete with chains. This was also explicitly evidenced by Simpsons, which operated alongside the pre-existing national network of small independent retailers who sold Simpson Ltd clothes. These agents were tied to the West End store not only through the garments, but through branding and window displays.

The management of Simpsons reassured the agents about the department store project in 1935 by describing how these places would relate to each other: ' "Simpson", becomes for you – your London shop. While your own personal business remains individual and untouched in its traditional character – you share with Simpsons the inestimable benefits of a "West End house" '.[25] These benefits which included access to its stock, use as a showroom, advice and training, and display templates. The West End anchor was explicitly sold to agents as a means of competing with chains:

> In nearly every sphere of retail today, the multiple store – heavily financed and heavily advertised – is spreading its tentacles throughout the country ... Against the superior financial and advertising strength of the multiple business, Simpsons are going to erect a strong nation-wide bulwark for you and all our agents – the keystone of which will be 'Simpson, Piccadilly'.[26]

This chapter argues that an acknowledgement of the special nature of the West End, of the metropolitan flagship, is not incompatible with a version of retail history which highlights the rise of the chain store, but it suggests a more complicated inter-war shopping landscape, and warns against the too hasty disposal of 'place' or 'metropolitan' as a means of understanding it.

Here it is worth considering the reasons for the crucial nature of this location for prestige stores in the 1930s. The West End of London was not an easy place to draw boundaries around, or to map, but then as now people were very clear about what it meant. It was London's centre of entertainment, shopping and fashionable living, luxurious yet also accessible: for the city gent and the office clerk (Edwards 2006a, 2006b). It existed in the popular imagination, in the many urban commentaries within newspapers, women's magazines and London guidebooks. As a guide of 1937 summarized,

> Since the last century, the term 'West End' has been regarded as a symbol of all that is most elegant in the capital: Royal Parks and Palaces; the 'town houses' of Society; great hotels; animated streets lined with fashionable shops; theatres; art galleries, and museums. If it is in the city that money is made, it is in the 'West End' that it is spent.
>
> (*London: A Combined Guidebook and Atlas*, 1937: 10)

The West End was the focal point for 1930s shopping cultures, a hub within local, national and international networks. Shopping that took place there was special and specific to that place; conferring value, status and meaning on both the activity and items bought; carefully constructed as an event, a source of pleasure, and a means of constructing a particular kind of consumer identity. As one West End retail professional wrote: 'In the case of the [provincial visitor], the names of the leading stores are ... such household words that it is remarkable how frequently they are one of the first places to be visited' (Neal 1932: 17).

The major West End stores were also hugely important in pulling in foreign tourists, and it is no accident that Simpsons advertised in publications such as the *Ocean Times*, for passengers on Atlantic liners. The 1930s was a period of growth in the British tourist industry, reaching a peak in 1937, the year of the coronation. Hence at the time of Simpsons' arrival on the West End stage, constructions of London through tourist texts, for an audience of national and international visitors, were becoming increasingly pervasive and London thus became a self-consciously 'tourist' city. A special 'British travel' issue of *Art and Industry* reported,

> Some years ago Great Britain was a comparatively untravelled country. Almost unawares a travel industry has sprung up with many agencies spread all over the world. Its pageantry, its traditional aspects, its stability in the midst of a disturbed state of affairs, are all the causes of a reawakening of interest in what a German writer not very long since called the 'unknown island ... London's shops are part of London's attractions. Almost every visitor makes a point of seeing what London offers the shopper.[27]

These networks were particularly important for a store like Simpsons, due to London's international reputation for traditional, masculine clothing. American *Vogue* addressed the following question:

What can I buy that is typically English? ... What clothes can I get here that are better than anything of the sort anywhere else?' ... Look in the men's shops. Not for nothing is London famed as the highest authority on men's fashions.[28]

Similarly, French *Vogue* noted the essential tradition and masculinity of the West End's shopping cultures,

Mayfair is not just an area of London, it is first and foremost a grand way of living. It's the shop windows that make you realize that London is the most civilized city in the world. London chic is masculine; women's fashion is considered an optional extra, a lesser art that shouldn't take centre stage.[29]

The careful positioning of the Simpsons flagship within this special location is also worth examining. Alexander Simpson explained, 'One hundred yards from Piccadilly Circus, and with a wide frontage on Piccadilly itself, there will rise during the next year a great, new, and modern, men's store ... There is probably no finer shop site than this in the entire world.'[30] It was placed very precisely in the tight cluster of streets in the heart of the West End around and between Oxford Street, Regent Street, Bond Street and Piccadilly that was acknowledged as 'London's most fashionable shopping district' (*London: What to See and Where to Stay*, 1930: 48). Its front entrance was on Piccadilly, close to Piccadilly Circus, between the National Provincial Bank and Lyons Popular café. This was at the beginning of the famous trail of major departments and other flagship stores, which reached up through Regent Street to Oxford Street. Piccadilly was also noted for its exclusive clubs and hotels, including the Piccadilly and the Ritz. These were situated amongst more weighty landmarks such as Burlington House with its host of learned societies, and also the London residences of figures such as the Dukes of York and Wellington. The guidebook *The World's Largest City* termed this street 'one of the world's most famous streets' and 'the great resort of the leisured and wealthy' (1938: 9).

Close to Piccadilly Circus, the store was also placed by London's arguably most iconic intersection at the junction of several busy streets: Shaftesbury Avenue, Haymarket, Regent Street and Piccadilly. It was a hub of traffic, consumption and cultural networks. It was home to the Criterion theatre and the old Swan and Edgar department store at the base of Regent Street. But it also functioned as the focus of a broader cultural network, as expressed by the guidebook *London: The World's Largest City*, 'Piccadilly Circus can be said to be the axel pin of the metropolis ... It is the place that all exiled English men and women abroad think of in their home-sick reveries; and so one may justly describe it as London's throbbing heart' (1938: 8). It also hosted Piccadilly Circus underground station, flagship in the high profile development of the Piccadilly Line. The station's interiors had been redesigned *c.*1928–30, by Adams, Holden and Pearson, using a fashionable 'moderne', visual vocabulary which connected it with fashionable West End shops like Simpson: smooth veneered surfaces, curved forms and the latest in atmospheric lighting (Saler 1999). The circus's statue of Eros, an important landmark and an emblem for the West End as a whole, was adopted as a key motif of Simpsons' advertising campaigns: cupid's arrow pointing the way to the store for the throngs of people. These connections were essential to attract the volume of dedicated customers and passers-by necessary to fill a store of Simpsons' proportions.

Simpsons' back door, however, addressed Jermyn Street, where its nearest neighbours were restaurants, bootmakers, tailors, the offices of solicitors and architects and residences of the well-to-do. This was part of the older route of masculine consumption which had its root in the masculine club land of St James's and stretched north to Savile Row, by way of Jermyn Street, Piccadilly Arcade and Burlington Arcade. Savile Row's thirty-nine properties were occupied by twenty-eight exclusive tailoring firms, accompanied by the occasional court dressmaker and club. The specialist businesses addressing more 'subsidiary' aspects of traditional elite masculine consumption were concentrated on Jermyn Street, Piccadilly and Burlington Arcades, and surrounding streets. For example, in the Burlington Arcade were a shirtmaker, four tobacconists, a fine art dealer, seven jewellers, seven hosiers and glovers, a heraldic stationer, a tie specialist, two bronze retailers, a milliner, a tailor, three bootmakers, an umbrella maker, an outfitter, a perfumier, a cutler, toy shop and a chocolate shop.[31] The business roll-call suggests a place where little had changed over the previous decades. They were also streets steeped in their broader history as a heartland of metropolitan masculinity, as H. V. Morton wrote of Jermyn Street, '... It is a street famed for its bachelor rooms and has housed, among many others, Newton, Gray, Scott and Thackeray' (Morton 1937). This route was fundamental to the West End's consumption patterns, and to London's worldwide reputation for masculine dress (Breward 1999).

The creation of a dual access enabled the store's internal circulation routes to tap directly into the street network, providing a direct cut-through from Piccadilly to Jermyn Street. Within this link, relationships between the old and new, the feminine and masculine could be renegotiated. It was this transformative capacity which differentiated this cut-through from Eagle Place just east of the store which made a similar spatial connection between Piccadilly and Jermyn Street. It also meant that it was different from the Piccadilly Arcade further West along Piccadilly, which housed traditional and primarily masculine businesses, maintaining continuity with rather than disrupting the old masculine shopping route as it jumped across Piccadilly between Jermyn Street and the Burlington Arcade. Positioning entrances on different streets in this way, although new for a West End man's shop, was an established department store technique used to exploit the benefits to business of addressing different routes.

However, 'back' entrances had a particular meaning in the context of the 1930s West End, when the balance between the different entrances and routes was shifting. A number of major West End stores appeared to be reorienting their buildings away from the main thoroughfares and towards similar minor streets. For example, the first stage of the Oxford Street John Lewis's rebuilding programme of 1937 was to create a prestige building addressing Cavendish Square. This was partly due to the protracted process of building up the 'island' site, negotiating with stubborn tenants. But it can also be read as a response to the disruption and chaos on the main streets, suggested by architect A. Trystan Edwards,

> Nothing is more tiring nor more discouraging to the would-be shopper than to be hustled by passers-by on a crowded pavement. It is notorious that Oxford Street and to a lesser extent Regent Street are losing their attractiveness owing to the discomfort experienced by pedestrians on the too narrow pavements, while more fortunate people who do their shopping by motor car find that there is insufficient room for vehicles to wait in the vicinity of the shops.
>
> (Edwards 1933: 61)

The commentator's point about parking perhaps gets closest to the truth: stores apparently believed that the West End's street network was being transformed by car ownership. The Westwoods advised,

> Proximity of squares where customers can park their cars is becoming increasingly important in site selection in central urban areas…. . Customers will patronize their shops where they can leave their cars even if it means travelling a greater distance to them. This is so important that at least one large London store has made arrangements with a near-by garage to park customers' cars free on production of a receipted bill.
>
> (Westwood and Westwood 1937: 17)

Display expert Hammond also clearly believed that shopping by car represented the way of the future, already being taken into account in North American retail design (Hammond 1930a: 38). It is important not to overplay this point: it was a long time before national mall-incrusted shopping networks developed, and the West End's arterial roads remained important shopping routes during the 1930s. However, these new ways of thinking about store positioning fed into the planning of new stores at this time: architects and owners were aware that they might soon have to operate as flagships within a rather different shopping geography.

This research, whilst acknowledging the development of chain stores in the inter-war period, which contributed to the construction of other kinds of national shopping networks with a multitude of suburban and provincial nodes, has made the argument that at this time such networks operated in tandem with an older, still potent and evolving, network of fashionable, metropolitan consumer cultures that centred on the West End. Here prestigious flagship stores like Simpsons proliferated, and it is clear that department stores still had a significant role to play. The dual trends of suburbanization and recentralization were a feature of commercial life and were indeed noted by the Greater London Regional Planning Committee in its report of 1933 (*Second Report of the Greater London Regional Planning Committee*, March 1933: 58).

In a time of some uncertainty about the future of British shopping geographies, 1930s retailers were still prepared to invest heavily in new West End flagships: understandably invoking the West End as a special place as often as possible within their advertisements. As a result, the area has been left a legacy of iconic stores – some reading as more 'modern' than others within the contemporary street scene, and all tied to the clothes and consumption cultures they were built to house. On the eve of opening, Alexander Simpson had written to his architect, 'I feel very much like the captain of a big new ship waiting for the pilot in charge of the tugs to get him out of the dock, so that I can sail spick and span on my maiden voyage.'[32] The challenge now is to understand and value these old flagships, as urban centres are reimagined for twenty-first century consumption, taking note of the risks and occasionally startling innovation that led to their building.

Notes

1 Memorandum, *c.*1935. Daks Simpson Archive.
2 For further discussion of the Simpsons consumer see Edwards (2003).
3 Letter from Alexander Simpson to Joseph Emberton, 29 August 1935, Daks Simpson Archive.
4 Discussed in a letter from Alexander Simpson to Joseph Emberton, 29 August 1935, Daks Simpson Archive.
5 Letter from Alexander Simpson to Joseph Emberton, 2 September 1935, Daks Simpson Archive.
6 *Daily Mail*, 30 April 1936.
7 Letter from Alexander Simpson to Mr Pearson, 1 January 1936. Daks Simpson Archive.
8 Review of Simpsons, *Art and Industry*, July 1936: 23.
9 Letter from Alexander Simpson to Joseph Emberton, 29 August 1935. Daks Simpson Archive.
10 Simpsons Advertisement, 'Sportsman's Paradise', *Evening Standard*, 26 May 1936: 11.
11 Simpsons Advertisement, 'Bill Bracken is at …', *Cook's Handbook*, 1938–9: 87.
12 Simpsons Advertisement, 'Daks Appeal', *Punch*, 11 May 1938.
13 Obituary for Alexander Simpson, *Sunday Express*, 16 May 1937.
14 'Simpson Advertising: a campaign of ideas', *Art and Industry*, June 1937: 245.
15 *The Scotsman*, 4 May 1936.
16 *Architect and Building News*, 8 May 1936.
17 Letter from Alexander Simpson to Joseph Emberton 20 May 1935. Daks Simpson Archive.
18 A detailed discussion of the relationship between British and International modernism is beyond the scope of this thesis, but is examined in more detail elsewhere, for example by Henry-Russell Hitchcock's essay 'Modern Architecture in England in *Modern Architecture in England*, Museum of Modern Art, New York, 1937: 25; Dean, *The Thirties*: 9; Stamp, *Britain in the Thirties*; Saler, *The Avant-Garde in Inter-war England*.
19 F. E. Bennett A.R.I.B.A. 'The Shop', *The Builder*, 1 February 1929: 240.
20 *Commercial Art*, August 1930: iv.
21 *Art and Industry*, July 1936: 18.
22 Memorandum *c.*1935. Daks Simpson Archive.
23 Minutes and staff magazines, Marks and Spencer Archive.
24 *Art and Industry*, July 1939: 13.

25 Memorandum *c.*1935. Daks Simpson Archive.
26 Ibid.
27 'Come to Britain!', *Art and Industry*, September 1936: 81, 86.
28 American *Vogue*, 21 June 1930: 54.
29 French *Vogue,* July 1938: 42.
30 Memorandum *c.*1935. Daks Simpson Archive.
31 *Kelly's Post Office London Directory*, 1936.
32 Letter from Alexander Simpson to Joseph Emberton, 20 April 1936. Daks Simpson Archive.

10 Wynn Las Vegas

A flagship destination resort

Nicky Ryan

Introduction

> In the next millennium, when people study the U.S. Empire, they won't be looking at buildings created by Frank Lloyd Wright or Frank Gehry. They'll be looking at our temples of pleasure, the buildings where we packed in as much America as would fit. And, somehow, Steve Wynn has done it in a way we won't be ashamed of.
>
> (Stein 2006)

In April 2005 entrepreneur Steve Wynn opened a new $2.7 billion, 2,716-room casino-hotel called Wynn Las Vegas. It is located on the Las Vegas Strip, a concentrated entertainment area of the city, five blocks wide and four and a half-miles long. The Strip is comprised of numerous themed 'megaresorts', huge hotels with multi-programmes that include casinos, theatres, restaurants, shopping malls, conference centres, and changing attractions (see Figure 10.1). Wynn, hailed by *Time* magazine as 'the gaming industry's most brilliant designer' (Stein 2006) was credited not only with introducing art, retail, and fine dining onto the Strip, but also

Figure 10.1   The Strip, Las Vegas (Photo: N. Ryan)

with setting the trend for themed hotels with the opening of the Mirage in 1989. He is also acknowledged as the developer responsible for moving the Strip upscale with the Bellagio in 1998, the first resort to offer luxury on an international scale. Having been forced to sell his company, Mirage Properties, to Kirk Kerkorian/ MGM Grand in a hostile takeover bid in 2000, Wynn's new hotel-casino marked his official return to the business of property development on the Strip. Wynn was a powerful member of a local growth coalition that espoused a pro-growth and pro-development ideology and his latest project was promoted as a new paradigm for luxury destinations that would revolutionize the Strip. The journal *Gaming Wire* (Stutz 2005) declared that 'Steve Wynn's openings are always a catalyst for something else' and prophesied that Wynn Las Vegas would initiate the next building boom. The emergence of numerous construction projects including plans for high-rise hotels and condo mixed-use developments, collectively referred to as 'the Manhattanization of Las Vegas', appeared to confirm this prediction.

This chapter will consider claims of flagship and paradigmatic status for Wynn Las Vegas and evaluate the ways in which Wynn's programmatic experiment offers innovations to the existing hotel-casino model. For a project to achieve flagship status, Bianchini *et al.* (1992: 245) argued that it must be a 'significant, high-profile and prestigious land and property development'. Mikunda (2004: 119) defined flagship buildings as 'business cards in the form of architecture' where the main purpose was corporate branding and image promotion. Buildings such as Wynn Las Vegas were designed to address both internal and external audiences and incorporated innovative technological and architectural features in order to construct an image of a progressive and 'cutting-edge' company. Wynn's hotel could be interpreted as a prominent corporate development which achieved both flagship and paradigmatic status through the use of experimental design to enhance brand identity.

Ritzer and Stillman (2001) argued that the casino-hotels of Las Vegas developed in the 1980s and 1990s were paradigmatic because they exemplified the processes that typify the 'new means of consumption'. This included 'rationalization', 'disen-chantment', 're-enchantment', 'spectacularization', 'simulation', 'implosion', and 'manipulations of time and space'. The casino-hotels of the Strip were buildings that concealed the realities of standardardized consumable space and economic enterprise beneath a façade of spectacular fantasy. Ritzer and Stillman argued that a paradigm must be the first of its kind and should serve as a model for subsequent structures *and* the processes undergirding a structure (2001: 84). The notion of Wynn Las Vegas as model and paradigm will be considered within the broader context of the development of the city. Las Vegas has been described by Rothman (2002) as the first city of entertainment, a test bed for radical ideas and the physical manifestation of a market-led ideology. The notion of Las Vegas as an urban laboratory, pioneering new trends that other places can adopt or adapt (Mikunda 2004: 93) gives the transformation of the Strip an international relevance.

Wynn Las Vegas can be interpreted as a cultural artefact with multiple meanings that are emblematic of temporal, spatial, political and social conditions concurrent with the hotel's production and consumption. The significance of Wynn's hotel is further underscored by its inauguration during the city's centenary celebrations. Wynn Las Vegas with its fifty storey arc-shaped bronze tower and lavish experiential features, not only symbolized the flagship status of Wynn Resorts Ltd. on the Strip, but provided a flagship for the city (see Figure 10.2). Powerful local business interests were transforming the image of Las Vegas in order to reframe the city as an upscale destination and sophisticated global metropolis. Wynn Las Vegas was deployed as a synecdoche, a marker of change for the city as it moved into a new transitional phase of growth.

The urban laboratory

> Las Vegas is the ultimate disposable city, shedding its old skin regularly as it fulfils its role as a mirror of popular culture.
>
> (Hess 1993)

Las Vegas has attracted interest from many writers due to its autogenesis and 'tradition of invention' (Douglass and Raento 2004). An analysis of the development of the city and its place within popular culture and critical writing situates Wynn's project within a specific historical and cultural context. Las Vegas is located in the middle of the Mojave Desert in Nevada and is metaphorically disconnected and 'marooned' from sprawling civilization by the surrounding sands. Historically cut off and isolated, the city has been described as 'a refuge from nature, but also

Figure 10.2   Wynn Las Vegas (Photo: N. Ryan)

from culture, from Protestant values and American ennui' (Farquharson 2001: 42). Five key phases of the city's growth have been identified by Gottdiener (1999) with phase one, lasting from 1861 to 1931 when mining, railroad and commercial interests from Los Angeles dominated the local economy. Phase two began in 1931 when gambling was legalized and continued until 1954, just before the local economy was transformed by casino gambling. Cheap electricity, the building of hotels and casinos, and Nevada's six-week residence requirement for uncontested divorce established Las Vegas as a major tourist destination with its 'Wild West' signifiers and frontier themes.

Phase three, between 1954 and 1969, saw the rise of gambling interests and mob involvement. Construction work filled the Strip and downtown 'Glitter Gulch' area with casino-resorts, and links with Hollywood's 'Rat Pack' developed the association of Las Vegas with celebrity and entertainment. The 1950s saw the growth of Las Vegas' convention industry and extensive real-estate development along the Strip, including glamorous hotels with neon signage such as the Flamingo, Desert Inn, the Dunes, the Hacienda, Tropicana and Stardust, offering spectacular stage shows and even golf courses. In the mid-1960s the construction of the themed hotels Circus, Caesar's Palace and the Aladdin Hotel reinforced the importance of the Strip as a site of tourism. The legitimating of activities such as gambling, prostitution and easy divorce helped make 'sin' a profitable enterprise.

The fourth phase from 1969 to 1987 witnessed the end of mob rule as the Corporate Gaming Act of 1969 allowed public corporations to purchase casinos, a decision, which transformed the look and financial operations of Las Vegas. It was during this period that Las Vegas, its image already well-established in popular culture through cinema and tourism became the subject of intellectual enquiry. In an article written following a visit to the city in 1965, journalist and author Tom Wolfe (1965: xvi) argued that it was Bugsy Siegel's lavish Flamingo Hotel that set the precedent for luxury themed gambling resorts, and which became not only *the* architectural style for all Las Vegas but for all of America. However, it was the publication of *Learning from Las Vegas* by architects Robert Venturi, Denise Scott Brown and Steven Izenour in 1972, which established the significance of Las Vegas within architectural discourse as a contemporary architectural icon and emblem of postmodernism. *Learning from Las Vegas* was an analysis of postwar populist American mass culture that argued for an architecture which used symbolism and allusion to create structures that expressed 'vitality' and 'fun' (p. 53). The decontextualization of the forms of Las Vegas and the aestheticization of the city caused some critics to accuse its authors of producing an uncritical celebration of consumer society. Las Vegas was positioned as 'other' to the prevailing architectural discourse of the 1960s, and was also perceived as 'other' within the popular imagination, a neon spectacle representing an escape from everyday life. For postmodern theorists such as Baudrillard (1983: 2), Las Vegas was a simulacrum, where the condition of hyperreality generated 'models of a real without origin or reality.' He compared it to a 'hologram' and 'mirage'

(1986), a depthless world of appearances, where everything was 'liquidated' and 'reabsorbed' into the surface.

Gottdeiner identified Las Vegas's fifth and current phase of growth as beginning in the late 1980s, and characterized by the dominance of corporate control. In 'MBA Vegas' gambling was renamed gaming, and large conglomerates developed leisure components that transformed the image of casino gambling into vacation entertainment. The legalization of gambling destroyed Las Vegas' monopoly of this leisure pursuit and necessitated the development of an alternative means of attracting tourists. The result was the advent and proliferation of the 'megaresorts', hotels with room counts of over 3,000 such as the Mirage, Excalibur, Treasure Island, and Luxor, all differentiated by fantasy themed environments. The majority of writing about Las Vegas produced at the end of the 1990s, focused on Las Vegas as a pleasure zone offering the varied seductions of money, sex, food, gambling, and nightlife. Boje (2001b: 81) categorized Las Vegas as the 'Postmodern City of Casinos and Simulation', emblematic of a transformation of the globalized spectacle of production and consumption. In his analysis of the postindustrial city as an entertainment hub, Hannigan (1998: 3–4) claimed that Las Vegas fulfilled all the characteristics of a 'fantasy city'. It was 'theme-o-centric', meaning that everything from individual entertainment venues to the image of the city itself formed part of a 'scripted theme' that bore little relationship to context; it was aggressively branded, it operated day and night; it mixed standard components into different configurations to create distinctive looking hotels; it was solipsistic, that is physically isolated from its neighbours; and postmodern in the sense that it was constructed around the technologies of simulation, virtual reality and spectacle. Similarly Dear (2000: 8) argued that the form of Las Vegas was 'increasingly determined by the demands of spectacle and consumption' and identified the city as a prototypical postmodern metropolis.

The most enduring conceptualization of Las Vegas appears to be that of an urban laboratory, a city constantly staging its own reinvention. Hess (1993: 117–18) constructed a view of the city as a pioneer of national and international trends, a model of American urbanism due to its architectural experimentation and the rise of hotels as mini-cities that rearranged the neighbourhoods of the traditional metropolis. For Sorkin (1999) Las Vegas was the 'designated city of the future' which offered an economic model for the next century – a post-industrial economy completely dominated by the service sector. In *Devil's Bargains* Rothman (2000) argued that the key to the city's survival was its malleability, the most critical feature of entertainment tourism. From sin city, entertainment centre, theme park to luxury destination, Las Vegas had consistently staged its own reinvention and remained a paradigm of a post-industrial service economy and model of entertainment tourism, a place where unskilled workers could earn a middle-class income with benefits and job security.

Literature written about Las Vegas in the 1980s and 1990s predominantly dwelt on the spectacular aspects of its gambling and tourism rather than on the urban challenges faced by a rapidly growing mercantile city. Las Vegas may have been theorized as the 'high capital of the society of spectacle' (Leach 1999: 70), a city of simulation and a phenomenon existing between reality and fiction, but even Eco (1998: 40) had to admit that it was rapidly becoming a 'real' city with residential areas, business, industry and convention centres. In what was the fastest growing city in America, growth was promoted as a constant source of interest by the media. Weibel (2001: 186) referred to Las Vegas as a 'post-public, private city' where tourists were more important than inhabitants, a city of consumption built on the principles of economy, money and profit. In a place where tourists numbered over 38 million in 2005, and inhabitants just under 2 million, their respective interests once seemingly aligned, appeared increasingly divergent particularly as the infrastructure of Las Vegas was failing to keep pace with the city's growth. Phenomenal growth posed challenges in terms of rising house prices, scarce public services, and a threat to the environment. An attempt to analyze the city's problems including its environmental crisis in relation to water supply, power and pollution and issues concerning traffic congestion, public debt and crime have more recently become the focus of attention for commentators on the city (see Davis 2000).

Variously characterized as a utopia (Hickey 1998), dystopia (Begout 2003), and heterotopia (Chaplin 2000), it would appear that Las Vegas was sufficiently multi-faceted for commentators to superimpose their own mythology upon the city. Key themes that emerge from an analysis of writings about Las Vegas are a fascination with the scenographic architecture of the city, a tension between the demands of tourism and a growing residential population, the implications for the environment resulting from rapid growth, and the power wielded by entertainment conglomerates in decisions about urban planning. For many visitors the concentrated entertainment infrastructure of the Strip *is* Las Vegas. Comprised of numerous multi-programmed competing hotels, the Strip was the battleground of private corporations such as MGM, Harrah's, Sands and Wynn Resorts Ltd., who competed in what Wynn (Ives 2005) described as 'twenty-four hour, seven days a week, violent hand-to-hand commercial combat'. This intense competition was what motivated casino-hotel owners to trial new attractions in order to differentiate their hotel from others on the Strip. However in the 'urban laboratory' of Las Vegas, experiments were quickly discarded if they failed to make a profit. As Rothman and Davis (2002: 14) argued, 'in Las Vegas, it is always about money, and in late capitalist postmodern America, there's nothing unusual about that except the frankness in acknowledging it'.

Wynn Las Vegas

Wynn has become the anti-Trump, hiding the bling, de-gilding the chandeliers, putting the Ferrari dealership in the back. The greatest creator of spectacle has redefined spectacle as an inner experience.

(Stein 2006)

This quotation from *Time* magazine formed part of a flattering synopsis of Wynn's career, thereby, justifying his inclusion in a list of the world's hundred most influential people. The article is noteworthy because it suggests that Wynn Las Vegas represented something fundamentally different from the majority of casino-hotels on the Strip. The 'myth' of Wynn as a legendary entrepreneur and formative influence on the development of Las Vegas, was well established in the media and academic literature. He was publicly credited with initiating a shift in the culture of Las Vegas from glitzy 'sin city', to a global entertainment resort offering a luxury experience at a middle class price (Rothman 2002: 24). This he had achieved by setting the trend for theming and by introducing leisure activities such as shopping and fine dining into the casino-hotel. The programmatic transformations that changed Las Vegas hotels into the mixed-use spaces of today are as significant as their iconographic transformation from 'decorated shed' to Disney-style themed 'architainment' (Klein 2004). It was the opening of the Mirage with over 3,000 rooms, 2,000 slot machines, and a spectacular fantasy environment that initiated the vogue for themed hotels. The hotel lobby included a tropical rain forest and a fifty foot long tropical fish tank, while outside there was a forest with waterfalls, lagoon and a volcano that erupted every fifteen minutes after dusk. Although theming had already existed in the form of Wild West, Arabian and Polynesian symbols, at the Mirage the themed narrative was extended to staff uniforms, restaurant cuisine, souvenirs and signage.

The luxury 'megaresorts' on the Strip cater for almost indistinguishable activities but achieve differentiation through their spectacular design rather than architectural authorship. Each hotel such as New York New York or the Luxor, has a discrete set of designed conditions which artificially differentiates their identical purpose. The meaning of these themed consumption spaces is produced through difference in the contrast between one casino theme and another. 'Metonymy and the juxtaposition of themes produces a spectacular system of signification' (Gottdeiner 1998: 13). The fantasy theme is developed through facades, the language of signs and pictures that connote a specific ideology or set of cultural meanings. By 2000 Las Vegas had become a city of hotels that mimicked other cities, a multitude of themed resorts borrowed from other places and other times. Like Disney's World Epcot Centre in Florida, the real world was captured and reintegrated into a synthetic universe where time was erased and all periods, all cultures, were accumulated into a single scenario. The hotels were 'scripted spaces' (Klein 2004) with Disney-style narratives and illusionistic effects, featuring the audience in the starring role. Individually the hotels were similar to what could be found in other American resorts such as Atlantic City, but grouped together they were spectacular. As Douglass and Raento (2004: 21) argued, the critical massing of simulacra in an unprecedented configuration 'constituted its own authentic reality', and made Las Vegas paradigmatic rather than parasitic. Collectively dazzling, this 'architainment' was designed to draw pedestrians in from the strip and to obscure the underlying function of profit.

Las Vegas has always been closely associated with hotels and according to the Las Vegas Convention and Visitors Authority website the city is home to seventeen of the twenty largest hotels in the United States. The 'megaresort' has its antecedent in the grand hotel tradition that emerged in America in the early nineteenth century. Hotels such as the Tremont in Boston (1829) and Astor House in New York (1836) established the hotel as a business enterprise and laboratory for new technologies (Albrecht 2002: 11). The evolution of the hotel is closely associated with the development of technology as the spectacular electric lighting of London's Savoy Hotel demonstrated when it opened in 1889. The sense of fantasy facilitated by new inventions was also evident in the Miami Beach hotels inspired by the glamour of Hollywood movies and designed by Morris Lapidus in the 1950s. The legacy of these developments can be seen in hotels such as Wynn's $2 billion Bellagio, which included a $40 million dancing fountain choreographed to a musical accompaniment. Concept architect Jerde Partnership developed the site plan of the project and the exteriors and some interior spaces, with the rest of the hotel, including the thirty-six storey tower block, designed by Wynn's in-house team Atlandia Design. This was not 'star' architecture in the manner of Frank Gehry's Guggenheim Museum Bilbao. At the Bellagio, the role and signature of the concept architect was absorbed into the broader scheme dictated by in-house multi-disciplinary teams. Wynn controlled all aspects of the design development of his hotels, just as Michael Eisner used to oversee all projects for the Disney Company. Davies (1999: 165) argued that in this respect, Wynn followed a pre-modern or Renaissance model when commissioning architecture where the architect deferred to the wisdom of the patron.

The concept for Wynn Las Vegas, like the Bellagio, was created by the Jerde Partnership but the detailed planning stage was coordinated by in-house architects DeRuyter of Wynn Design and Development. With its fifty storey arc-shaped bronze hotel tower, man-made mountain, waterfall, gardens, golf course, art gallery, casino, shops, cafés, theatres, and convention rooms, Wynn Las Vegas was a hybrid space programmed to deliver a range of spectacular experiences. The key 'innovations' introduced at Wynn Las Vegas included the omission of an obvious theme or front stage attraction, hotel branding based on the personality of its owner, an attempt to raise the level of luxury and the concept of a more metropolitan sophisticated resort design. If the Bellagio 'brought luxury living to the level of fine art' (Wynn quoted by Twitchell 2002: 229) then according to its owner, Wynn Las Vegas was 'how God would do it if he had money' (Wynn quoted by Francis 2005). Luxury, argued Braudel (1967), is a relative concept and the idea of what constitutes luxury changes over time and in relation to different societies but the value attached to luxury is a crucial component in any society's self-understanding. The sign value of Wynn Las Vegas can best be understood in relation to the other casino-hotels on the strip where its apparent lack of theme and understated luxury communicated differentiation and distinction. The rejection of an open model resort for an inner-looking closed version appeared to be motivated by economics as much as aesthetics, the intention being to drive people into the building to spend rather than provide a free sidewalk spectacle. The hotel offered no external core attraction such as the volcano at the Mirage, the pirate ship at Treasure Island or the choreographed fountain display at the Bellagio. The mountain and landscaping on the Las Vegas Boulevard were conceptualized as 'back of stage' with the theatrical spectacle comprising the resort design itself.

In spite of its size, the hotel was deliberately designed to an intimate scale, substituting small-scale 'neighbourhoods' for large and dramatic spaces, thereby avoiding the gigantism of many competing resorts. Customization was an important design element, which was executed through the design of restaurants that reflected the personalities of the nineteen chefs in house, and the creation of sensual spaces through the use of colour, texture and custom made fixtures and furnishings (see Figure 10.3). The majority of hotels on the Strip are comprised of the same components but what creates difference, according to Wynn, is the artistry involved in their arrangement. Corporate promotional material for Wynn Las Vegas focused on the hotel rooms, emphasizing high tech equipment, lavish decorations and breathtaking views. The strapline of an advert for the hotel stated that, 'It took Michelangelo four years to complete the Sistine Chapel. Your room took five' (LVCVA website), suggesting that a room at Wynn Las Vegas was on a par with one of the greatest masterpieces of the Renaissance. The implication was that Wynn, whose signature defined the room's rarity, had replaced the creative genius of Michelangelo. Through a process of symbolic 'transubstantiation', the application of Wynn's logo had transformed the hotel into a work of art (Bourdieu and Delsaut 1975). At the Bellagio, Wynn commissioned artist Dale Chihuly to create a central feature for the lobby which resulted in the $10 million hand-blown multi-coloured glass chandelier *Fiori di Como*. At Wynn Las Vegas the focal point was a bar. Aside from the economic concern of converting sightseers into customers, the

Figure 10.3   Wynn Las Vegas lobby (Photo: N. Ryan)

implication was that celebrity art is unnecessary because the new hotel itself 'is an environmental theatre – like a famous painting you can walk into' (Wynn quoted by Francis 2005). At Wynn Las Vegas what appeared to be on offer was no Disney-style encounter but an *art experience*.

Wynn Las Vegas opened with a small art gallery and adjacent larger gallery shop. Having introduced fine art as an attraction on the Strip with the Bellagio Gallery of Fine Art, which had attracted 1,800 visitors per day, Wynn assumed that he would have a similar level of success with his new art venture. The decision to exhibit art in the Bellagio, according to founding curator Libby Lumpkin, was not 'a shrewd business enterprise in itself; it was intended to enhance and set the tone for the elegant, upscale hotel – sort of the jewel in the crown' (Lumpkin 2006). Wynn began buying for the Bellagio collection in 1996 and acquired an art collection then valued at $350 million. He and his wife Elaine are recognized as two of the most important patrons of the arts in Las Vegas, funding exhibitions, music and dance performance as well as building up a substantial collection of fine art. At the Bellagio, Wynn managed to negotiate an arrangement whereby the resort paid him rental fees to display his collection, paid his insurance, property and sales tax, in return for allowing the public access to the paintings. He was therefore able to fund his art purchases while gaining $40,000 per day in entry charges, which paid for the cost of operating the gallery. He could display the art, the value of which increased through exhibition and associated publicity, while retaining the right to sell any pieces should he choose to do so. For Wynn being a patron of local cultural events and accumulating an art collection, proved to be a judicious strategy for dealing with federal tax laws, a potentially lucrative source of investment and a means to accrue 'cultural capital' (Bourdieu 1984) and improve his standing in the community. The Wynn Gallery was a for-profit space, dark and vault-like with paintings spot lit and protected behind rails. Within the heavily guarded gallery, audio guides delivered Wynn's personal narrative about the art pieces, stressing their authenticity and economic value. The story of art presented at Wynn Las Vegas was that of a single collector's vision where everything was for sale. However, unable to attract a sufficient number of visitors to make it economically viable, in 2006 the gallery was replaced by a men's shoe shop.

The contemporary exterior of Wynn Las Vegas, a dynamic arc of curtain glass wall bearing the signature of its owner, resembled an office block rather than the 'funhouse urbanism' (Hawthorne 2005) of Las Vegas. The corporate headquarters of Wynn Resorts Ltd. was a flagship building that signified a politics of space representing Wynn's economic, political and cultural status in the city. The aim of flagship buildings according to Mikunda (2004: 119) was 'image building, public relations and brand and corporate advertising'. Flagships are three-dimensional logos, prominent and photogenic symbols used on publicity material, postcards, and corporate communications. They function as promotional signs of the corporation and sometimes the city, as in the case of Wynn Las Vegas which formed a significant element of the urban skyline. A frequently reproduced image of Wynn Las Vegas is the view photographed from the Strip looking up at the bronze reflective tower, its imposing form softened by the foliage, water features and cluster of small buildings in the foreground. One of the most striking features of the design is the Wynn logo, the distinguishing mark of the hotel's creator. Based on Steve Wynn's autograph, it precisely underlined the status of this building as a 'signature' resort. This was the latest architectural statement from his company, a blueprint for future corporate developments such as his hotel-casino in Macau (see Stein 2005). Immortalized in a triptych by Andy Warhol (1983), fêted by *Time* magazine, Wynn was already a brand in his own right. The use of the signature logo and invented company crest throughout the building was designed to reinforce his authorial omnipresence.

The Manhattanization of Las Vegas

> 2005 will be remembered as a transitional period for Las Vegas. It saw a legend return and the groundwork laid for a transformation of the Las Vegas Strip.
>
> (Schwarz 2006)

Wynn was the legend referred to in this quotation from the *Las Vegas Business Press*. The cult of personality celebrated by the media could in part be explained by a nostalgic yearning for the 'heroic' characters that had shaped early Las Vegas, such as Bugsy Siegel and Howard Hughes. As massive conglomerates such as MGM began to buy up the majority of the Strip, Wynn stood out as a 'visionary' entrepreneur whose buildings reflected the scale of his personal ambition. Wynn has been characterized as a 'new economic Medici' (Davies 1999: 175) drawing parallels with the family of bankers who in Renaissance Florence enhanced their reputation, social status and ultimately political power through their patronage of art and architecture. In the case of Wynn, his property development gave him economic power and membership of a powerful business elite, and his role as a patron of the arts enhanced his respectability and social standing. The predominantly favourable media coverage Wynn received was due as much to his litigious reputation and status as the 'most feared and the most powerful man in the State', as to his architectural innovations. Critics such as John Smith (2001) have challenged the myth of Wynn's contribution to the development of the city, and proposed an alternative narrative that questioned the legitimacy of some of his business dealings. Wynn's patronage of the arts served to communicate an image of the property owner as a philanthropist with an interest in the wider community, deflecting criticism away from political activities, which often advanced casino interests at the expense of public welfare.

Wynn's latest casino-hotel was significant not only because it took five years to build, was the most expensive property on the Strip and its progress was veiled in secrecy, but it was the first major building on the Strip after a downturn in business following the destruction of New York's Twin Towers in 2001. With its contemporary-looking arc-shaped curtain glass wall and lavish interiors, it appeared to embody the city's latest reincarnation. The abstract, mirrored façade of Wynn's tower block provided a model and benchmark for the new condominiums planned or under construction on the Strip. What Wynn (quoted by Stein, 2005) described in *Time* magazine as the 'most understated overstated hotel in the world', signalled a move away from kitsch to a more sophisticated metropolitan sensibility that reflected the changing demographics of the city. Wynn Las Vegas could be classified as a flagship project not only because it was a high-profile, prestigious large-scale corporate development but also because it appeared to play 'an influential and catalytic role in urban regeneration' (Bianchini *et al.* 1992: 245). The catalytic role of flagship developments was crucial because building projects 'only justify their flagship status if they succeed in attracting a 'flotilla' of other developments in their wake' (p. 246).

The numerous construction sites on the Strip populated by cranes, diggers and a predominantly Latino workforce provided the physical evidence of this 'flotilla', and several websites were launched to chart Las Vegas' real estate transformation. One such website *Manhattanization Las Vegas* (www.manhattanization.com), described itself as an online magazine 'dedicated to the vertical growth of the Las Vegas marketplace', while *Vegas Today and Tomorrow* (www.vegastodayandtomorrow.com) stated that its aim was to track 'the current building boom and future urban projects in Las Vegas'. On its home page the latter claimed that,

> Vegas has been expanding skyward since 2005 when Steve Wynn launched the latest and largest building-boom Vegas has ever seen. More than 110 high-rise, condo, hotel, mixed-use and other major projects in the Las Vegas area are in various stages of planning, development and construction [...] Transportation projects, public facilities and high-rise residences are being built among new markets, galleries, shops, clubs and bistros. The Las Vegas Strip is filling in and stretching out with projects, all boasting the latest in new-urban concepts, architecture, design and technology.

Whether the 110 building projects identified above could directly be attributed to Steve Wynn's influence was questionable but his reputation as successful entrepreneur and pioneer of new trends was important. It was Wynn's personal status that caused the media to interpret Wynn Las Vegas as a signal of rising confidence in the city's property market.

In Las Vegas, growth and property development is a constant source of interest to both the media and public. In spite of the fact that many of the projects reported in the press failed due to rising material costs and the low supply of qualified labour, the media continued to promote 'high-rise fever'. In particular, prestigious developments such as MGM/Mirage's City Center, costing over $7 billion, were widely reported and promoted as mixed-use spaces that would provide an authentic city centre, a real urban district. Following Wynn's lead, MGM/Mirage rejected the theme-park design of the 1990s, but unlike Wynn opted instead to work with celebrity architects such as Rafael Viñoly, Norman Foster, Art Gensler, James Cheng, Cesar Pelli and Kohn Pedersen Fox. These 'star' architects were briefed to design megaresorts, boutique hotels, condominium towers, retail, theatres, nightclubs and convention space 'with limitless boundaries, exploring unique and modern ideas' (www.vegastodayandtomorrow.com). New architecture incorporating cutting-edge design was used by private corporations such as MGM and Wynn Resorts Ltd. to mark out and maintain brand distinction in the increasingly competitive Las Vegas marketplace. As Sklair (2005) has argued, in the culture-ideology of consumerism, iconicity is a resource for struggles in meaning and power.

Images of the rapidly changing cityscape of Las Vegas were disseminated internationally through photographs and computer renderings via the internet, newspapers and architectural magazines. The transformation of city cultures through the projection of new images designed to make them more attractive to visitors, investors and consumers can take a number of forms. Crane *et al.* (2002) have outlined three strategies for reframing national and local cultures; the retooling of urban neighbourhoods by increasing opportunities for tourism and commerce, Disneyfication, and 'postmodern upscaling' where the arts are used to attract an elite international audience. In the case of Las Vegas it could be argued that all three strategies have been employed in the city's re-imaging as demonstrated by the increase in leisure facilities, the theming of hotels and the introduction of fine art galleries onto the Strip. Andrew Smith (2005: 399) defines re-imaging as 'the deliberate (re)presentation and (re)configuration of a city's image to accrue economic, cultural and political capital'. This can involve conventional place-marketing techniques using slogans, logos and promotional literature or more subtle strategies such as the hosting of events and construction of iconic buildings. Gottdeiner (1986: 208) suggested that the most influential constructed images of the city are those produced by local growth coalitions consisting of private-sector business, community leaders and government officials. Unlike the urban images found in local authority discourse which he considered to be largely irrelevant, 'urban regimes' were able to fundamentally alter a city's image through the creation of privately funded property developments.

The meaning of Las Vegas was being re-written by a local growth coalition that included casino executives, real estate developers and the media, a business elite that espoused a pro-growth and pro-development ideology. Casino owners like Wynn were able to exert a powerful political influence and shape public policy in the interests of land developers and the gaming industry. Through campaign contributions and by influencing voter registration among thousands of employees, members of this coalition actively bankrolled political candidates for office and exerted control across Nevada government at all levels (Moehring 2002: 81). This corporate control of the political system ensured the maintenance of low property taxes and high sales taxes which benefited developers and the casinos but which failed to provide adequate state funding for infrastructure and public projects. Zukin (1995: 2–3) has argued that 'those who create images stamp a collective identity [...] By accepting these spaces without questioning their representations of urban life, we risk succumbing to a visually seductive, privatized culture'. She claimed that in the process of re-imaging a city or place, an identity could be created that concealed an ideology often at odds with the interests of local inhabitants. Beneath the gloss of media rhetoric about the benefits of growth and Las Vegas becoming an exciting, modern, liveable city, there remained a clear divide between the Strip, the locus of power, and the residential suburbs. For local officials, Wynn's new megaresort transformed the dormant northern end of the Strip, inspired new resort construction, and provided an effective symbol of world demand for the city's latest entertainment spectacle. However, the additional real estate construction it stimulated could only result in more traffic congestion, smog, crime and increasing pressure on social services. As Moehring (2002: 95) has argued, 'paradoxically, while gambling continues to create new jobs and attract new residents to Las Vegas, the political economy of gambling threatens the city's future as well as the state's'.

Conclusion

> This pure – virtually empty – sign – is ineluctable, *because it means everything*.
>
> (Barthes 1979)

The media reception of the highly anticipated Wynn Las Vegas was generally positive but there were reservations (for example see Hawthorne or Gorman 2005). The majority of critics agreed that the hotel was intricately crafted and in terms of the Strip possessed an unusual degree of intimacy and understated luxury, but it wasn't significantly better or different from its predecessors. Wynn Las Vegas did not appear to signify a leap in terms of flagship hotel-casino design as the Mirage did in 1989 or the Bellagio in 1998. Rather it was an evolution or 'refinement' (Rothman 2006) of the typical multi-programmed resort model. Wynn's project could be seen as the pinnacle of the Strip megaresort genre and 'a new benchmark for the size of resorts the market will bear' (Smith 2005) but it was not a new paradigm. Claims that it laid the groundwork for a transformation of the Strip could be substantiated in that it redefined a new standard in terms of sophisticated design, customization, luxury and service that many of the new condominiums and mixed-use spaces currently in development sought to match. Wynn moved away from a culture of kitsch and 'infantilism' (Belk 2000) towards a more understated form of luxury that used fine art as part of its signifying practices.

The iconic Desert Inn hotel had been imploded and replaced with an updated model in what Sorkin (1999) described as a celebration of temporality, 'waste elevated to symbolic exchange'. Wynn Las Vegas as an event, that is the staging of the processes of destruction and construction, was as important as the building itself and was emblematic of the image of permanent change associated with the city. Any symbol is partial and selective and Wynn's new resort failed to address the wider challenges affecting the future of Las Vegas as a whole. In a city with the lowest ratio of public spaces and parks per capita, the hotel's closed model neither added outdoor civic space nor enhanced the pedestrian experience of the Strip. Even in the hotel atrium public seating was replaced by a waitress-service bar, thereby exchanging free contemplation for economic transaction. Moreover when environmental issues in relation to water and electricity were hotly debated, the overall design of Wynn Las Vegas incorporated no eco-friendly features but wasted resources in spectacular style.

Wynn Las Vegas fulfilled the criteria for flagship status because it was a development in its own right, a marshalling point for further investment, and a promotional tool for an area or city (Smythe 1994: 5). The significance of Wynn's project resided less in the implications of its subtle differences for resort design, but rather in its symbolic role in mediating corporate identity and as a flagship for the city with its potential to stimulate economic growth and add incremental demand for tourism. Wynn Las Vegas signalled the rebirth of Wynn's property interests on the Strip, and was a synecdoche, a metaphor for the re-invention of Las Vegas from middle-class leisure destination to high-end luxury resort and sophisticated adult destination.

11 High-end 'factory outlets'

New showcases of German carmakers

Dion Kooijman

Introduction: new flagships, new metaphors

German automobile manufacturers have been busy revitalizing their relations with their customer base by designing and developing new showrooms and flagship stores. In many cases these include museums, restaurants and other leisure attractions under the same roof. Autostadt from Volkswagen, located near Wolfsburg in Germany, is a good example. It was built in 2000 to present all the brands of the Volkswagen family. But other German carmakers also have their conspicuous projects. Mercedes opened a brand new museum near its production facilities in Stuttgart. BMW followed in 2007 with its BMW-Welt in the centre of Munich.

Marketing and 'brand experience' are at the core of the business motives. The Volkswagen group literally states on its website: 'as communications platform of the Volkswagen group, the Autostadt is the interface between customer and global company' (www.autostadt.de, 2007). The business chain is undergoing a shake-up, resulting in the emergence of a new spatial network of consumer activities. Producers are looking for distribution opportunities and at the same time the consumption sphere is filled with 'leisure' and 'experiences'. At stake here are not the well-known factory outlets, disconnected from both production sites and shopping areas, selling previous years' stock leftovers at discount prices. Autostadt, BMW-Welt and others are – on the contrary – high-end consumption places, often linked with the carmakers' production facilities and dominated by consumption of the brand. This chapter sheds some historical light on these new cathedrals of consumption, and notes that this metaphor is wearing thin in places.

Shop types that have arisen since the beginning of the nineteenth century such as shopping arcades, department stores and even shopping malls have often been compared to cathedrals and palaces (Gardner and Sheppard 1989; Crawford 1992; Falk and Campbell 1997; Crossick and Jaumain 1999). There is much to be said for that, for they imitate their religious and aristocratic forebears with large, high-ceilinged interiors and lavish decorations. Milan's gigantic Galleria, the immense dome of the Printemps store in central Paris and the huge atrium in the Mall of America near Minneapolis USA all represent this approach in their different ways. They are retail spaces you literally have to look up to, just like churches and palaces. Palaces and cathedrals were obvious metaphors for shops like these. They made new socio-economic developments acceptable to the developer, the retailer and the consuming public alike. Metaphors serve often enough as lubricants of social change.

The American sociologist Richard Sennett (1990) analysed medieval cathedrals in terms of social boundaries. The cathedral represented a safe haven of order for the congregation amid the chaos of the surrounding town. As we know, the faithful get their reward only after death. The social unity which in Sennett's view has been lost is thus restored posthumously. With regard to the consumption of goods in today's shops, this question takes on somewhat earthly dimensions. The vertical relationship between the worshipper and his God has tipped over to a horizontal one between the consumer and the product on the shelf. The satisfaction of needs is no longer a postponed state of bliss but an immediate one – except in that the goods must first be paid for at the checkout. The spacious arcade, the heavenly vaulting of the department store and the cavernous shopping mall atrium are no more than backdrops for that climax. These imposing retail spaces are often literally within our grasp; they have become functional spaces which no longer force us to look up at them. The moving stairway has made it possible to traverse the space with serenity, so that we may easily imagine ourselves as omnipotent beings in the post-modern retail atrium; having reached the top floor we gaze down on our own sort and thus on ourselves.[1]

The function of the metaphorical form of language must here be sought primarily in what Sennett has termed an 'adjacent attraction'. The architecture is

Figure 11.1   The green environment of Autostadt near Wolfsburg, Germany (Photo: Dion Kooijman, Delft)

required to compensate for the 'poor' (in other words, standardized) products of industrial manufacturing (Sennett 1977). The attractor thus consists primarily of the shop rather than the products it sells, although much the same could of course be said about the packaging of those products. The use-value of the products has been suspended for a while. A more detailed analysis of the cathedral metaphor reveals that the analogy with shop types often falls flat. The familiar guise of the metaphor has often enough served as a disguise for genuine social innovation.

The brief for the Munich firm Henn Architekten was to make Wolfsburg attractive to potential Volkswagen purchasers (Henn 2004). Their answer was Autostadt. A metaphor is at play here as before, but now it is one that links the 'city' ('Stadt' in German) to vehicle consumption. Wolfsburg houses Volkswagen's main factory, the largest car plant in the world with a daily output of some 3,500 to 4,000 cars. The town of Wolfsburg is pre-eminently a home for Volkswagen employees and has little to offer non-residents. The requirement for something 'extra' was inspired largely by the marketing objectives of the vehicle marque. A brand image consists nowadays of emotion and subjective experience. Emotion here means the non-rational aspects of buying behaviour, while subjective experience relates to the extensive perceptions constructed around the brand. An emphasis on the experience is an attempt to disconnect consumption from daily preoccupations and to redefine it as a leisure activity. The marketeers agree that there is little ground to be gained on competitors in technical respects, but emotions and experiences can make all the difference.

The management gurus Joseph Pine and James Gilmore (1999) set the tone for this in their book *The Experience Economy*.[2] Consider car advertising: the message is nowadays seldom about horsepower or top speed, but instead about accessories such as navigation systems, the leisure uses of the vehicle or simply a sexy image. German car manufacturers like Volkswagen, BMW and Mercedes-Benz have since the 1950s been offering purchasers the option to collect their new vehicles from the factory in person, and today 35 per cent of German customers take advantage of this opportunity. All that was required, in effect, was to dress up the logistic happening; and the use of a city metaphor was the first step in this direction. However, Pine and Gilmore are obviously speculating about social evolution. Experiences are fourth in a chain of developmental stages. They have emerged after commodities, goods/products, and services have come into use. Each new stage makes the former obsolete. Pine and Gilmore also stated that the trade of experiences will make the escape from price competition possible. The history of retail however has showed a quite different, multi-layered development and not the absolute extremes Pine and Gilmore have propositioned.

Consumer-shareholders

Autostadt is a different kind of consumption space from the above-mentioned shopping arcades, department stores and shopping malls. To start with, it is not a conventional (separate) retail outlet but one which is tied to a single manufacturer. It no longer involves shopkeepers selling goods on their own account and at their own risk, but manufacturers who have taken over the retail function. This is remarkable in that a separate economic branch of retailing has been the favoured trading model for some 200 years; the distribution of consumer goods was believed to take place most efficiently without the interference of manufacturers. Nearly all the familiar shops and formulas are based on this principle. During the last two decades we have become familiar with the so-called factory outlet stores and factory outlet centres, distribution extensions of several producers, but what is conspicuous is the high-end quality of Autostadt. Autostadt is a flagship, but one of a manufacturer involved in retailing.

A second phenomenon of growing importance is what I would term the consumer-shareholder. Consumption has taken control over production. Market researchers are constantly probing for details of consumer preferences and hammering them into new or modified products and formulas. The marketing is carried out along the new borders of life-style representing a plethora of niches and segments (Cohen 2003; Gartman 2004). Already in the late 1920s, the car industry became consumer directed. But, at that time, this new orientation was towards a mass market. In the 1970s and 1980s different and separated markets showed up. It all happens at breakneck speed, and is referred to nowadays as a demand-driven market. In the process, consumers have considerably expanded their territory in recent years – not only as to the volume of goods consumed but also in that consumption has become the construction material for the current identity and a criterion of many social activities. We not only consume products and shops, for example, but TV programmes and political parties. The consumer has usurped the citizen; it would seem (Sorkin 1992).

Michael Sorkin was one of the first scholars who recognized the confluence of city and consumption. His edited book, *Variations of a Theme Park* (1992) saw this new phenomenon analysed in depth. Several authors noted the nearly endless duplication of images in leisure and retail spaces, which is relevant considering metaphors as specific examples of duplication. Boyer (1992) suggested that a 'feeling of social insecurity seems to breed a love of simulation'. Images of e.g. a heroic past offer 'a reassuring anchor'. Crawford (1992:12) indicated a close, more fundamental, relationship between consumption and identity: 'If the world is understood through commodities, then personal identity depends on one's ability to compose a coherent self-image through the selection of a distinct personal set of commodities'. For similar lines of thought, see Benson (2000) and Lasch (1984). (For our own attempt with respect to consumption psychology and architecture, see Kooijman, and Sierksma 2007.)

In cases where consumers participate in the financial risk of an enterprise, they are often also shareholders. There are plenty of those around nowadays. Manuel Castells (2001) draws a picture of a 'management elite' of employees who participate in the future of their employing company. In my view, this is symptomatic of a much more widespread phenomenon. To start with, those of us who fill in our own income tax returns in the Netherlands (taxation policy since 2002) know that the taxman assumes a fictional return of 4 per cent on capital. Modest though this amount is, ordinary savings accounts rarely offer an

Figure 11.2   Collection by new car owners, Mercedes-Benz, Sindelfingen, Germany
(Photo: H. van der Veen, Delft)

interest rate as high as that. Only investment in equity holds out the prospect
of a higher return. Shares in vehicle companies, which may be concealed in an
equity fund from a bank or insurance company, are one possibility. Incidentally,
the professionals have already recognized for some years how influential small
investors can be on the ups and downs of the financial markets, having been
responsible for triggering a number of crises. These crises can in turn have a
crucial impact on individual investors. James Farrell (2003) observes considerable
dissavings in American households, probably the combined effect of high-level
consumption and the devaluation of shares.

Autostadt

The economy and consumption have in effect been short-circuited in several
ways. A hybrid conglomerate of demand and supply factors has developed, each
showing certain hybrid features in its own right. After all, the carmakers have set
up shop; and the consumer shops around – often uninhibited by brand loyalty – for
goods as diverse as cars, leisure packages and shares. The Wolfsburg Autostadt
raises many questions. What consequences will Autostadt have for geographic
space? What similarities and differences are there between the German carmakers
Volkswagen, Audi, Mercedes, BMW and Porsche? In what ways are the shopping
for identity and the shopping for cars – still an expensive good – linked? How do
architects and other design disciplines adapt to the car manufacturers' policies?

Perhaps the most important question, however, is to what extent does marketing dominate the architecture and urban design of consumption spaces?

Autostadt consists of ten buildings in park-like surroundings. This green environment gives Autostadt a rather suburban character. The Autostadt 'city' is situated opposite the railway station and alongside Volkswagen's existing manufacturing facility. Each of the company's marques has its own building: Audi, Bentley, Lamborghini, Seat, Skoda and Volkswagen itself are presented separately. There is also a museum giving an overview of Volkswagen history. If you are properly guided – by someone else or through your own knowledge – there is indeed something to learn here. The new vehicles awaiting collection by their new owners are parked in two transparent cylinders, each as tall as a block of flats. A miniature railway conveys interested visitors on a behind-the-scenes tour of the Volkswagen factory. The marque thereby demonstrates that it has nothing to hide (Barnstone 2004). The architecture of the individual buildings underlines this principle by draping itself in glass curtain walls. There is also a hotel at the edge of the park to accommodate multi-day visits.

Autostadt's 'adjacent attraction' starts, however, at the entrance hall, which is linked to the railway station by a footbridge. Here it is not only the cathedral-like height that impresses but also the depth. A glass floor offers a view underfoot of colourfully rotating globes of the world. Those who are not yet satisfied by the visual consumption of this spectacular space are free to turn left towards the shop or right towards the restaurant. The tour for new car owners follows a route from the impressive entrance lobby to the *Kundenzentrum* (customer centre) where the purchaser finally takes possession of his or her new vehicle. On the way it passes the *Zeithaus* (museum) and the pavilions for individual marques. All this is free of charge for new car purchasers; tourists and museum visitors have to pay.

Autostadt was created for the 2 million temporary 'residents' who pass through annually. The planned volume of visitors made it imperative to design it for efficiency. A well-planned visitor route and smooth flow patterns were major considerations. To this end, the designers carefully studied existing examples such as Disneyland, Futuroscope and Niketown. But at heart, the well-designed visitor route is like that in a supermarket. The guided tour traverses the park clockwise; the guide has his group of visitors in his supermarket trolley, so to speak, and wheels them along the shelves of the marque pavilions. A cluster of 20 to 30 visitors passes every 45 minutes. At the end of the tour, the new car awaits in the *Kundenzentrum*. The new owners gather on a platform and gaze down on the assembled vehicles. They are then summoned one by one to descend and take possession. The customer is king or God, if only for the moment.

Glass

Volkswagen's 3D marketing is not restricted to Autostadt. Autostadt is more or less a theme park for quite a number of visitors. All the brands are present. The marketing message, here, is directed to potential future consumers (children accompanied by their parents) or to current customers (owners collecting their new cars at the factory). Of course these two groups are often combined in one visit. The company has strengthened its ties with its customers in two other ways as well. In Dresden, the company built the *Gläserne Manifaktur* (The Glass Factory), a stylish glass box in which they construct the Phaeton (VW's top of the range model) on an assembly line floored with parquet (including the conveyor). Gläserne Manifaktur is a special factory, representing the high-end of a market segment and combining the spheres of both production and consumption. The building has turned production into a real experience, according to the VW company. In the centre of Berlin, too, at the corner of Unter den Linden and Friedrichstrasse, there is *VW Forum*: a showroom for all the company's current models – once again with large areas of glass. VW Forum is not just an ordinary showroom, but also showing the presence of the brand in the centre of a big city.

Glass is a material that both separates and connects. Large panes of clear glass began appearing as shop display windows from the mid-nineteenth century onwards (Pevsner 1976; Van Der Grinten 1980). Glazing optically connects the consumer with the product; in other words, it puts wealth within grasping distance if only visually. Besides shutting out all kinds of climatic inconvenience, the glass window delays actual possession of the goods until the purchaser has paid for them. Some 150 years ago, when the department stores first began to turn their whole premises into shop displays, shoppers sometimes proved incapable of distinguishing between the two above mentioned aspects of glass. Retailers complained frequently about shoplifting. The specific knowledge, social value

Figure 11.3   Conveyer belt and parquet-paved floor of Gläserne Manifaktur, Dresden, Germany (Photo: H. van der Veen, Delft)

and custom needed to distinguish visual from economic possession was not yet universal.

The glass walls of the Gläserne Manifaktur disclose a comprehensive functional programme: the reception lobby, the restaurant, the glass cylinder containing cars ready for handover and, of course, the assembly plant. The involvement of the customer is a bit different from in Autostadt. The choice of engine, upholstery and colours are linked with an exclusive visit to this factory that takes place before the act of ordering. In Autostadt the visit of the factory is not determinative for the buying of the car; most visitors see the factory after they decided for brand and type of car. In the Volkswagen flagship in Dresden the glass is intended to convey a message: Volkswagen is making a show of its concern for 'sustainability' and its culture of employee job satisfaction. Sustainability has been put to effect in the principle of the assembly plant, and the car components are delivered to the plant on the non-polluting *Strassenbahn* (tram). Working in teams on a rotating scheme reduces the monotony of work for the employees and allegedly raises job satisfaction. The professed principles are emphasized by the quasi-domestic styling of the parquet-clad production line. The 5,000 square metres on the conveyer belt is indiscernible from the total of 25,000 square metres of parquet in this factory. 'What you see is what you get' is now a familiar slogan, but it's only actually true when you lack the relevant knowledge. The components delivered to the plant are fabricated elsewhere in 'normal', smelly factories. The clean electric tram, once out of the town, is relieved of its task by polluting diesel lorries. Even the most honest of purchasers is thus transformed into an environmental felon.

The other German car marques have similar projects (see Table 11.1 for an overview.[3]). Audi was first in 1989, constructing its 'Audi Forum' on the outskirts of Ingolstadt. The project combines the *Selbstabhohlung* (car handover centre) with a museum, a theatre, and exhibition area, a shop, a restaurant and a factory tour. Since 1996, the hangar format of the *Kundenzentrum* has become the architectural hallmark of all dealers worldwide. Henn Architekten took on most of the designing work for Audi as well as for Volkswagen's Autostadt and the Gläserne Manifaktur. Porsche built a factory near Leipzig for its Cayenne and Carrera GT models. Customers are free to test-drive the cars on the factory's own race circuit. Van Gerkan, Marg and Partners, renowned for many station designs, sketched a building shaped like a pulpit (Meyhöfer 2003). Once again the ecclesiastical metaphor comes into play, now with the consumer as preacher.

BMW and Mercedes are examples of German flagship projects of recent years. The Dutch architect Ben van Berkel of UN Studio designed a new museum building for Mercedes in the shape of a double helix, uniting the myth of Mercedes with the company's collection; and the collection has a great deal to offer, not least because Benz is widely considered the inventor of the modern automobile. The design recalls that of the Guggenheim in New York. The visitor starts at the top where the oldest vehicles are on show, and descends via spiralling ramps to the earthbound level of today's models. The Van Berkel's project had its opening mid-2006. For BMW, Coop Himmelblau designed a building that almost floats on air. The glass in this case emphasizes the immateriality of the marque. The ideas of

Table 11.1 Overview of 'factory outlets' of German car brands

Brand	Name	Main characteristics	Location	Year
Audi (Volkswagen)	Audi Forum	Car handover centre, museum	Ingolstadt	1989
BMW	BMW Welt	Restaurant/theatre, exhibition space, shops, car handover centre, (2008) (renovated museum)	Munich	2007
Porsche	Customer Center	Racetrack, car handover centre	Leipzig	2002
Mercedes	Mercedes Welt	(New) museum, restaurant theatre, car handover centre	Stuttgart	2006
Volkswagen	Gläserne Manifaktur	Production space, restaurant/ theatre, car handover centre	Dresden	2001
Volkswagen	Autostadt	Car handover centre, museum, restaurant/theatre	Wolfsburg	2000
Volkswagen	VW Forum	Showroom	Berlin	2001

Note
All brands are looking for a complete package of services: delivery space, museum, restaurant etc. Everything must be there. The main characteristics of the project are listed in the first position. All locations are in Germany

the above-mentioned Pine and Gilmore are here almost literally illustrated. New BMWs are handed over to their purchasers in this building; the particular place is called 'the première'. Already the brand is promising the day of the car collection as 'the most beautiful day in your world'. But the theatre and exhibition space were important as well to give the building a 'public' and more social function. The design of Coop Himmelblau has been in use since the end of 2007 and the refurbished museum reopened in June 2008.

All the German examples consist of the car handover centre in combination with something else. This 'something else' depends on the brand. Porsche sticks to its (perceived) brand core: driving fast. Volkwagen Gläserne Manifaktur to the (responsible) production itself. A museum in nearly all cases is an important cultural addition as shown by Audi, BMW, Volkswagen's Autostadt and Mercedes Benz. One can ask oneself whether the designs – perhaps with the Gläserne Manifaktur and the racetrack of Porsche as exceptions – really are about making choices. Nearly everything is there, so a match between consumer and brand can happen easily. The parallel between product design and the architecture of the brands is conspicuous. All the manufacturers are now making the same types of cars: a small city car, a family saloon, a businessman's car, a sports car, an estate car, a van and so on. Even Porsche is differentiating at high speed. Beside its 'classical' Carrera, there is a roadster (Boxter), a sports car (Cayman) and an SUV (Cayenne). In today's confluence of consumption and identity, loyalty seems more linked to the type of the car than to the social standing of the brand. The uncertainty of the brand and the uncertainty of the consumer can hardly be bridged by marketing.

Whatever the differences, all car brands offer a factory tour. This is an important distinction with other 'high-end' outlets such as Cadbury (1990), Philips' Evoluon (between 1966 and 1989) and Legoland. Cadbury's World near Birmingham in the United Kingdom is about the history and craftsmanship of chocolate making. The Philips Evoluon project was about the history of science and technology and the role of the company in that. It closed its door because the costs were considered too high. Legoland is the 'homo ludens' version of the serious world of science and technology. The first leisure park was built in the vicinity of the factory in Denmark (from 1968 onwards); the United Kingdom, Germany and the United States have their own Legolands. The leisure parks experienced similar exploitation problems, and today the company, Lego, only has a share in Legoland. Cadbury, Evoluon and Legoland can certainly be understood as early examples of 3D-marketing like the German car industry, but they did not and do not offer the transparency of a factory visit. The leisure site and the production site are just in the same area, but the relationship can hardly be experienced by consumers.

Mobility

Despite the social theming in the projects of the German carmakers, the designs still strongly underscore the idea of mobility. Mobility here applies not only to driving cars (obviously) but also to leading streams of visitors around the vehicle museums and other buildings. The design has to guarantee the function of the buildings as (often mass) consumption projects. The individual architects have their own emphases in this regard. Ben van Berkel stresses 'the dynamic and integral spatial concept' as the selection criterion (the phrase is quoted from his website). For the Austrian architect Coop Himmelblau and BMW, BMW Welt is intended as a 'portal' to all the company's other functions. This is not so much a matter of mobility as of the related accessibility. The metaphor of mobility is, to put it bluntly, taken very literally in each case. This may well be the most significant difference from the cathedrals and palaces of bygone eras, and even from the arcades, department stores and malls of the last century and a half, because in those cases other meanings are additionally involved. Those consumptive spaces are not limited to 'mobility' in their meaning. This abstract characteristic of a theme like 'mobility' is probably the only way in which a brand can 'communicate' through architecture. Recent research indicates that architecture – its monumentality and choice of materials – hardly support the recognition of a brand (Kooijman and Sierksma 2005).[4] Logos and perhaps colours are considered more effective.

The car makers are bringing about a rearrangement of spatial activities. They draw consumptive activities in towards themselves, with the result that consumers consume and enjoy recreation in different places and at different times. This change also results in realignment within the business chain. The dealers may be less concerned with marketing, and the transportation of new vehicles by road between the factory and the sales point is less frequent. Yet, dealers throughout the world are confronted with ever more severe regulations about the presentation of the models and the architecture of the building. Different cities consequently

Figure 11.4   The design by Ben van Berkel for Mercedes World, Stuttgart (Source: UN Studio, Amsterdam)

become important within the pattern and distribution of consumption: Wolfsburg and Dresden in the case of Volkswagen; Ingolstadt and Zwickau (Audi); Bremen, Regensburg and Stuttgart (Mercedes Benz); Munich (BMW); and Stuttgart and Leipzig (Porsche).[5] New characteristics are thereby added to the existing network of cities with its countless meanings – Berlin as the 'city of politics', Stuttgart and Leipzig as 'commercial centres', Dresden, Leipzig and Munich as 'cultural cities'. All these cities enter into a relationship with one or more car manufacturers and vice versa. Existing urban structures are not written off. On the contrary, existing cultural values are intensified as far as possible. Car marques also try to do something for the city. Several marques explicitly flirt with the city's cultural significance. Examples of such new combinations include Dresden-Volkswagen and Munich-BMW. Both these cities are famed for their musical and artistic life, and a tour of the factory is conveniently combined with a night at the opera or a museum visit. The 'adjacent attraction' is in this case already part of the existing context. The German car companies comply in this sense with the tradition of consumer cathedrals that has developed since the mid-nineteenth century. There is one important difference however: the manufacturers now claim a significant presence in the consumptive realm.

The spatial effects are expected to be identifiable on various levels and scales. First, the developments are taking place at the national scale of Germany. The sharing of functions between manufacturers and dealers is undergoing many changes on that scale. The market positioning of marques is primarily local. This is not so much a matter of industrial upscaling (i.e. fewer but larger dealers); this kind of scale growth is taking place in every country. The German marques lead a life in other countries which is different from that in Germany. A Porsche, for example, costs twice as much in the Netherlands as in Germany. This means that the marque has to be surrounded with a mystique of wealth that does not strictly accord with the engineering under the bonnet. Architecture here once again facilitates a milieu of luxury that casts a sumptuous light on the marque itself. For the Dutch Porsche facility, the Amsterdam agency Qua decided on a 'pit stop' which harbours such brand attributes such as 'history', 'passion', 'reputation', 'dreams come true' and 'me'. No less than 12 brand attributes (each a combination of a pithy description and an image) are central to all the marketing presentation and design of Dutch Porsche. For Porsche, and also for Audi and for Volkswagen's Phaeton, architecture has played an explicit part in construction of the brand image. In the case of Mercedes Benz and BMW, architecture plays at first sight a much more modest role; in these instances, the evolution of the brand and its physical context was crucial. But Mercedes and BMW also cherish the expectation that the prominent designs now being constructed will have a long-term effect on the image of the whole building stock. From a global standpoint, the interviewed representatives of the companies anticipate that the buildings will show more 'movement'.

Conclusions: transparent ambitions

Without exception these factories and cities have huge ambitions. They want to be cultural, rich, high-end, responsible for the environment, historical, authentic, unique, etc. The use of glass may show one or more of these listed characteristics. There is hardly any metaphorical use of the material left here. 'What you see is what you get'. But not a single critical or negative characteristic has been mentioned, of course (Gold and Ward 1994: 2). There is also a promise of a participatory relationship between the consumer and the brand, but this promise does not differ much from the one connected with the glass shop windows of the mid-nineteenth century. Today the architecture of the building has to contribute to brand awareness. Both the brand pavilions and even the landscaped nature of Autostadt have to express the 'personality' of the brands (see Table 10.2). And because of the importance of brand awareness through architecture, car brands are also imposing adapted regulations on dealers worldwide.

One can only speculate about the importance of consumption for the construction of identities. Phenomena like compulsive shopping and de-shopping are already linked to psychological problems. Research shows that the act of shopping only produces a kind of satisfaction during a short period of time. One can easily understand that fashion goods are more applicable for this behaviour than e.g. cars. But research even showed that there is a correlation between the choice of a car type and psychological and social uncertainty. And this uncertainty is precisely the definition of 'experience' by the German sociologist Schulze (Schulze 2000; Benson 2000; Bradsher 2002). For Schulze the Experience Society represents an inner directed society with people uncertain about what they want, quite different from its forebear the Modern Society inhabited by strong egos busy with shaping

Table 11.2 Brand pavilions in Autostadt

Brand	Values	Design and themed nature
Bentley	Aristocratic understatement	Plant-covered hill, like a jewel in its setting. English oak
Lamborgini	Unsubdued strength and pure automotive emotion	Black cube. Sweet chestnut tree
Skoda	Security and honesty	Faceted pavilion, fanning out from the centre. Lime tree from Bohemia
Seat	Southern gaiety, innovation and quality	Sensually-sweeping, brilliantly white sculpture
Audi	Design and elegance, selective exquisiteness	Interlocking rings
Volkswagen	Classic modernity, evolution through democracy and perfection	Glass cube and sphere. Birchl

Source: Press release Volkswagen AG, Architecture of Autostadt, June 2000

the external conditions to get what they already want. Schulze's definition is quite different from the definition of the cited Pine and Gilmore; the latter have stated the experience economy as a new phase in a developing civil society. However, compulsive shopping and de-shopping hardly support that proposition of positive growth.

On one hand the experience economy tries to reach the already existing emotionality of consumers. The use of glass not only makes the brand visible, but sets the consumer in the spotlight too. Even this seems not enough. There now follow some quotes from a recent article about place branding: 'Place branding aims to *create* deep-rooted and genuine changes in the make-up of a place'. Also: 'It has been driven by a political ambition to *change* the way people in the area live and reflect on their identity'. And: 'This plan builds on the intention to create and communicate the brand from the *inside out'* (the italics are mine) (Pederson 2004). Again, the aforementioned Pine and Gilmore had initially formulated this ambition the first time. Their book contains no doubt relevant trends and cases about the importance of leisure in society today. But experiences represent just a provisional phase; they are after what they called 'transformations'. A change of individuals is their ultimate goal. 'With transformations, *the customer is the product'* (Pine and Gilmore 1999: 172). They also stated that 'theatre' and 'stage-set' are not metaphors for the experience economy but models. Transparency, then, implies imposed behaviour.[6]

Notes

1 Gardner and Shepperd (1989) follow, at first sight, a similar track of reasoning. The 'cathedral' has been considered as a metaphor, but within the sphere of consumption the relationship between the consumer and his 'God' is different. What is important,

they stated, is the 'participatory' relationship (p. 125) between the consumer and the shop and this participation represents (more) 'democracy'. A few comments: (1) The hypothesis of democracy with respect to consumption and shopping has been researched and falsified by Lizabeth Cohen (2003) in her book about mass consumption in the United States. Mass consumption has always had the meaning of economic buying power, but no real political representation was implied. (2) Several analyses have made clear that the result of post-modern consumption is moving towards the direction of 'doing' instead of 'having', meaning that the shopping process itself has become more important than the goods purchased (Davis 1966; Crawford 1992; Kooijman 1999; Benson 2000). The issues of compulsive buying, the phenomenon of 'de-shopping', the importance of shopping for personal and group identities are important indications of this trend. (3) What is 'participatory' is the involvement in life-style groups and specific market-segments; I will elaborate the issue with the concept of 'consumer-shareholder' and the analyses of Autostadt and Gläserne Manifaktur.

2   The comparison with a supermarket, here, is rather more than just a metaphor. The design has provided the well-known efficient shop layout. The American supermarket Piggly Wiggly may be considered as the prototype: turnstiles at the beginning and end of the store impose the one-way direction, and the positioning of the shelves at an angle of 90 degrees of the store front provides the cashier maximum overview. The store opened in 1917 and its design was patented in 1920 (Kooijman, op cit.). Ikea stores illustrate that this type of shop layout is not restricted to supermarkets. We see the same kind of efficiency in leisure parks and projects like Autostadt.

3   My source of data was the interviews I conducted with representatives of various German vehicle manufacturers in February and March 2004. I visited the projects of Volkswagen in Wolfsburg, Dresden and Berlin in May 2003. For the Dutch situation and contribution, I benefited greatly from interviews with Porsche in Leusden, BMW in Leidschendam and Breda, Mercedes Benz in The Hague and Nieuwegein, Volkswagen/Audi (Wittebrug) in The Hague, design agency Qua in Amsterdam, and Ben van Berkel of UN Studio in Amsterdam.

4   The proposition of a distant relationship between architecture and (car) branding grew from our own research about car showrooms in the Netherlands (Kooijman and Sierksma 2005). In other words, architecture cannot represent (like logos can) a specific brand. A recent master's thesis about fashion shops concludes in the same way: Tiemensma (2007) found out that only a rather small amount of design/spatial variables are contributing to the recognition of specific (fashion) brands. Architectural characteristics are probably only playing a role on a more general level.

5   Most of the countries have different (well-known) combinations of industry and cities. Though the industrial characteristics have changed or even disappeared, the combination is often still 'branding' the city. Spain has e.g. Valencia-Ford, Valladolid-Renault and Zaragoza-General Motors. Sorkin (1992) mentioned three characteristics of the post-modern theming: placeless, cocooning, surveillance and control, and simulations. One may conclude about a uniform strategy among various cities, but most of the examples in this chapter, however, do not show a placeless characteristic (see also Holcomb 1994).

6   I started this chapter with the common use of metaphors in the history of retail and more specific metaphor of 'cathedrals'. Pine and Gilmore did not state literally that customers and behaviour can be produced. But with the expression 'The customer is the product', they are pretty close. They eventually left the production issue to God. 'What could be the ultimate customer-as-product? The utmost would be *perfection*, the perfect human being. According to our own worldview, there can be no sixth economic offering, because perfecting people falls under the province of God, the Author and Perfecter of our faith rather than in the domain of human business' (Pine and Gilmore 1999: 206).

12 What is a flagship supermarket?

An analysis of supermarket flagships in a historical context

Audrey Kirby

Introduction

A dictionary definition suggests that 'flagship' can be interpreted as 'a single item from a related group considered as the most important, often in establishing a public image' (Collins English Dictionary 1986). It can be argued that the architectural design of a number of supermarket buildings in the UK are intended to 'establish a public image' for the company that has developed them. This chapter will explore the concept of flagship stores in the context of supermarket commerce and the architectural design of supermarket developments. The main focus is on a series of landmark stores produced by Sainsbury's during the 1980s and the significance of their designs, their origins and antecedents. These will be discussed in the context of supermarket buildings produced by other grocery retailers in the past twenty years.

Branding and buildings

Architecture alone rarely becomes the symbol of a brand. The application of a logo or company name is in most cases essential to conveying identity. However, some buildings become a brand in their own right through public interest, for example the Pompidou Centre or the Swiss Re 'Gherkin' in London. Venturi suggests that 'the sign is more important than the architecture. This is reflected in the proprietor's budget' (Venturi *et al.* 1998: 13). With a few notable exceptions this comment is particularly relevant to supermarket buildings, many of which are difficult to identify without the company name or logo.

However, architectural design is capable of reinforcing corporate identity. Roman imperial supremacy was impressed upon subject nations through recognizably Roman buildings, that replaced local styles. Subsequently, other powerful institutions have used buildings to distinguish themselves from the population. The monastic orders of the early Middle Ages 'used architecture to impress upon monks the supremacy of their order' (Forty 1986: 222). Corporate business headquarters can be impelling symbols of corporate virtues and managerial intentions (Berg and Kreiner 1990). The nineteenth century saw advances in store design, with increasingly expansive and opulent department stores identifying their retail owners. In the same way large modernist or unique supermarket buildings represent the attitudes, status and power of the companies whose products they house.

The nineteenth century also saw the arrival of branding as a technique to endow a household product with special characteristics including its name, packaging and advertising that offered reliability and consistency to the consumer (Lury 1996). The recognition of company logos evolved from this point and that the role of advertising became a way of building an image around a particular brand name version of a product (Klein 2005). The relationship between branding and retail design suggests that 'brands signal our membership of an 'in' group. They are the tools with which we build status ... brands build emotions, promise happiness and provide kicks' (Riewoldt 2002: 8).

Lamacraft (1989) emphasizes the importance of architecture in conveying brand identity. Buildings should have 'something to say' and architectural design 'harnessed to serve the purpose of transmitting messages in a marketing environment' (Brauer 2002: 7). Riewoldt echoes this view, by proposing 'Brandscaping' as the deliberate three-dimensional design of brand settings, and an increasingly important aspect of retail architecture (Riewoldt 2002). This approach transforms the brand into a location and the image of the brand is communicated through the architecture and design of the building. In the retail industry, the store can be a three-dimensional brand statement that embodies the personality of the retailer. But such are the dynamics of the industry, that the status of many supermarket flagship buildings is likely to be temporal: a company's most recent innovative design being described as a 'flagship' building, only to be replaced by a larger more radical structure at a later date.

Origins and antecedents in the UK

The antecedents of the present day supermarkets in Britain can be traced to medieval fairs and street markets. Market traders were unwilling to invest in fixed shop premises and stalls were often provided by market owners, or were made to be easily transported and assembled by the traders themselves (Winstanley 1983). Covered markets subsequently made a colourful and contentious component of the retail scene (Winstanley 1983). Although markets of both varieties came to be supplemented and largely superseded by specialist grocery stores, their legacy of choice and freshness is retained in the visual imagery of grocery superstores. Jack Cohen founded Tesco following his experience with selling from postwar market stalls, while Morrison's interior designs include simulated market stalls.

The origins of supermarket trading in the UK can be found in the retail systems established in the USA in the early part of the twentieth century. After the Second World War food retailers in the UK who had seen self-service retailing working in the United States realized the potential of the system and began to experiment with similar ideas. The claim to be the first self-service store in the UK is controversial, the difficulty lying in the definition of 'self-service'. David Grieg briefly converted his Turnpike Lane branch to self-service in 1932. An attempt was made to introduce the system during the Second World War. Harold Wicker, said to be 'father of British self-service', in 1942 converted a small section of an Essex department store into a self-service grocers (Corina 1972). The Co-op was the first company to design a shop specifically for self-service, at Kingskerswell in September 1949 (Westwood and Westwood 1952). At the time the Co-op's marketing strength and well-established in-house architectural team may have given them an advantage over their competitors (Morrison 2003). The first purpose-built Sainsbury's is recorded as being opened in 1952 in Eastbourne (Williams 1994).

Most early shop layouts were purpose designed for each location to fit into a pre-existing shop unit. A typical 1960s high street grocery store would have been part of a mixed development with retail units on the ground floor and offices above. The frontage to the street was created using a fully glazed shop front with a tiled façade above, providing a backing for the store signage (Morrison 2003). Buildings could also be converted, as retailers sought larger premises to accommodate their expanding product ranges. Town centre cinema buildings were ideal for this purpose. Tesco converted a cinema in Malden in 1956, and Morrisons, following their cinema conversion in Bradford converted a bowling alley into a self-service supermarket in the mid-1960s (Seth and Randall 1999).

By the early 1970s larger supermarket companies began to experiment with out-of-town developments. The design of these initially echoed the first high street stores, maintaining the large glass windows in a single-storey, pre-fabricated steel framed building on a site which now necessarily included a car park (see below). Sainsbury's opened their first purpose-built out-of-town 'flagship' store at Coldham's Lane, near Cambridge in December 1974 (Williams 1994).

Supermarket flagships in the USA

The appearance and purpose of supermarket architecture, although diverse in style and concept can be usefully assessed through work of the postmodern architect, Robert Venturi. Venturi's concept of postmodernism advocates a rejection of modernist simplicity and the adoption of a collage style composed of an eclectic mixture of historic references (Glancey 1998). In his seminal work 'Learning from Las Vegas', Venturi *et al.* (1998) explain the symbolism and impact of popular culture on architectural styles and suggests that architects should be more receptive to popular tastes and values.

Venturi's work gives credence to the study of a style of architecture which, like the architecture of supermarkets, is generally considered to be outside the boundaries of academic interest. Commenting on the architecture of Las Vegas, he writes:

> We believe a careful documentation and analysis of its physical form is as important to architects and urbanists today as were the studies of medieval Europe and ancient Rome and Greece to earlier generations. Such a study will help to define a new type of urban form emerging in America and

Europe, radically different from that we have known; one that we have been ill-equipped to deal with and that, from ignorance, we define today as urban sprawl.

(Venturi *et al*. 1998: 1)

In this context, the symbolism of architecture, criticized as ugly and ordinary, should not be discounted and, indeed, its significance must be acknowledged. He cites historical instances of architecture developed from the commonplace or mundane, the influence of folk art on fine art, conventional rustic architecture on eighteenth-century architects and industrial buildings on early modern designers.

The Best Supermarket, built in 1975 in Houston, Texas and described by James Wines, its architect, as 'de-architecture' is notable in postmodern commentary as one of a series of unconventional store designs. Its crumbled features impressed Charles Jencks (1979: 32) by demonstrating the 'simultaneous existence of entropy and order. The public fascination with disaster and ruins is also a motive. The extreme contrast of BEST and "worst" is no doubt also intended.' These buildings can certainly be defined as flagship stores in that their eccentric designs established a strong, if transient, identity for the company.

There was an observable humour too, in the architectural design as 'the idea was quite funny in a Beavis and Butthead kind of way' (Glancey 1998: 289). Charles Jencks found S.I.T.E.'s third store project for Best Supermarkets compelling:

Every morning at 9.00am this front door slides open for shoppers, but unlike other push-button apertures it takes part of the building with it, forty-five tons of jagged-edged engineering brick. The handling of the 'ripped joint' is carefully realistic; it follows the angle of shear which might occur in an earthquake, and a few bricks are missing near the points of violence.

(Jencks 1979: 31)

The Best buildings certainly broke the mould of conventional, and for postmodernists at least, boring, supermarket design. Although their playful and quirky designs were unsustainable, the buildings set a precedent for supermarkets that escaped the efficient, rectangular modernist 'box' and pointed to distinctive and individualistic approaches to brand identity communicated through the building.

Flagship supermarkets in Britain

By the 1980s the supermarket developments in the UK had increased dramatically both in size and number (Seth and Randall 1999). The competition for town centre and edge of town sites became acute; demand increased and sites available for development in these areas dwindled. Competition for space and the growing public disquiet at the decline of high street retailing placed local planning authorities in a dominant position and able to demand architectural designs and site landscaping that would appease public opposition. Seth and Randall (1999:

226) record that 'the planning authorities have insisted on high building standards, so the cheap, large sheds typical of continental or US hypermarkets are not an option for the UK grocers'.

Public concern regarding the hegemony of supermarket trading resulted in local authorities becoming unwilling to accept inappropriate developments that would result in local dissent. This was particularly the case in areas or sites that were considered to be architecturally or geographically of special merit.

The 'Essex Barn'

The Essex Barn style marked a significant turning point in the design of supermarket buildings and lasted, in various permutations, for almost twenty years. The origin of this ubiquitous building form was an Essex superstore designed for Asda by Alcock in 1977–8. Although not regarded at the time as a blueprint for a 'flagship' store, in retrospect it was an important generic design. Based on the design of a medieval tithe barn, its initial purpose was to blend in with the surrounding rural landscape. Such harmony also required careful attention to detail. Sainsbury's journal reported in 1991 that their store in Rustington designed with 'country-style, high gables and roof tower looks immediately at home amid the greenery of the Sussex countryside' (J.S. Journal 1991a: 9). Similarly the company's store in Larkfield was constructed from 'Staffordshire blue bricks' and was deemed to be an 'attractive addition to the Kent countryside' (J.S. Journal 1991a: 11).

Possibly the style provided customers with a classless feeling of comfort, security, wholesomeness and prosperity, selling a nostalgia for a past that probably never existed. It certainly became popular with local planning authorities as it generally roused least protest from civic and community groups. Many authorities and shoppers still view this concept as the most suitable for a supermarket development. For some, it became the 'traditional' supermarket design.

Although using many of the ideals of quality construction and functionality that were adopted by modernist architects, their architectural design was based on the concept of a rural idyll that employed traditional building crafts and local materials combined with a high standard of craftsmanship (Fleming *et al.* 1966). In the same way that designers in the nineteenth and early twentieth centuries felt threatened by the effects of the industrial revolution, it is possible that by the 1970s there was a suspicion that vernacular traditions were being lost to innovative technology, mass housing developments and destructive urban regeneration schemes. Samuel suggests that

> brick represents a craft material in an age of mass production. In recoil from the 'faceless' buildings of functional architecture, they invest brickwork with almost human qualities. It is tactile, textured and grainy where modern surfaces are flat. It is individual and quirky where modernism's surfaces are flat.

(Samuel 1994: 120)

The popularity of designers such as Laura Ashley that supported a fashion for nostalgia and rural imagery, coincided with the increased national interest in preserving, and making available to the public, buildings and collections that were starting to be regarded as the national heritage. The expansion of the tourist industry also reinforced an interest in historical heritage, that by its nature discouraged modernist architecture, already damaged by disfiguring cheap developments of the 1960s.

Neo-modernism and Sainbury's flagship designs

The Essex Barn style provided out-of-town food retailers in particular, with a design that was accepted by local government planners and consumers. It enabled new superstores to be built quickly and to showcase larger ranges of merchandise, services and facilities as company flagships. However, the wave of out-of-town development during the 1980s, and the consequent visual prevalence of the 'Essex Barn' led to Sainsbury's decision to focus attention on the architectural design of their stores. A series of landmark stores resulted by the end of the next decade in a portfolio of buildings designed by high profile architects. Several of these stores received design awards and gained Sainsbury's a reputation for architectural innovation. This was in part due to the appointment of Colin Amery, the *Financial Times* architectural critic who advised and encouraged the directors to be adventurous in their architectural projects.

The commissioning of high-profile architects to design a portfolio of flagship stores was intended to reinforce the company emphasis on quality in all things (Williams 1994). Lamacraft in her *Financial Times* survey reported that

> Sainsbury's uses architecture and design to differentiate itself from rival food multiples and enhance the separateness of its brand. It wants its customers to equate the quality of the built environment with the quality of the products inside. By taking a local approach to the design of each of its stores, Sainsbury's creates a sense of community ownership that would be impossible with a rigid Sainsbury's formula ... Whereas until recently supermarket architecture in the UK was characterised by vernacular 'barns ' and red brick clock towers, Sainsbury's has taken a boldly diverse approach, commissioning some of the biggest architectural names.
>
> (Lamacraft 1998: 10–11)

The first of Sainsbury's flagship stores was designed by Ahrend Burton and Koralek in 1984 on a site close to Canterbury cathedral. The architecture was designed to echo the spire of the medieval cathedral and involved the use of exposed structural beams and masts as decorative features. It was said to resemble the exoskeleton of an insect (Williams 1994). An architectural review observed that 'Sainsbury's supermarket buildings have always stood out from the rest of the barnyard crowd. Increasingly they are gaining a reputation for stores that look a little out of the ordinary' (Hardingham 1996: 324). Distinctiveness was found in 'the brightly coloured structure (that) will give the building a strong visual identity and will make it a clearly recognizable landmark' (Architects Journal 1982: 46).

The store was also a landmark design in its implications for the possibilities concerning the design of supermarket structures as prestigious flagship buildings. This exploration away from the accepted, by then 'traditional', store design was without doubt intended to reinforce and establish the company brand. At a period of increasing competition from rivals, the company now seemed anxious to demonstrate that it could supplement its reputation with high quality buildings.

Terry Farrell's 1994 design for the edge of town development in Harlow was given an RIBA award in 1995 for its innovative postmodern design. The store, which is linked to the city centre by a pedestrian cycleway, is designed as three large white cubes with arcades beneath. Between the cubes are cylindrical blue towers and a flight of steps leading to the north entrance. The cut-out primary coloured corners of the cubes are illuminated at night (Hardingham 1996).

Another Sainsbury's flagship store built in 1994 in Canley, near Coventry, was designed by Lifschutz Davidson and is dominated by illuminated winged canopies that cover the petrol station and provide a shelter over the glass front elevation of the store. Hardingham describes the construction of the canopy 'tubular supports are spanned by steel aerofoil frames across the top with an opaque PVC-coated polyester fabric stretched cover. On the underside is a PVC-coated polyester mesh which, when illuminated reveals the profiles of the frames inside' (Hardingham 1996). The shape and construction of the canopies was inspired by the Sopwith Pup aircraft, which were once constructed on the site (Hardingham 1996 Blueprint February 1994).

Flagship stores could also be designed for urban locations. Nicholas Grimshaw's high-tech design, including the 'flagship' supermarket in Camden High Street, London, incorporated workshops, canalside housing and 300 car parking spaces located beneath the store, accessed by a travelator. In answer to the brief which stipulated a column-free interior, Grimshaw designed a central span supported by 'steel cantilevered elements counterbalanced by a steel tie at the back of the pavement line' (Building Design 1986: 10).

The building was specifically designed to occupy the site formerly occupied by the listed Aerated Bread Company; the bays of the front elevation of the store are designed to mirror the width of the listed Georgian houses opposite (Williams 1994). Despite enthusiastic praise from the architectural press, the public were not so impressed, with reports that 'inevitably the overt, or as the architect calls it, "heroic" high-tech appearance of the building has provoked concern among local residents and community groups' (Architects Journal 1986: 29).

The flagship store in Clapham High Street, designed by Chetwood, is an infill development sandwiched between a Victorian church and high street shops. The building is high-tech in design with tubular steel supports framing the entrance to the side of the building and because the local authority were insistent that a blank wall the length of the building should not face the high street, Chetwood installed a 20 × 3 metre £400,000 armour-plated video wall, used to advertise Sainsbury's products and display local information. In the same year a video installation won the prestigious Turner Prize. Although looking stunning at night, problems with sunlight and dirt detract from the video effect during the day.

A concern with the landscape was once more evident in Sainsbury's 1994 Plymouth flagship store, designed by Dixon and Jones. The design conceived as being part of a landscape was set to the side of a semi-circular car park bordered by small trees and dense shrubbery. The building is faced with red brick, apart from the front elevation which is faced with stainless steel panels. The sail-like structures that form the dramatic front canopy were initially designed by then Ove Arup engineer Peter Rice who had also worked on the design for the Sidney Opera House. Hardingham includes the store in her architectural guide and records that although the store itself is unremarkable, the canopy and façade of the store are 'undoubtedly the key features' (Hardingham 1996: 254). Describing the sails she suggests that they appear different from different angles: 'from the motorway above they are sails, from the car park and to the side they are like sections of a spine, and from underneath they make up the underbelly of a snake' (Hardingham 1996: 254).

Sainsbury's Millennium store at Greenwich is probably the best known of this group of flagship stores. The site was won controversially amidst fierce competition from the other major supermarket companies. The design represents the peak of Sainsbury's foray into high-profile architectural design. Sainsbury's bid for and capture of what was at the time, a prestigious site illustrates the attitude of the company towards its perceived corporate status and identity at the end of the twentieth century.

Designed by Chetwood Associates, it was innovative in its use of natural light and recycled energy systems. Costing almost twice as much as conventional stores, its much publicized 'green features' were seen as setting a precedent for future supermarket design and the energy saving properties of the building were widely promoted. The *Building Design* journal (1998) reported that

> Landscaped earth bonding shelters the concrete side walls. Water at a constant 10°C abstracted from a borehole will be used to absorb heat produced by refrigeration units, making them work more efficiently. Electricity for the store is generated by an on-site combined heat and power plant. The saw-toothed roof is 30 per cent glazed. The remainder is metal-clad and heavily insulated with wood-wool to maximise thermal performance.
>
> (Gardner 1998: 28)

The building was originally (1998) conceived as a generic 'green' design that would be a format for future supermarket buildings. Close attention to and emphasis on 'green issues' was likely to be a popular element in any planning proposal. Sainsbury's emphasized that 'our aim is to deliver the MOST ENVIRONMENTALLY RESPONSIBLE SUPERMARKET IN BRITAIN' (their capital letters) (Sainsbury 1997). A Bream rating of 75 is claimed for the proposed store, 25 being a more usual score for a 'modern superstore' (Sainsbury 1997).

The store was the subject of a major publicity campaign by Sainsbury's from its conception, and the company's bid for the Greenwich Millennium site, to its opening in 1999, concurred with the opening of the Millennium Dome and the festivities associated with the event. Sainsbury's lavish publicity material, often quoted verbatim, was used extensively by the press and media. Emphasis was placed on the originality of the design whose innovative approach was welcomed by the media as a deviation from the commonly perceived basic rectangular box shape of standard stores. Sainsbury's also used the store to launch their new bright orange design scheme, which gave an additional boost to the publicity launch.

In their comprehensive presentation document for the project development Sainsbury's proposed that the landscaping scheme will create a diverse environmentally responsible landscape. The area behind the store it is suggested, will not only shield the service yard but will in addition 'provide an area where there is the potential to work with local schools and community groups to manage and study the area' (Sainsbury Archive). English Partnerships' literature describes the store landscaping as comprising various habitats including woodland, wildflower meadow, wetland pond and reed bed that will be watered with recycled water from the roof of the building. Unfortunately many of the apparently sustainable features proved to be 'green wash' and the store itself now (2006) appears sadly neglected.

In retrospect this building has not fulfilled its much publicized potential as a flagship and as a paradigm for future supermarket buildings, and it remains a one-off in the field of supermarket architecture. It perhaps represents the peak of Sainsbury's foray into high profile architectural design, Sainsbury's bid for and capture of what was at the time a prestigious site, illustrates the attitude of the company towards its perceived corporate status and identity at the end of the twentieth century. The 'green' features of the building collectively gave the structure its high profile status and emphasized the company's much publicized apparent concern for the environment. The store itself is small and was so costly to build and maintain, that despite its energy saving features, it could be defined as being part of Sainsbury's advertising programme rather than a working supermarket, and might be described as a 'loss leader'. As such it is an important trace in defining the phenomenon of supermarket buildings, their meaning and their historical significance.

The implications of the failures of the building, both in terms of economic, retail and design issues, were not lost on Sainsbury's or their rival supermarket companies. As discussed above, what was seen eventually as an eccentric and costly attempt to demonstrate the company's prestigious position, was soon dismissed as a building that had briefly served a purpose, but subsequently became a forgotten asset too costly to maintain. Although most recently other companies are responding to the problems posed by climate change, the Greenwich design as an example of a sustainable building, has had little impact on store design or company policies. This is particularly the case in the planning of stores which might relegate economic or retail issues, by ignoring tried and tested methods of practice, in order to acquire sites or reinforce brand image.

Tesco's flagship store designs

Sainsbury's demonstrated that distinctive new designs could gain acceptance and approval by consumers and influential audiences in government, the media, building and planning professionals. They also provided alternative forms to the relatively expensive brick-built Essex Barn style. These advantages led to Tesco's mid-1990s introduction of innovative modernist or neo-modernist designs into their portfolio of new stores. Flagship supermarkets at Sheffield, Swansea and Cromwell Road, London, all exhibited this changing approach to supermarket architectural design, which provided an innovative environment for both customers and staff. The designs could be of award-winning quality, earning approval and recognition from professional bodies; the Sheffield store, with its distinctive waveform roof won a RIBA award in 1997 (Tesco archive).

Tesco's flagship design for their store in Ludlow, in 1995, presented the company with circuitous problems of both architectural design and further complex issues of branding. By the 1970s the increase in car ownership and the promotion of tourism had changed the status of Ludlow from a close knit prosperous community to a marketable commodity in the heritage industry.

The town's architecture is nationally recognized in its 500 listed buildings (Lloyd 1999). Its castle, medieval buildings, burgage plots and royal associations became part of the town's corporate, or civic, identity. The town's history represents a major part of what could be described as its 'brand' as a tourist attraction. Civic identity and civic pride dictated that the design of any development within the town would be subject to close scrutiny by both local and national authorities and local inhabitants. The unpopularity of supermarket companies, who were perceived as having destroyed high street retailing, meant that the architectural design of a building, proposed to occupy an ancient cattle market site, would be of paramount importance.

Although Tesco at this time occupied the premier position in supermarket retailing the company brand was still associated with its origins as a brash working class 'pile 'em high sell 'em cheap' business (Morrison 2003). Olins referring to Tesco's corporate identity writes that 'it was seen to have a genuine character, a genuine corporate identity, which emanated, of course, from its founder' (Olins 1978: 80). Local opinions voiced at other public enquiries suggest that if Sainsbury's or Waitrose had secured the site the opposition would almost certainly have been less dramatic.

The design of the building is an interpretation of the townscape and roofscape of Ludlow, and is a transition between the historic form and a contemporary modernist design, deliberately avoiding pastiche interpretation of the 'burgage' plots of the town's historic buildings. Referring to the earlier proposals for the site CABE conclude that '... perseverance in the face of many obstacles can result in architectural excellence, even in a type of building which usually has no design merits at all. It demonstrates that a large modern building can be designed so as to sit comfortably in an historic town' (CABE 2001: 28). Two previous schemes had been rejected at planning inquiries on the grounds of unsuitable design. CABE acknowledges the problem and recalls that 'The central problem to be tackled in this project was that of designing a large modern building which would sit well on a prominent site in an unspoilt historic town where virtually all the other buildings are considerably smaller' (CABE 2001: 28).

Although there was clearly a physical problem of size and scale, the problem of convincing two strongly branded bodies that they could become compatible was almost certainly an equally difficult challenge. Explaining the psychological aspect of branding, Coomber suggests that 'Brands are about hearts and minds (Coomber 2002: 12). He quotes futurist Watts Wacker who suggests that 'a brand is a promise, and, in the end you have to keep your promises' (Coomber 2002: 12). The challenge at Ludlow was for Tesco to demonstrate through their architectural design that their brand could be re-branded to fit the Ludlow 'promise'.

A major problem in developing the site, lay in the size of the store. In fact the store is not large for a modern supermarket but the design, particularly of the roof profile, does reduce the visual weight of the store. In addition the extensive use of glazing on both sides of the building not only reduces the bulky appearance characteristic of a 'traditional' supermarket, but has the effect of reducing the structure's visibility through the reflections of surrounding buildings and landscape. The CABE report quotes Caird as saying in 2001, 'We believe that after many years of frustration and indecision the outcome has been a building which fits well into Ludlow and which we can be proud of' (CABE 2001: 28).

Ultimately Tesco was forced to engage a high profile architect, Sir Richard Cormac, to design the store in order to secure the site. However, unlike Sainsbury's, Tesco did not repeat this commissioning exercise, and did not take up the opportunity to raise the prestige of their brand profile through unique or at least, distinctive designs. The implications of this lengthy struggle to develop a supermarket on a sensitive site, in a historically significant town, suggests that although economically unsound in the planning and design stages, the end result was justifiable, particularly in respect of excluding rival stores. The fact that CABE gave public approval to a design by a company normally criticized for its brash, often ugly, buildings demonstrates both the power of public protest but also the eventual public acceptance of a modern store design.

The reuse of flagship buildings

The reuse of many listed or flagship buildings for supermarket use, was a result of competition between supermarket companies for sites on which to develop new stores. Local authorities responsible for the restoration of important buildings were happy to allow supermarket companies to acquire prime sites for development, which included the restoration and use of a building that could not be demolished.

Many of these eminent buildings were flagships in their own right through the prestige of their design and past existence, thereby passing on their particular character and status to their new retail inhabitant.

The re-use of prestigious buildings could include valuable adjacent space. In 1982 Sainsbury's restored the disused, but architecturally listed Green Street railway station in Bath. The station building serves as the main pedestrian entrance to the supermarket but is not incorporated into the store, which was located to the rear of the listed train shed. The covered link, an orange tinted curved roof, between the station and the store echo the vaulted roof of the station. The forecourt and surrounding yards provided plenty of easily adapted parking space.

In 1993 Tesco famously restored the listed Art Deco Hoover Building in West London. The architects Lyons Sleeman and Hoare created a scheme which restored the main building fronting the A40 road for office use; while the supermarket building to the rear was designed with Art Deco detail that echoed the original 1930s design by Wallis Gilbert and Partners (*Architects Journal* 1993: 37). Other notable developments of listed buildings include St George's church Wolverhampton converted by Sainsbury's in 1988, Morrison's conversion of a military barracks in Hillsborough (1991), Tesco's restoration and adaptation of a former Water Authority building in Baldock, and Sainsbury's conversion of a mill in Streatham, London. In many cases (Wolverhampton, and Streatham) the restored building does not house the commercial sales area of the store. More usually it provides a social space for a coffee shop or memorable entrance hall.

The implications of reuse have become more significant in the light of present issues regarding climate change and global warming. In the past the adaptation of buildings for supermarket use has been, on the part of the supermarket companies, almost solely in order to acquire important sites for trading ahead of commercial rivals. It is possible that the reuse of existing buildings will be encouraged and planning permission made easier if structures can be shown to have a sustainable future. This could provide new sites for development and facilitate placement in existing high streets.

Conclusions

It can be argued that the Sainsbury's flagship stores discussed in this chapter were all developed on sensitive or prestigious sites that allowed respective local authorities to demand high profile buildings. Despite the company's intention to 'reinforce the company emphasis on quality in all things' (Williams 1994), many of these stores, particularly Greenwich, have not since their inception been well maintained and are showing signs of neglect.

As flagship buildings these stores were received with enthusiasm by the architectural press who welcomed them as a break away from the hegemony of the 'Essex Barn' design that became prevalent in the 1980s. However none of the designs became a template for later stores, largely due to the high cost of their unique construction, but possibly because their originality set a standard for other companies and 'raised the bar' in terms of quality in the eyes of local authority planners. Like other flagship buildings they were without doubt intended both to raise the status of the company, and to reassure shareholders. However, it is also clear that their impact as flagships was temporal and, like all supermarket design, by nature ephemeral.

Glancey writing in *The Guardian* records that Richard Cormac was asked to design a store for Sainsbury's. His proposal included the design of the store interior, which was rejected on the grounds that 'his job was to style the façade. In other words, the architect was effectively designing a giant advertising poster and pasting it over a shopping shed' (Glancey 1998: 12).

Supermarket architecture in general is ephemeral and short lived. In the context of retail history many flagship buildings have ceased to retain their status as their importance and originality have been superseded by new and more prestigious architectural designs and powerful brand initiatives. However, the sometimes controversial listing of buildings by English Heritage has protected the flagship status of many structures, particularly those constructed in the recent past, which would otherwise have been lost, for example, Erno Goldfinger's Trellick Tower and Sir Giles Gilbert Scott's Bankside Power Station, now the Tate Modern. Supermarket buildings attached to important or significant buildings, for example Tesco and the Hoover Building London, Sainsbury's and St George's Church Wolverhampton, are likely to be regarded as having flagship status for as long as they remain related to these recognized flagship buildings.

It is a matter of conjecture as to whether in the future any of Sainsbury's purpose built flagship designs will be recognized as deserving listed status. Such recognition, while adding to the brand's distinction and historically marking the structure as important and worthy of conservation, would present a major burden in terms of maintenance costs attached to a building not designed for permanent recognition and flagship branding.

In the future, supermarket architectural design is likely to focus on sustainable development and energy saving technology. While Sainsbury's flagship Millennium store in Greenwich did not stand as a generic design for future store developments, flagship stores are likely to be those combining authentic concern for the environment and current thinking on branding and consumer culture.

13 Virtual flagships

Tim Jackson

Introduction

This chapter aims to synthesize existing knowledge of flagship retailing with an analysis of fast evolving virtual environments facilitated by the Internet. In this respect the chapter is exploratory and conceptual in parts, drawing from observations, interviews and the author's consultancy experience in the field of luxury branding. A key objective is to suggest that the notion of the flagship as a real-world retail format can evolve into a new shopping arena in a virtual world.

Well-discussed notions of the term flagship include ideas of superiority, communication and innovation, and the term crosses into retailing by signifying a brand's best store. In a similar way to product ranging in the fashion industry, where buyers make decisions about 'good, better and best' levels of product options within a category, so retailers operate stores of varying size, target turnovers and in locations of varying prestige. However, the term flagship is also widely used to refer to products and brands to denote superiority. For example, Zara is often referred to as Inditex's flagship brand, and car manufacturers apply the same description to specific prestige marques. Superiority may manifest itself in a variety of ways and in the luxury market will often be linked to brand status and positioning. Fundamental differences exist in expectations of design innovation and cost between the development of flagship stores in the luxury and mass markets. The latter may also feature differences between retailers and brand, which follow very different business models. Brands are likely to invest more money in design innovation across products and communications, since they don't normally possess a significant retail network. Over the last ten years many brands have discovered the value of selective directly operated stores as vehicles for brand communication.

Shopping and emotion

The concept of a flagship mirrors the evolution of shopping, which has developed from a mundane functional experience driven by necessity, to one in which many shoppers enjoy the experience as much as the products they buy. An experiential approach emphasizes the importance of affect on consumers and the need to extend product functionality to the delivery of experiences. Typical of this approach, Gobé's 'Ten Commandments of Emotional Branding' recommends that brands change their perspective from product to experience, identity to personality and function to feeling (2001). The importance of consumers' feelings in branding is supported by Wally Olins (2003), who describes how 'a consumer's relationship to a brand is as much to do with what it makes him feel as to how it performs'. Flagship stores are designed with innovation and the generation of an exciting consumer experience in mind.

The significance of stores as communicators of brand identity and status is especially important at the luxury end of the fashion market. Tom Ford famously made the point that although product is key, 'a dress does not exist in a void, it exists in a world and its context can radically alter its effect or its success or its appropriateness' (2001). The re-positioning and branding of Selfridges in the 1990s under the management of Vittorio Radice was similarly guided by the principle of enhancing the consumer shopping experience. Radice described shopping as 'the moment of freedom for individuals' and believed that the shopping experience is central to retailers' success, famously stating that place is more important than the product (Radice 2002). Other luxury brands also see the role of stores as more than simply housing for products. Christian Blanckaert at Hermès considers it important for Hermès stores to be places of theatre (Blanckaert 2002) and a number of Italian luxury brands have extended their successes in store design, to designing and building their own hotels. These become spaces where consumers can experience alternative dimensions of the brand.

Store design

Innovative store design is important to many fashion and luxury brands as a differentiator and means of enhancing and focusing the shopping experience for customers. More so than other retail spaces, the concept of a flagship store reflects the idea that sales are best achieved by not over merchandising with product and space- filling tactics. Sales are generated as a result of greater consumer involvement and emotional connection with a brand, and from engaging with the retail space and experiencing exquisite service. In many respects this implies characteristics of flagship stores that are different from standard physical stores. Frequently flagship store designs are inspired by art, create an innovative space, inviting a change of pace in the shopping experience for consumers and an opportunity for the brand to be seen as something different and opposed to the ordinary.

The location of flagship stores is often as important as the design itself. In Tokyo the 'must-be-in' location of Ginza hosts some of the most extravagant stores built by luxury brands. Hermès, Louis Vuitton, Chanel and Gucci each have extravagant and innovatively designed and constructed flagship stores in this area. High levels of service, exclusive products and innovative merchandising have been key to the store's success. Great attention is paid to the selling ceremony, with bags shown to clients on rolled-out pads. Such attention to the finest detail is characteristic of the flagship store experience, 'from the materials to such small details as silk robes in the fitting rooms, monogrammed leather shoehorns, credit-card trays, and even specially made seats for dogs, so that customers can enjoy shopping with their canine companions' (Jackson 2007).The opening of concept stores in London by Swarovski asserts their luxury credentials through their design statement, in which the Crystal Forest architecture forms a showcase that reflects the 'infinite possibilities of crystal and illustrates a deep affinity with the natural world' (Swarovski 2008).

The significance of such store developments on the streetscapes of global destination cities has been underlined by Yves Carcelle, CEO of Louis Vuitton, when he observed:

> I think we were the first one to participate in the reshaping of the cities where we are; if you look at the history of cities you have the church and the cathedrals, the princes and kings and their palaces and unfortunately, for a long period of time there was nothing; today I think the luxury industry is participating in the reshaping of the centre of cities.
>
> (Jackson 2007)

However, retail expansion can lead to a situation where innovative design and exclusivity is diluted by the roll-out of the same or similar looking stores. A standardized store appearance may conflict with the consumer's expectation of individual attention and customized experience. This concern prompted Prada to hire consultancies H&deM and OMA to conceive what subsequently became its epicentre stores. In this context the virtual flagship store should contribute to the distinctive presence of the retailer through its online location, design and service.

The flagship store and the spaces it contains – and flagship stores tend to expand their open spaces – can create a sense of the virtual. These spaces are used for circulation, browsing, and above all for interacting with the store as brand, rather than transacting with products, and are themselves virtual. Without a defined role they mediate both commercial transactions and leisure based consumption, creating synergies between real space and virtual space.

The merging of physical and virtual worlds is evident in the increasing use by retailers of instore information technologies to communicate and at best, interact with consumers. Technologies offer opportunities for retailers that know how to cope with the user-driven revolution. However, it is only in the past few years that businesses have started using them to engage with consumers. Widgets can be storefront windows for selling products and services for digital billboards to which customized advertisements can be attached (Ante *et al.* 2007). Designer fashion brands such as Prada (in New York) and Shiseido (in Tokyo) allow consumers access to detailed product information through in-store RFID readers. Such advances mean that it is now possible to tag any physical object with data and allow co-creation of products and services with consumers and point to many creative possibilities in the retail environment (Dyke 2007). In the real world, Apple has installed genius bars at its flagship stores, where specialists provide technical services, and by harnessing the enthusiasm of its customer base, effectively turns its consumers into its sales force. At USA PRO's flagship store in London, virtual sales assistants in the changing rooms help with consumer decision making. As the real world of retailing develops its points of interactivity with consumers, both between other objects and other users, so a shared experience has become an important part of the web. Consequently, consumer generated content and enhanced interaction will be at the front of online commercial development.

Online retailing

Websites have made significant advances since the 1990s, when creatively designed website concepts could not be supported by limited online connectivity and the home computer technology used by consumers. Complex, image-laden sites of early online fashion retailers, such as Boo.com effectively required a higher broadband capability to achieve reasonable download speed and improved higher processing and memory capacity on users' computers than tended to be available. Rapid developments in both these fields have enabled consumers to immerse themselves in the Internet for both shopping and entertainment. As consumer confidence grows, so brands have turned their attention to how to engage creatively with customers.

A significant amount of research interest has been focused upon consumers' actual experiences of Internet retailing and the degree to which these will affect their overall assessment of the online shopping process. Online sites provide convenient access to information, services and products, with an increasing number of consumers researching online before purchasing offline. A number of websites compete as online clubs to share information. These provide a shopping box of tools that help consumers to identify, locate and compare products from e-retailers (Dennis 2004).

The relationship between dwell time at the website, or in the store, and consumer expenditure was identified in an early stage of website development, when the concepts of stickiness and 'two clicks to access' concepts were considered important aspects of site design and navigation. Ease of use, perceived control, interactivity and shopping enjoyment have been related to site quality, customer loyalty and intention to continue shopping online (Wolfingbarger and Hilly 2003). Szymanski and Hise (2000) investigated the impact that customers' specific experience of convenience, merchandising, site design and security might have on their overall satisfaction with a particular website. Site aesthetics serve two functions; they provide visitors with a positive experience and they can render customers' surfing experience enjoyable. Other frequently mentioned usability aspects include effective navigation, customer facing functionality, user friendliness response speed and easy checkout (Yang *et al*. 2003).

The antecedents of loyalty, such as service quality, trust, value and satisfaction, have been significant in the consumer experience (Harris and Goode 2004; Rafiq and Fulford 2005). Other researchers have undertaken detailed studies of consumers' experiences of single aspects of retailers' online offerings, and the influence of e-tail store image (Wilde *et al.* 2004) or 'store layout' (Vrechopoulos *et al.* 2004), on their online behaviour. It is noticeable that the majority of studies focus primarily on the consumer experience of the website rather than on elements of the offline encounter, such as marketing communications, call-centre operations, service responsiveness, order delivery/fulfilment and after sales service. Indeed Jiang and Rosenbloom (2005) conclude that research relating to experiences and encounter-specific satisfaction is sparse and the contribution of after-delivery satisfaction in an e-retail context is virtually unknown (Doherty and Ellis-Chadwick 2006).

Virtual environments

A virtual environment may be described as an interactive computer-simulated location. Such environments are typically visual experiences with audio capabilities but at their most developed may include haptic systems facilitating a range of tactile options. A central problem is how to deliver online, the kind of unique experience that goes beyond a graphical interface. There remains a tendency for brands to plan their online presence in terms of a two-dimensional medium, and for online retailers to rely on brand building through visual experiences. A more expansive notion of an environment where people can interact on a larger and more diverse scale, has evolved around the success of Massive Multiplayer Online Role-playing Games. In these environments communication between users has ranged from text, graphical icons, visual gesture, sound, and rarely, forms using touch and balanced senses. Nevertheless they point to new opportunities for online flagship stores based on social networking.

Familiarity with the Internet is such that social networking sites are becoming an increasingly popular medium, complementing or even substituting for, email messaging. Two significant drivers are the expectations of younger consumers, and the available media for personalized communications. Communication tools that include message boards, audio clips, blogs and live scheduled chat facility, are now commonly used by individuals. These features present opportunities for online brands to engage with their consumers and an integrated approach to communication provides many points of interaction. Scheduled chat sessions with celebrities, downloads of music and video clips, interactive question and answers provide audio-visual levels of communication. A 'Try that style' drag and drop visual tool enables readers to make up outfits on a model and extends the level of interactivity. This level of technology application is hardly cutting-edge for regular readers of teen magazines and yet it is significantly ahead of most fashion online retailers.

Interactive sites can overcome the undesired aspects of an overt commercial presence and intrusive marketing techniques. The migration from MySpace to Facebook arose in part, because networkers grew tired of unsolicited advertisements and the explicit intrusion of strangers into what they understood to be their personal space. Online marketers need to facilitate virtual word of mouth appeal to new customers through pay-per-click solutions, improved search engine optimization and adapted viral techniques. Thus video clips can be forwarded but not necessarily traditional messages; in effect, the customer controls the relationship.

At the most developed end of the virtual environment are virtual worlds, which also vary hugely in terms of sophistication and complexity, with some replicating real world life and providing an arena in which consumers can indulge their fantasies. Virtual worlds that offer an alternative reality, such as Second Life, aim to replicate real life through operating systems that replicate the constraints of the real world, such as time and commercial exchange. Second Life has sought to recreate the physical shopping experience by combining 3D environments with avatars, and the opportunity has been taken up by retailers across a wide range of sectors. Dior and Mercedes Benz have explored the three-dimensional world of Second Life, with Mercedes Benz opening a showroom to launch its C class car, and other retailers showcasing their products and services in distinctive sites. The business model has yet to be established, and in this sense it may mirror the commercial development of the Internet in general. Nevertheless social forecasters predict that virtual (v)-commerce, with its 3D stores, will replace e-commerce (SIRC 2006) and companies that install virtual replicas of real-world stores are missing the point. As the virtual world develops so it will develop codes of behaviour that resemble real world ones and online community values will become more important. In the short term, there are lessons to be learned by companies committed to engagement with virtual communities, and to collaboration and communication with other members in emerging online societies.

The online flagship store

There are few examples of a virtual flagship store and so predictions are based on the emergence of hybrid models combining real-world flagship stores and virtual-world interactive spaces which host virtual stores. Nevertheless, some guidelines exist for online designer stores and there is clear evidence that virtual stores can compete successfully with their real counterparts as both the online Saks and Armani Exchange sites outsell all but the top stores in their chains. Faster connections, improved photography, and designer brand labels are important factors behind the growth in sales. Market positioning is important too, and delivering exclusivity is evidently easier when the products it sells are inherently exclusive. Companies such as CoutureLab.com promise the delivery of personalized attention, while 20limited.com is a designer fashion site that features only twenty products at a time and reflects both a focus on telling the stories behind the items it is selling combined with an 'extremely product centric' approach. The site is designed as a gallery rather than a shop, and creates a sense of the real time Sotheby's or Christie's auction houses, rather than a traditional luxury brand site (Birchall 2007). The most successful luxury e-commerce sites, including NiemanMarcus.com and Net-a-Porter have embraced the fact that shopping online for luxury goods needs to move the customer experience forward.

Larger online stores contain more features to help customers find their needs, search for more information on the products, evaluate alternative products and get help after they have purchased products from that store. Moreover, larger stores tend to have more design features to help customers find what they want (Huang and Christopher 2003) and editorial features to help improve the shopping experience. Online store designers should investigate development opportunities from existing provision, for example, by using enhanced image capability, interaction with garments through drag and drop features, where digital images of real clothes can be modelled, and zoom capabilities to enhance the image of products and click to talk services. The aim is to achieve a higher level of visual and interactive experience through 3D and 360 degree views of the product range and to provide facilities to exchange and comment on them (Euromonitor 2007). Gucci's website already provides this type of all round view and Louis Vuitton's site provides the opportunity to manipulate an image so that the viewer can zoom in to see product details. Following Lagerfeld, more designer fashion brands have taken to webcasting their runway shows. An online flagship should assess the value of these features through all its electronic and mobile commercial environments while maintaining a focus on transactional convenience and accessibility.

A key consideration for any brand developing a virtual flagship will be to define what additional brand benefits online flagship stores can deliver compared to real life flagship stores. One important potential benefit is that they frequently showcase products and practices in innovatively designed environments. The virtual world provides both opportunities to extend these activities and redefine their 3D characteristics to provide similar or alternative benefits. An influential representation of a virtual flagship is the Armani store, where the designer replicated his Milan store in Second Life in September 2007 to sell virtual Armani clothing and accessories for avatars: it makes itself more accessible through the web. A similar idea is for the retailer to develop different versions of company websites to attract and facilitate interactions with different visitors.

Clothing and accessories are the obvious way for avatars to differentiate themselves. Following the styling of the owner, a real-world consumer, an avatar wears specific designs in Second Life that convey taste and status in a similar way to that in the real world. The operator of the avatar is open therefore to brand choice of both in-world Second Life designers and brands and real-world brands that have 'set-up' in the virtual world. The latter may serve as an entry point into the brand back in the real world. This is a significant issue for innovator or early adopter brands since these characteristics are common among Second Life residents. Crucially the link between a young person routinely using relatively advanced technology in their daily social and entertainment activities and operating within a virtual world is not very great. In addition, as shopping is a social activity, concerning exchange in the broadest and richest sense (Hughes 2007), so online service deserves closer attention. This suggests that a further undeveloped aspect of virtual stores is the presence of staff in the virtual space, and the hiring and training of employees to act as avatars is an opportunity, if expensive and time-consuming, to create warm and welcoming spaces.

At an operational level, Ralph Lauren's polo.com is an efficient and designer-led example of how men's online shopping can improve on the real store shopping experience. In the physical world, classic polo shirts are colour coded and stacked high, which has a negative impact on accessibility and convenience. At Polo.com by contrast, product selection is reduced to a three click process that takes no more than ten minutes. The fit can be selected, slim, classic, vintage, and tried on by clicking onto a male model whose polo and penny logo change colour accordingly, with a two week delivery for custom orders (Sherwood 2007). The Ralph Lauren style guide online magazine provides clear, concise tutorials on the finer points of modern dressing.

Retailers in sectors other than fashion and luxury products, provide further insights into flagship store development. Amazon has the advantage of a strong brand and remains strongly focused on customer satisfaction, a particularly important factor in online retailing where the relationship between consumer and retailer is extremely pared down. Amazon's high customer satisfaction ratings prove important in its increasingly direct competition with eBay. The boundaries between auction sites and retail sites become more blurred as Amazon turn to selling more used goods, and eBay selling many new branded goods.

The website at John Lewis offers more guidance to furniture shoppers for achieving certain looks in their homes and the new website provides more inspiring photography that demonstrates furniture in room settings. Sony's PlayStation 3 unit enables users to get access to a specially created virtual world that is also compatible with MP3 music players and digital cameras. Mass customization and personalization provide other online flagship opportunities for retailers to take to create an individualized fit. Both Nike and Converse offer customers a degree of customization with their shoes and other complementary products but the same process lends itself to more exclusive products and services.

Other experiential brand leaders fail to maximize their impact online. The Disney store website is brightly coloured to appeal to children and offers a wide range of brand merchandise from toys to clothes. However, the site could make more of the Disney theme park entertainment concept and the company could and should be pushing the boundaries further in terms of escapism and sensory immersion. Customers are continually aware that this is a store for purchasing goods rather than a shopping entertainment concept. Similarly the Nike website reinforces the presence of the brand in its physical environment, but it has done little in the virtual world to take the level of absorption further by engaging all the senses in an entertainment experience (Ross and Kent 2004).

Personal space has become far more fluid freed of the constraints of conventional architecture by mobile phones, international travel and memory storage and global Internet communities. Law (2006) defines cyberspace as the straightforward 'symbiotic balance between architecture, spaces and technology', and the Electronic Arts Experience retail showroom demonstrates how a building within a building can create a freestanding retail cyberstructure that uses the concept of the game itself to form the space inhabited by customers. The result is a hybrid environment that combines materiality of the real and digital of the virtual world. It harnesses technology to generate the most cost-effective and simple solutions, in which reality is exaggerated to create a hyper-real environment.

The concept of interactivity and the ways in which interactive components of a flagship store can differentiate between online stores, require further analysis. Blogs are interactive in the sense that they can be navigated, and provide opportunities to move in and around the site. A forum is yet more interactive. Real-life flagship characteristics translate into the virtual world through the creation of a presence in cyberspace and the extent to which it is a transactional website. What is required is an alternative name that reflects how brands use social networking sites to provide a meeting place.

Conclusion

As website developments adopt more of the characteristics of social networking sites, so they begin to mimic aspects of real-world store interaction. What is beginning to change is the increasing facility to engage synchronously with staff via the website. The UK skincare brand Liz Earle (uk.lizearle.com) offers a scheduled chat facility on its site so that customers can hold a live conversation with a skincare expert and/or a member of the brand's customer care management. Such synchronous contact through a site effectively removes a long standing barrier that has differentiated real-world (bricks and mortar) shopping from online shopping. Given that most mass-market retailing experiences are based on self-service, this could develop into a scenario where online provides an opportunity to receive more informed support from retail staff than in a real-world store.

In addition live contact removes some of the uncertainty associated with remote buying as questions can be asked and answered immediately. The component elements of increased customer sophistication and access, found in advanced 'touch' technologies, live and delayed social interaction, hi-image mobile and interactive visual technologies can combine to deliver a high specification, interactive, online shopping experience. 3D V-commerce is ready to expand its inworld existence and become the next retailing frontier.

Afterword

Tony Kent

The most visible aspect of the flagship concept and certainly one that defines its place is its physical presence. Buildings in general are a common element in the relationship between the organization and its environment. They can be seen as symbolic artefacts that reflect the organization inhabiting them. Emphasis on their internal and external surfaces may be understood as a purposeful adaptation to postmodern society; what counts is as much its appearance, and thus its credibility, as its performance.

The flagship building is designed to communicate, and designers and architects have an essential role in exploring this function in iconic and signature buildings. Less well observed has been the retail industry's interest in distinctive buildings and the ways in which architecture has been used to create retail stores and individual visual identities. Edwards highlights past investment in prestigious architecture and retailers' use of such iconic places, invoking London's West End in their advertisements. As she rightly points out, there is a challenge to understand and value these flagship stores, 'as urban centers are re-imagined for twenty-first century consumption'. One such re-imagining has taken place in nearby Regent Street. The sense of place is visually striking from the regularity and quality of the street's architecture. The pillars and columns of the facades are monumental, their features combining to create a sense of permanence that appeals to the visitor's sense of an ideal, well-ordered shopping street. While planning requirements and a new, possibly enforced sense of history have determined some interior designs, others use the architecture itself to define their brand. Cultural quarters have purpose-designed or adapted spaces to create a sense of identity and a focus for cultural and artistic activities. This aspect of the flagship concepts finds a resonance with the function of design, to 'connect to the past with a reassuring familiarity, while surprising users with its inventiveness' (Liedtka and Mintzberg 2006: 10).

Commitment to a flagship project forms one dimension of strategic planning and management. This is most evident in the use of flagship stores in the internationalization of designer brands, where they both support geographical expansion and raise the brand's profile. The development and maintenance costs of flagship, their financial and non-tangible contributions to profitability and balance sheet, are not fully understood. There are dangers that arise from the failure of a flagship and the subsequent potential negative effects on the core organizational activities. Consequently, the strategic implications of using flagships need to be assessed in more detail. Adapting a strategic approach that analyses the physical and reputational resource of the flagship will enhance organizational capacity to build competitive advantage. For organizations operating from multiple sites, there is a need to measure its function as a place for experimentation with new products, designs, operations and brands and their influence on other less prestigious trading units. The influence of a flagship is felt elsewhere in the market, as competitors respond to the challenges posed by new concepts and operations, and opportunities exist to model and analyse this specific environment.

A distinctive feature of the flagship is that it will fulfil a more or less clearly thought out marketing communications function. Fresher, more desirable and more spectacular visual images have often been demanded to enhance the value of the brand (Olins 1990). Communication of a consistent retailer identity, through exteriors and interiors, is the outcome of the design process in which consumerist, psychological, and aesthetic elements are drawn together (Din 2000). Bitner (1992) records that the physical environment 'may be very influential in communicating the firm's image …'. A number of elements, including colour and music, can inform users about the organization. Spatial design and physical symbolic artefacts influence the formation of individual identities, and relate to the image of the organization and buildings it occupies. Interpretation of the built physical symbolic artefacts in these processes engages with individuals' emotions. The exclusive image of the flagship is enhanced or eroded by the balance or imbalance achieved in the processes of identity and image formation.

The application of architecture and design can create distinctive environments in often less explicitly prestigious places. 'Store as design' has come to relate consumer behavioural needs to functionality and branding, and for out of town superstores at least, inside-out store design gave further emphasis to the maximization of interior sales space and to the development of retailer brands and services. For food retailers, the flagship superstore creates a functional space in, and around, which a branded identity can be supported. These are transient flagship stores responding to marketing initiatives, 'food as fashion', and the enabling power of rapidly evolving operational methods. As long as food retailers continue to exploit commercial opportunities through new store openings, the latest flagship store will showcase new products, services and technologies, and their internal selling spaces will be organized around these elements. In these stores, extracting additional value from selling spaces is always paramount, and an unresolved tension exists between costs and the distinctiveness of architecture as an element of the brand.

The concept of internal spaces serving a more abstract social purpose concerns their use and design in the building itself, and their extension into the surrounding environment, typically the street, mall or area. The hybridity of usage was typified by the concept of the third space which emerged during the 1980s, as experience-oriented marketing turned to stores and also museums, restaurants and hotels. It saw the creation of public spaces that were neither home nor work. Through their sensuality and homeliness they came to be perceived as personal habitats where the brand's 'core function is complemented by an emotional extra of almost equal value' (Mikunda 2004: 4).

As spaces for consumption, play or enjoyment, flagships provide an important medium for socialization and interaction, as well as arenas for synthesizing leisure and consumption. Flagship shopping malls epitomize this synthesis, as their scale provides more focused opportunities. However, Dennis citing Howard (2007) in his earlier chapter observes that leisure is underpinned by a revolution in food consumption, evident in the growth in bars and restaurants, rather than 'retailtainment'. Leisure led flagship developments are the exception in the UK, and open up opportunities for further US lifestyle centre development. Such spaces afford retailers the opportunity to engage in co-creation with consumers and stimulate peer-to-peer communication.

Flagship concepts should, at least, be inspiring and create spaces for memorable experiences. This is partly to do with size but also to do with their porpose. Flagship developments tend to be characterized by their large internal spaces, which provide opportunities for commercial transactions with products and services. But they are also experiential environments, where shopping and leisure are combined formally, and less formally. However some stores create memorable experiences through the intimate use of space. The cube-shaped Clube Chocolate in São Paulo is '... not so much a micro-department store phenomenon but a different – almost intimate – attitude to luxury shopping, one that serves ... fresh, unique products on every visit and a diverse shopping experience, all wrapped up in an aesthetically pleasing and social environment' (Harkin 2004: 9). Smaller spaces afford opportunities to create idealized room settings, drawing on positive emotions about home and leisure, personal identity and branding. Such an approach is typified by the Levi girls' store, which 'combines the feel of a girl's bedroom with the sophistication of a boutique shop' (Marketing 2004: 21). This use of 'space as communication' is particularly significant for youth markets which seek out authenticity and prize honesty and integrity in products, services and their communication.

Sustainable memorable experiences can arise from these spaces, both large and small where products, physical and virtual environments engage our senses through the visual but also touch and sound, and to a lesser degree, smell and taste. This emphasis on sensory engagement supports the concepts of experiential marketing developed in the 1990s by Pine and Gilmore (1999) as a means to achieve a high level of differentiation and added value. In their definition of the concept, an effective marketing experience is interactive and physical but also delivered through a powerful emotional or sensory experience. It is an orchestrated presentation, event, advertisement, acknowledgement, that causes people to relate to the message, connect with its appeal and experience a sense of excitement, pleasure or satisfaction (Marconi 2005). While the general application of experiential marketing principles may have been accepted as a short lived approach – an aspect of the experience economy – the concepts remain relevant to the flagship sector.

The flagship concept engages with creativity, in a sense left unresolved by Pine and Gilmore. Creative spaces can be understood within a context of more substantial and located places. Of particular concern to designers as they move between closure and adaptation in each project is the extent to which design can ever be said to be complete, and, how businesses can adapt to change and continuity concurrently. Great designs, in the view of Liedtka and Mintzberg, are typified by simplicity and emotional engagement, combining the new and familiar. Moreover, individualized design can be contrasted with commodification of retail architectural practice as the 'perception design' of shopping experiences, their enthusiasms and escapism (Kelly 2006; Frampton 2006). Wynn Las Vegas demonstrates the influence of the hotel flagship as a marker of change, through its carefully controlled design, understated luxury and absence of overt, or commoditized theming. It explains how the city has been used as a test-bed for radical ideas, as an urban laboratory comparatively unrestrained by government regulation.

Interactivity and experimentation present further creative challenges. Static spatial configurations can create 'product museums', while flexibility enables stores to adapt and change to meet commercial and social needs. The unconventional design of Niketown blurs the boundaries between promotional, sales and educational spaces where customers can spend time with the brand as a leisure activity (Peñazola 1999). The Eden project has been discussed in terms of being too alive and too fertile to be merely called a flagship, with its connotations of solid buildings and urban landscapes; rather it is a unique living and growing entity. More recent developments include the Apple store, currently trading from 30,000 square feet over two floors in London. Its use of large, open internal spaces, minimal stock densities, opportunities for interaction with products and services, and its high flow of visitors and customers have made it a model for other stores in the same street. At a more luxurious extreme, Nokia's Vertu concept reflects the brand's core identity of luxury and personal communication. These spaces combine human contact and personal communication, and through their in-store technologies enable a 'richness' of personal encounters to extend to online communities (Lindstrom 2003; Lammiman and Syrett 2004).

Virtual environments provide opportunities to change and expand the concept of the flagship location. As a meeting place rather than showcase, it enables social interactions to extend beyond by the physical environment. An intention to create an enjoyable place should be a distinctive feature of the flagship concept. It can be educational or somewhere to play but interaction should remain an essential element. While the visual sense has been in the primacy for the postmodern consumer, here other senses can be more fully engaged. The virtual world expands the opportunities for real world flagship projects.

The preceding discussion has identified different appearances and uses of flagship concepts and places, and touches on the question of who is engaged with flagships. Governments, both centrally and locally, directly and through agencies, often create and use flagship developments to regenerate post-industrial areas. The mega-project becomes a reliable focus in place-marketing plans. Dennis proposes that the planned shopping mall can act as a magnet for regeneration and as a beacon to investors, to provide additional finance to extend and sustain the scheme, but also to provide cultural investment though creative and cultural activity. Less frequently, government policy turns to the promotion of existing centres. The Vienna cultural quarter raises the profile of the city as an international cultural tourism centre. Elsewhere, distinctive modern architecture can provide a very purposeful destination for tourists; Chicago and more recently Dubai and Shanghai, provide well-documented visual spectacles. 'Architourism' is observed by Schwarzer (2005: 17) in large cities around the world where 'striking buildings by signature architects can act as touristic cash cows'.

However the need for prestigious, distinctive and expensive buildings is increasingly questioned in the interests of the local community. Social and commercial activities combine within the flagship but their effect extends too, beyond the immediate environment. The DCMS suggests that cultural excellence should be balanced with community needs, and at worst an iconic building can have a detrimental impact. Therefore policy makers need to assess their impact through quantitative and softer measures. Smyth (1994) asks whether flagship developments are just an expensive way of effectively promoting urban regeneration: a fundamental tool for unlocking latent demand in the local economy; or a symbol. Critically, in this context, there must be an evaluation of the flagship's ability to deliver the required benefits to attract further consumption and investment.

The discussion creates new opportunities to examine the consumption of experiences. In the future, we may be obliged to consume fewer things (products) as sustainability and availability issues become more significant. Such limitations address the extent to which the consumption of things can be augmented and even replaced with sensory experiences. In addition, as flagship projects are observed to create memorable experiences, so in the future, researchers will assess the opportunities to replicate these in less prestigious places. Already, restrictions on developing out of town sites have resulted in closer attention being paid to urban locations and the creative re-use of sites. This has an impact on marketing strategy, by creating opportunities to demonstrate environmental responsibility. The ability to develop a distinctive brand identity through the architectural design of supermarkets has yet to be fully exploited.

Consequently, the significance of flagship projects will engage a wider population and its access to the enjoyment and use of experiences. As such, they provide transferability and diffusion, diversity and accessibility. 'Intelligent' and 'consumer responsive' environments may emerge. Increasingly use of space blurs the distinction between places of consumption, between different types of store, hotel and cultural centre, and on a larger scale, areas and cities. Intelligent environments, adopting new information and communication technologies may render a physical flagship redundant, or transform the nature of space and time to create new forms of experience.

The retail environment remains both complex and dynamic, and while both modern and postmodern flagship designs appear experimental, they point to more altruistically inspired opportunities. Environmental and government planning agenda will require careful assessment of development opportunities. In part this will be in the form of greater re-use of buildings, and brownfield sites and create relationships between present and future developments and the inherited prestige of the former occupants, their history and visual appearance. In part too, new flagships featuring integrated environmental designs, and seen experimentally at Sainsbury's store in Greenwich, will encapsulate environmental concerns for sustainability.

References

Aaker, D. and Joachimsthaler, E. (2000) *Brand Leadership*, New York: The Free Press.

Adburgham, A. (1979) *Shopping in Style: London from the Restoration to Edwardian Elegance*, London: Thames and Hudson.

Ahonen, T. and Moore, A. (2005) *Communities Dominate Brands: Business and Marketing Challenges for the 21st Century*, London: Futuretext.

Aitcheson, C. and Evans, T. (2003) 'The cultural industries and a model of sustainable regeneration: manufacturing "Pop" in the Rhondda valleys of South Wales', *Leisure*, 8 (3): 133–44.

Albrecht, D. (2002) *New Hotels for Global Nomads*, London: Merrell.

Allegra (2002) *Shopping Centres in the UK*, London: Allegra Strategies.

Allegra Strategies (2005) *Project Flagship*, London: Allegra Strategies.

Amendola, G. (1995) 'Public spaces and city regeneration', in *Culture and Neighbourhoods (1): Concepts and References*, Strasbourg: Council of Europe Publishing.

Ang, S. H., Leong, S. M. and Lim, J. (1997) 'The mediating influence of pleasure and arousal on layout and signage effects', *Journal of Retailing and Consumer Services*, 4 (1): 13–24.

Anon. (2006) 'Diesel drives upmarket with Bond Street flagship store', *Drapers*, 22 April, London.

Ante, S. E., Green, H. and Holahan, C. (2007) 'The next small thing', *Business Week*, 23 July, Info. Tech: The Web, 4043: 58.

Architect's Journal (1982) *Canterbury Choice*,13 October: 44–46.

Architect's Journal (1986) *Superstore Solutions*, 6 August: 29–36.

Architect's Journal (1993) 'New lease of life for the Hoover factory', 27 January: 37–46.

Argyris, C. and Schön, D. (1989) 'Participatory action research and action science compared: a commentary', *American Behavioural Scientist*, 32 (5): 612–23.

Arnould, E. J. (1998) 'Daring consumer-oriented ethnography', in B. Stern (ed.) *Representing Consumers: Voices, Views and Visions*, London: Routledge.

Augé, M. (1995) *Non-places: Introduction to an Anthropology of Supermodernity*, trans. J. Howe, London: Verso.

Babin, B.J., Darden, W. R. and Griffin, M. (1994) 'Work and/or fun: measuring hedonic and utilitarian shopping value', *Journal of Consumer Research*, 20: 644–656.

Baker, J., Grewal, D., Parasuraman. A. and Voss, G. B. (2002) The influence of multiple store environment cues on perceived merchandise value and patronage intentions,' *Journal of Marketing*, 66 (2): 120–141.

Barnstone, D. A. (2004) 'Transparency in postwar German politics and architecture', dissertation, Delft University of Technology.

Baron, S., Davies, B. and Swindley, D. (1991) *The Macmillan Dictionary of Retailing*, London: Macmillan.

Barthes, R. (1973) *Mythologies*, trans. A. Lavers, London: Paladin.

Bassett, K., Griffiths, R. and Smith, I. (2002) 'Testing governance: partnerships, planning and conflict in waterfront regeneration', *Urban Studies*, 39 (10): 1757–75.

Barthes, R. (1979) *The Eiffel Tower and Other Mythologies*, New York: Noonday Press.

Bathurst, A. (2007), quoted in 'Nokia secures its next flagship store in São Paulo'. Available online at: www.theretailbulletin.com (accessed 26 October 2007).

Baudrillard, J. (1983) *Simulations*, New York: Semiotext(e).

Baudrillard, J. (1986) *America*, London: Verso.

Baudrillard, J. (2001) 'Simulacra and simulations', in M. Poster (ed.) *Selected Writings*, Cambridge: Polity Press.

Baumol, W. and Baumol, H. (1994) 'On the economics of musical composition in Mozart's Vienna', in J. M. Morris (ed.) *On Mozart*, Cambridge: Cambridge University Press.

BBC News, (2001) 'Dome boss pinpoints failures' (cited 31 January 2007). Available online at: http://news.bbc.co.uk/1/hi/uk/1449701.stm (accessed 12 July 2007).

BBC News, (2005) 'Eden is favourite modern building' (cited 11 June 2007). Available online at: http://news.bbc.co.uk/1/hi/england/cornwall/4522840.stm (accessed 20 July 2007).

BDP (1992) *The Effects of Major Out-of-Town Retail Development: A Literature Review for the Department of the Environment*, London: BDP Planning and Oxford Institute of Retail Management/HMSO.

Becker, F. (1990) *The Total Workplace: Facilities Management and Elastic Organisation*, New York: Praeger Press, in Swann, P., and Birke, D. (2005) 'How do creativity and design enhance business performance? A framework for interpreting the evidence', London: Department for Trade and Industry.

Begout, B. (2003) *Zeropolis: The Experience of Las Vegas*, London: Reaktion.

Belk, B. (2000) 'May the farce be with you: on Las Vegas and consumer infantalization', *Consumption, Markets and Culture*, 4: 101–124.

Bellizzi, J. A., Crowley, A. E. and Hasty, R. W. (1983) 'The effect of color in store design', *Journal of Retailing*, 59 (1): 21–45.

Benjamin, W. (2000) *The Arcades Project*, trans. H. Eiland and K. McLaughlin, Cambridge, MA: Harvard University Press.

Benson, A. L. (ed.) (2000) *I Shop, Therefore I am: Compulsive Buying and the Search for Self*, Oxford: Jason Aronson.

Benton, C. (1995) *A Different World: Émigré Architects in Britain 1928–1956*, London: RIBA.

Berg, P. O. and Kreiner, K. (1990) 'Corporate Architecture: turning physical settings into symbolic resources', in P. Gagliardi (ed.) *Symbols and Artifacts: Views of the Corporate Landscape*, New York: Aldine de Gruyter.

Beverland, M. and Morrison, M. (2003) 'Experience-brand "fit": a contingent model', Paper presented at the Society of Marketing Advances Conference, New Orleans, 5 November.

Bianchini, F. (1995) 'Cultural consideration in inner city regeneration', in *Culture and Neighbourhoods 1, Concepts and References*, Strasbourg: Council of Europe Publishing.

Bianchini, F., Dawson, J. and Evans, R. (1992) 'Flagship projects in urban regeneration', in P. Healey, S. Davoudi, M. O'Toole, S. Tavsanoglu and D. Usher (eds) *Rebuilding the City: Property-Led Urban Regeneration*, London: E & F. N. Spon.

Birch, E. L. (2002) 'Having a longer view on downtown living', *Journal of the American Planning Association*, 68 (Winter): 5–17.

Birchall, J. (2007) 'Weaving the web around exclusive brand sales', *FT Report, Business of Luxury*, 4 June: 3.

Bitner, M. J. (1992) 'Servicescapes: the impact of physical surrounding on customers and employees', *Journal of Marketing*, 56: 57–71.

Blanckaert, C. (2002) 'Fashion 2002 – luxury unlimited', International Herald conference presentation, Paris: George V Hotel.

Blewitt, J. (2004) 'The Eden project – making a connection', *Museum and Society*, 2 (3): 175–89.

Blum, A. (2005) 'The mall goes under cover: it now looks like a city street', *Slate*, Wednesday, April 6, 2005. Available online at: http://slate.com/id/2116246/(accessed 26 September, 2007).

Boje, D. M. (2001a) *Narrative Methods for Organizational and Communication Research*, London: Sage.

Boje, D. M. (2001b) 'Introduction to deconstructing Las Vegas', *M@n@gement* (4): 79–82.

Boulding, K. E. (1956) *The Image*, Ann Arbor MI: University of Michigan.

Bourdieu, P. (1984) *Distinction: A Social Critique of the Judgement of Taste*, London: Routledge.

Bourdieu, P. (1991) *Language and Symbolic Power*, Cambridge, MA: Harvard University Press.

Bourdieu, P. and Delsaut, Y. (1975) 'Le couturier et sa griffe: contribution à une théorie de la magie', *Actes de la Recherche en Sciences Sociales*, 1: 7–36.

Bourn, J. (2001) 'Reinforcing positive approaches to risk management in government', *Third Annual Lecture*, London: The Institute of Risk Management.

Bowlby, R. (1985) *Just Looking: Consumer Culture in Dreiser, Gissing and Zola*, London: Methuen.

Boyer, M. C. (1992) 'Cities for sale: merchandising history at South Street Seaport', in Sorkin, M. (ed.) *Variations on a Theme Park. The New American City and the End of Public Space*, New York: The Noonday Press.

Bradsher, K. (2002) *High and Mighty. The Dangerous Rise of the SUV*, New York: Public Affairs.

Brambilla, R. and Longo, G. (1977) *For Pedestrians Only*, New York NY: Watson-Guptill.

Braudel, F. (1967) *Capitalism and Material Life, 1400–1800*, New York: Harper Torchbooks.

Brauer, G. (ed.) (2002) *Architecture as Brand Communication*, Basel: Birkhäuser.

Breward, C. (1999) *The Hidden Consumer: Masculinities, Fashion and City life, 1860–1914*, Manchester: Manchester University Press.

Breward, C. (2003) *Fashion: Oxford History of Art series*, Oxford: Oxford University Press.

Brooks, A. C. and Kushner, R. J. (2003) 'Cultural districts and urban development', *International Journal of Arts Management*, 3 (2): 4–15.

Brown, A., O'Connor, J. and Cohen, S. (2000) 'Local music policies within a global music industry: Cultural Quarters in Manchester and Sheffield', *Geoform*, 31 (4): 437–51.

Brown, S. (1992) *Retail Location: A Micro-Scale Perspective*, Aldershot: Avebury.

Bruner, J. (1990) *Acts of Meaning*, Boston, MA: Harvard University Press.

Building Design (1986) *Chain Reaction*, 8: August: 10–11.

BURA (2002) 'Retail and regeneration – perfect partners?' Conference Report, British Urban Regeneration Association and the British Retail Consortium.

Burgoon, J. K. and Saine, T. (1978) *The Unspoken Dialogue: An introduction to Nonverbal Communication*, Boston, MA: Houghton Mifflin.

CABE (2001) *Building in Context: New Development in Historic Areas*, London: CABE and English Heritage.

Canter, D. (1977) *The Psychology of Place*, New York: St Martin's Press.

Careri, F. V. (2001) *Walkscapes: Walking as an Aesthetic Practice*, Barcelona: Editoral Gustavo Gili.

Carriere, J.-P. and Demazière, C. (2002) 'Urban planning and flagship development projects: lessons from EXPO 98, Lisbon', *Planning Practice and Research*, 17 (1): 69–79.

Caru, A. and Cova, B. (2003) 'Revisiting consumption experience: a more humble but complete view of the concept', *Marketing Theory*, 3 (2): 267–86.

Cassill, N. L., Li, J. and Wang Y. (2004), 'A comparative study of new fashion outlets in the Shanghai apparel market', *Journal of Fashion Marketing and Management*, 8 (2): 66–75.

Castells, M. (2001) *The Internet Galaxy: Reflections on the Internet, Business, and Society*, Oxford: Oxford University Press.

Castells, M., Fernandez-Ardevol, M., Qiu, J. L. and Sey, A. (2007) *Mobile Communication and Society: A Global Perspective*, Cambridge, MA: MIT Press.

Census of Population (1991), London: HMSO.

Chaplin, S. (2000) 'Heterotopia deserta: Las Vegas and other spaces', in I. Borden and J. Rendell (eds) *Intersections: Architectural Histories and Critical Theories*, London: Routledge.

Chebat, J.-C. and Michon, R. (2003) 'Impact of ambient odors on mall shoppers' emotions, cognition and spending: a test of competitive causal theories', *Journal of Business Research*, 56: 529–539.

Chia, R. (1996) 'The problem of reflexivity in organizational research: towards a postmodern science of organization', *Organization*, 3 (1): 31–59.

Childressa, M. D. and Braswell, B. R. (2006) 'Using massively multiplayer online role-playing games for online learning', *Distance Education*, 27 (2): 187–96.

Chmielewska, E. (2005) 'Logos or the resonance of branding: a close reading of the iconosphere of Warsaw', *Space and Culture*, 8 (4): 349–80.

Christaller, W. (1933) *Central Places in Southern Germany*, translated by C. Baskin (1966), Englewood Cliffs, NJ: Prentice-Hall.

Clark, D. (1982) *Urban Geography*, London: Croom Helm.

Clegg, A. (2006) 'Hot shops: retail revamps'. Available online at: www.brandchannel.com (accessed 21 April 2006).

Clements, A. (2000) 'French Connection keeps it simple', *Retail Week*, 3 November, London.

Coble, S. (2007) quoted in R. Warrington, 'Its all go at Uniqlo', *City AM*, 6 November.

Cohen, l. (2003) *A Consumers' Republic: The Politics of Mass Consumption in Post-War America*, New York: Vintage Books.

Colomina, B. (1994) *Privacy and Publicity: Modern Architecture as Mass Media*, Cambridge, MA: MIT Press.

Colquhoun, I. (1995) *Urban Regeneration, An International Perspective*, London: Batsford.

Cook, I. (2004) 'Waterfront regeneration, gentrification and the entrepreneurial state: the redevelopment of Gunwharf Quays, Portsmouth', SPA working Paper, 51 (July), School of Geography, University of Manchester.

Coomber, S. (2002) *Branding*, London: Clipstone Publishing.

Corina, M. (1972) *Pile it High Sell it Cheap*, London: Weidenfeld and Nicolson.

Coyne, R. (1995) *Designing Information Technology in the Postmodern Age: From Method to Metaphor*, Cambridge, MA: MIT Press.

Coyne, R. (1999) *Technoromanticism: Digital Narrative, Holism, and the Romance of the Real*, Cambridge, MA: MIT Press.

Coyne, R. (2006) 'Space without ground', in M. Bain (ed.) *Architecture in Scotland*, Glasgow: The Lighthouse Trust.

Coyne, R. and Stewart, J. (2007) 'Orienting the future: design strategies for non-place', in T. Inns (ed.) *Design for the 21st Century*, London: Gower Ashgate.

Coyne, R. and Triggs, J. (2007) 'Training for practice-based research: adaptation, integration and diversity', in T. Bianchi, (ed.) *Creativity or Conformity: Building Cultures of Creativity in Higher Education*, 8–10 January, Cardiff: University of Wales Institute Cardiff.

Crane, D., Kawashima, N. and Kawasaki, K. (eds) (2002) *Global Culture: Arts, Media, Policy, and Globalisation*, London: Routledge.

Crary, J. (1999) *Suspensions of Perception: Attention, Spectacle, and Modern Culture*, Cambridge, MA: MIT Press.

Crawford, M. (1992) 'The world in a shopping mall', in M. Sorkin, (ed.) *Variations on a Theme Park. The New American City and the End of Public Space*, New York: The Noonday Press.

Crossick, G. and Jaumain, S. (eds) (1999) *Cathedrals of Consumption. The European Department store, 1850–1939*, Aldershot: Ashgate.

Csikszentmihalyi, M. (1997) *Finding Flow*, New York: Perseus Books.

Csikszentmihalyi, M. (1999) 'Implications of a systems perspective', in R. J. Sternberg, (ed.) *Handbook of Creativity*, Cambridge: Cambridge University Press.

Csikszentmihalyi, M. and Rochberg-Halton, E. (1981) *The Meaning of Things: Domestic Symbols and the Self*, Cambridge: Cambridge University Press.

Cushman and Wakefield Healy and Baker (2004) *Main Streets Across the World 2004*, London: CWHB.

Czerny, A. (2007) 'Uniqlo to double UK sales with Oxford Street shops', *Drapers*, 10: November.

Davies, P. (1999) 'The landscape of luxury', in J. Hill, (ed.) *Occupying Architecture: Between the Architect and the User*, London: Routledge.

Davies, R. L. and Bennison, D. J. (1979) *British Town Centre Shopping Schemes: A Statistical Digest. Report U11*. Reading: Unit for Retail Planning Information.

Davis, D. (1966) *A History of Shopping*, London: Routledge and Kegan Paul.

Davis, M. (2000) 'The strip versus nature', in *Metropolis Now. Urban Cultures in Global Cities*, Vienna: Springer.

Dawson, J. A. (1979) *The Marketing Environment*, London: Croom Helm.

DCMS (1999) Draft Guidance for Local Cultural Strategies, London: DCMS.

DCMS (2004) 'Culture at the heart of regeneration', *Summary of Responses*, London: Department for Culture, Media and Sport. Available online at: http://www.culture.gov. uk/NR/rdonlyres/8667CB79-7686-4266-9723-8B93131C9D23/0/cathr_summary_of_responses.pdf (accessed 7August 2007).

Dear, M. (2000) *The Postmodern Urban Condition*, Oxford: Blackwell.

Debord, G. (1983) *The Society of the Spectacle*, Detroit, MI: Black and Red.

Deffner, A. (2000) 'Cultural Industries in Athens: spatial transformations during the nineties'. In Papers of the *6th World Leisure Congress: Leisure and Human Development*, Bilbao: Deusto University.

Deffner, A. D. and Labrianidis, L. (2005) 'Planning culture and time in a mega-event: Thessaloniki as the European city of culture', *International Planning Studies*, 10 (3/4): 241–64.

De Frantz, M. (2005) 'From Cultural regeneration to discursive governance: constructing the flagship of the "Museumsquartier Vienna" as a plural symbol of change', *International Journal of Urban and Regional Research*, 291, Pt. 1: 50–66.

Dennis, C. E. (2004) *E-Retailing*, Basingstoke: Palgrave.

Dennis, C. E. and Newman, A. J. (2005) 'Manipulation of stimuli in a retail setting: a study into the effects of Captive Audience Network screens on shopping center customers', *Brunel Business School Working Paper Series: Special Issue on Marketing*, Brunel University, 2.

Dennis, C. E., Marsland, D. and Cockett, W. (2002) 'Central place practice: shopping centre attractiveness measures, hinterland boundaries and the UK retail hierarchy', *Journal of Retailing and Consumer Services*, 9 (4):185–99.

Dennis, C. E., Newman, A. J. and King, T. (2006) 'Brand image and shoppers' choices of shopping destinations: a study of an outer London (UK) town', Proceedings of the 13th Recent Advances in Retailing and Services Science Conference, Budapest: EIRASS, June.

Dennis, C. E. Newman, A. J. and King, T. (2007) 'Evaluating micro dimensions of brand image: a study of an outer London (UK) town', 14th International Conference on Recent Advances in Retailing and Services Science, San Francisco, June.

Des Rosiers, F., Lagana, A., Thierault, M. and Baudoin, M. 'Shopping centres and house values: an empirical investigation', *Journal of Property Valuation and Investment*, 14 (4): 411–62.

Dibbell, J. (2007) 'The life of the Chinese gold farmer', *New York Times*, 17 June. Available online at: http://www.nytimes.com/2007/2006/2017/magazine/2017lootfarmers-t.html (accessed 10 October 2007).

Dickens Heath Village Centre (2007) Available online at: http://www.dickensheathvillage.com/ (accessed 26 September 2007).

Din, R. (2000) *New Retail*, London: Conran Octopus.

Doherty, N. F. and Ellis-Chadwick, F. E. (2006) 'New perspectives in internet retailing: a review and strategic critique of the field', *International Journal of Retail and Distribution Management*, 34 (4/5): 411–28.

Domosh, M. (1996) 'The feminised retail landscape: gender ideology and consumer culture in nineteenth-century New York City', in N. Wrigley and M. Lowe (eds) *Retailing, Consumption and Capital: Towards the New Retail Geography*, Harlow: Longman.

Donovan, R. and Rossiter, J. (1982) 'Store atmosphere: an environmental psychological approach', *Journal of Retailing*, 58 (spring): 38–57.

Donovan, R. J., Rossiter, J. R., Marcoolyn, G. and Nesdale, A. (1994) 'Store atmosphere and purchasing behavior', *Journal of Retailing*, 70 (3): 283–294.

Douglass, W. and Raento, P. (2004) 'The tradition of invention: conceiving Las Vegas', *Annals of Tourism Research*, 31: 7–23.

Doyle, A., Moore, C., Doherty A-M. and Hamilton, M. (2008) 'Brand context and control: the role of the flagship store in the B&B Italia', *International Journal of Retail and Distribution Management*, 36 (7): 551–563.

Dubé, L. and Morin, S. (2001), 'Background music pleasure and store evaluation: intensity effects and psychological mechanisms', *Journal of Business Research*, 54 (2): 107–113.

Dybedal, P. (2000) 'Theme parks as flagship attractions in peripheral areas', *Annals of Tourism Research*, 27 (1): 250–2.

Dyke, M. (2007) 'When worlds collide', *Campaign*, Digital essays; 29 June: 37.

Eco, U. (1986) *Travels in Hyperreality*, trans. W. Weaver, San Diego, CA: Harcourt Brace Jovanovich.

Edelman, M. (1977) *Political Language: Words that Succeed and Politics that Fail*, New York: Academic Press.

Edwards, A. T. (1933) *The Architecture of Shops*, London: Chapman and Hall.

Edwards, B. (2003) 'A man's world? Masculinity and metropolitan modernity and Simpson, Piccadilly', in D. Gilbert, D. Matless and B. Short (eds) *Geographies of British Modernity*, Oxford: Blackwell.

Edwards, B. (2006a) 'The fashionable maps of 1930s Vogue', *Fashion Theory*, 10 (1/2).

Edwards, B. (2006b) 'West End shopping with *Vogue*: 1930s geographies of metropolitan consumption', in J. Benson, and L. Ugolini (eds) *Cultures of Selling: Perspectives on Consumption and Society Since 1700*, Aldershot: Ashgate.

Elliot, S. (2004) 'Don't call it a store, call it an ad with walls', *New York Times*, Section G, 7 December: 6.

Elsbach, K. D. (2004) 'Interpreting workplace identities: the role of office décor', *Journal of Organizational Behaviour*, 25: 99–128.

Euromonitor (2007) 'Corporate summary: global retailing strategies for meeting the demands of modern consumers', Report, 3 October, London: Euromonitor International PLC.

Evans, G. (2003) 'Hard-branding the cultural city – from Prado to Prada', *International Journal of Urban and Regional Research*, 27 (2): 417–40.

Evans, G. (2004) 'Measuring impact, culture and regeneration', *Arts Professional*, 4 October: 5–6.

Evans, G. (2005) 'Measure for measure: evaluating the evidence of culture's contribution to regeneration', *Urban Studies*, 42 (5/6): 959–83.

Evans, J., Bridson, K., Byrom, J. and Medway, D. (2005) Retail internationalisation: drivers, impediments and business strategy, Proceedings of the 13th International EAERCD Conference on Research in the Distributive Trades, University of Lund.

Falk, P. and Campbell, C. (eds) (1997) *The Shopping Experience*, London: Sage Publications.

Farquharson, A. (ed.) (2001) *The Magic Hour: The Convergence of Art and Las Vegas*, Ostfildern: Hatje Cantz.

Farrell, J. F. (2003) *One Nation under Goods: Malls and the Seductions of American Shopping*, London/Washington, DC: Smithsonian Institution Press.

Feinberg, R., Stanton, J., Keen, C., Kim, I.-S., Hokama, L. and de Ruyter, K. (2000) 'Attraction as a determinant of mall choice', Proceedings of the 11th International Conference on Retailing and Services Science, Eindhoven: European Institute of Retailing and Services Science.

Fernie, J., Moore, C. M. and Lawrie, A. (1998) 'A tale of two cities: an examination of fashion designer retailing within London and New York', *Journal of Product and Brand Management*, October, 7 (5): 366–78.

Fernie, J., Moore, C., Lawrie, A. and Hallsworth, A. (1997) 'The internationalization of the high fashion brand: the case of central London', *Journal of Product and Brand Management*, 6 (3): 151–62.

Ferrari, M. and Ives, S. (2005) Las Vegas: *An Unconventional History*, New York NY: Bullfinch.

Field, M. (1997) 'Shopping as a way of life', *Blueprint*, 135: 28–30.

Finn, A. and Louvière, J. J. (1996) 'Shopping centre image, consideration and choice: anchor store contribution', *Journal of Business Research*, 35: 241–51.

Fiske, J. (1989) *Reading the Popular*, London: Unwin Hyman.

Fitzpatrick, M. (2007) 'Fast retailing plans Paris flagship'. Available online at: www.just-style.com (accessed 12 October 2007).

Fitzsimmons, D. S. (1995) 'Planning promotion: city reimaging in the 1980s and 1990s', in W. J. Neill, D. S. Fitzsimmons and B. Murtagh (eds) *Reimaging the Pariah City: Urban Development in Belfast and Detroit*, Aldershot: Avebury.

Fleming, J., Honour, H. and Pevsner, N. (1991) *Dictionary of Architecture*, 4th edn, London: Penguin Books.

Floor, K. (2006) *Branding a Store*, London: Kogan Page.

Ford, L. R. (1994) *Cities and Buildings: Skyscrapers, Skid Rows and Suburbs*, Baltimore, MD: Johns Hopkins University Press.

Ford, T. (2001) 'Fashion 2001: the business of luxury', International Herald conference', presentation, Paris: George V Hotel.

Forshaw, A. and Bergstrom, T. (1983) *The Markets of London*, London: Penguin.

Forty, A. (1986) *Objects of Desire*, London:Thames and Hudson.

Foster, A. (2006) 'Sold out in six minutes', *London Evening Standard*, 28 April: 31.

Foster, L. (2004) 'Elegantly waisted – Ermenegildo Zegna', *Drapers*, 21 August: 24–26.

Foxell, E. and Kent, A. M. (2006) 'The role of the flagship store in retail branding', Proceedings of the British Academy of Management Conference, Belfast.

Frampton, K. (2006), 'The work of architecture in the age of commodification', *Harvard Design Review*, Regeneration, 23 (Fall/Winter): 65.

Francis, P. (2005) 'Steve Wynn interview with Paula Francis', *Eyewitness News*, 28 April.

Frayling, C. (1993) *Research in Art and Design: Royal College of Art Research Papers Series* (1), London: Royal College of Art.

Frey, B. S. (1998), 'Superstar museums: an economic analysis', *Journal of Cultural Economics*, 22 (2/3): 113–125.

Fussell, P. (1983) *Class*, New York; Ballantine Books.

Gardner, C. and Sheppard, J. (1989) *Consuming Passion. The Rise of Retail Culture*, London: Unwin Hyman.

Gardner, G. (1998) 'Supermarket sweeps clean', *Building Design*, News in Focus, 22 May: 7.

Garreau, J. (1991) *Edge City: Life on the New Frontier*, Anchor: New York.

Gartman, D. (2004) 'Three ages of the automobile: the cultural logics of the car', *Theory, Culture and Society*, 21 (4/5): 169–96.

Gilbert, D. (2000) 'Urban outfitting: the city and the spaces of fashion culture', in S. Bruzzi and P. Church Gibson (eds) *Fashion Cultures: Theories, Explorations and Analysis*, London: Routledge.

Gilmore, J. H. and Pine, B. J. (2002) 'Customer experience places: the new offering frontier', *Strategy and Leadership*, 30 (4): 4–11.

Girin, J. (1987) 'Le siege vertical et communiquer dans un tour de bureaux', *Annales des Mines-Gerer et Comprendre*, 9: 4–14.

Glancey, J. (1998) 'How would you fit Tesco into this little corner of olde England?', Arts Architecture section, *The Guardian*, 27 April: 13–12.

Goad Plans/OXIRM (1991) *The New Guide to Shopping Centres of Great Britain*, London: Hillier Parker.

Gobé, M. (2001) *Emotional Branding: The New Paradigm for Connecting Brands to People*, Oxford: Windsor.

Gold, J. R. and Ward, S. V. (eds) (1994) *Place Promotion. The Use of Publicity and Marketing to Sell Towns and Regions*, Chichester: John Wiley and Sons.

Golden, L. G. and Zimmerman, D. A. (1986), *Effective Retailing*, Boston MA: Houghton Mifflin.

Gopal, D. (2003) 'Promoting retail to revitalize downtowns: an examination of the business improvement district idea', *Department of Urban Studies and Planning*, Boston, MA: MIT Press.

Gorman, T. (2005) 'At Wynn's namesake, he's on par with himself', *Los Angeles Times*, 5 July.

Gosling, D. and Maitland, B. (1976) *Design and Planning of Retail Systems*, London: Architectural Press.

Gottdeiner, M. (1986) 'Culture, ideology, and the sign of the city', in M. Gottdeiner and A. Lagopoulos (eds) *The City and the Sign: An introduction to Urban Semiotics*, New York: Columbia University Press.

Gottdeiner, M. (1998) 'Consumption spaces and spaces of consumption', in S. Chaplin and E. Holding (eds) *Consuming Architecture*, London: Wiley-Academy.

Gottdeiner, M. (1999) *Las Vegas: The Social Production of an All-American City*, Oxford: Blackwell.

Goulding, C. (2005) 'Grounded theory, ethnography and phenomenology: a comparative analysis of three qualitative strategies for marketing research', *European Journal of Marketing*, 39 (3/4): 294–308.

Graham, S. and Marvin, S. (2001) *Splintering Urbanism: Networked Infrastructures, Technological Mobilities and the Urban Condition*, London: Routledge.

Greenland, S. J. and McGoldrick, P. J. (1994) 'Modelling the impact of designed space: atmospherics, attitudes and behaviour', *International Review of Retail, Distribution and Consumer Research*, 4 (1): 1–16.

Greenwich (2000) 'Millennium Dome original planning proposals' (cited 1 March 2007). Available online at: http://www.greenwich20000.co.uk/millennium/experience/exhibition-plans.htm.

Guardian, The (2007) 'In praise of the millennium wheel', 27 February: 32.

Guy, C. M. (1994) *The Retail Development Process: Location, Property and Planning*, London: Routledge.

Guy, C. M. (1998) 'Classification of retail stores and shopping centres: some methodological issues', *Geojournal*, 45: 255–64.

Guy, C. M. (1999) 'Retail location analysis', in M. Pacione (ed.) *Applied Geography: Principles and Practice*, London: Routledge.

Guy, C. M. and Ducket, M. (2003) 'Small retailers in an inner city community: a case study of Adamstown, Cardiff', *International Journal of Retail and Distribution Management*, 31 (8): 401–7.

Hall, L. (2007) 'Karen Millen on hunt for Paris flagship', *Drapers*, 1 September.

Hallsworth, A. (2000), 'Britain's local loyalty cards – an unmanageable revolution', *International Journal of New Product Development & Innovation Management*, 2 (2): 133–144.

Hammond, A. E. (1930a) *Multiple Shop Organisation*, London: Sir Isaac Pitman and Sons.

Hammond, A. E. (ed.) (c.1930b) *Men's Wear Display: A Practical Work on Window Showmanship and Interior Planning and Equipment*, London: Caxton.

Hankins, K. (2002) 'The restructuring of retail capital and the high street', *Tijdschrift voor Economische en Sociale Geografie*, 93 (1): 34–46.

Hannigan, J. (1998) *Fantasy City: Pleasure and Profit in the Postmodern Metropolis*, London: Routledge.

Hannigan, J. (2004) 'Diversity without tears: marketing the multicultural in the gentrified city', paper presented at the seminar on '*Takeaway Cultures*', December, Barcelona: Centre de Cultura Contemporania.

Hardingham, S. (1996) *England – A Guide to Recent Architecture*, London: Ellipsis.

Harkin, F. (2004) 'Stores that trade on club style', *Financial Times, FT Weekend - Shopping*; September 18, Saturday: 9.

Harris, L. C. and Goode, M. M. H. (2004) 'The four levels of loyalty and the pivotal role of trust: a study of online service dynamics', *Journal of Retailing*, 80 (2): 139–58.

Hatch, M. J. and Shultz, M. (2002) 'The dynamics of organizational identity', *Human Relations*, 55 (8): 989–1018.

Hawthorne, C. (2005) 'A glitch in the glitz', *Los Angeles Times*, 9 May.

Heidegger, M. (1977) 'The age of the world picture', *The Question Concerning Technology and Other Essays*, New York: Harper and Row.

Heim, M. (1998) *Virtual Realism*, Oxford: Oxford University Press.

Henn Architekten (2004) *Interview with Günter Henn and Jan Esche*, Munich, 14 February.

Hess, A. (1993) *Viva Las Vegas*, San Francisco, CA: Chronicle Books.

Hickey, D. (1998) 'Dialectical utopias: on Sante Fe and Las Vegas', *Harvard Design Magazine*, 4 Winter/Spring.

Hildebrandt, L. (1988) 'Store image and the prediction of performance in retailing', *Journal of Business Research*, 17: 91–100.

Hoel, P. G. and Jessen, R. J. (1982) *Basic Statistics for Business and Economics*, New York: Wiley.

Hoffmann, H. (1930) *Modern Interiors*, London: Studio.

Holbrook, M. B. and Hirschman, E. C. (1982) 'The experiential aspects of consumption: consumer, fantasies, feelings and fun', *Journal of Consumer Research*, 9: 132–40.

Holcomb, B. (1994) 'City make-overs: marketing the post-industrial city', in J. R. Gold and S. V. Ward (eds) *Place Promotion. The Use of Publicity and Marketing to Sell Towns and Regions*, Chichester: John Wiley and Sons.

Hollander, S. C. (1970), *Multinational Retailing*, East Lansing, MI: Michigan State University.

Holt, D. B. (2002) 'Why do brands cause trouble? A dialectical theory of consumer culture and branding', *Journal of Consumer Research*, 29: 70–90.

Horbert, C. (2005) 'Urbane fashion in the "glass whale"', *Shops and Stores*, April, Cologne: EHI.

Hospers, G.-J. and van Dalm, R. (2005) 'How to create a creative city? The viewpoints of Richard Florida and Jane Jacobs', *Foresight*, 7 (4) : 8–12.

House of Commons (2000) 'The Millennium Dome', Report by the Comptroller and Auditor General, House of Commons 936, Session 1999–2000, London, 9 November.

House of Commons (2000) 'The Millennium Dome', Hansard written answers, 28 February (pt. 23).

House of Lords (2000) 'Millennium Dome', House of Lords Debates, 29 November.

Howard, E. (1993) 'Assessing the impact of shopping centre development: the Meadowhall case', *Journal of Property Research*, 10: 97–119.

Howard, E. (1997) 'The management of shopping centres: conflict or collaboration?', *The International Review of Retail, Distribution and Consumer Research*, 7 (3): 263–286.

Howard, E. (2007) 'New shopping centres: is leisure the answer?', *International Journal of Retail and Distribution Management*, 35 (8): 661–672.

Huang, A. S. and Christopher, D. (2003) 'Planning an effective internet retail store', *Market Intelligence and Planning*, 21 (4): 230–8.

Huang, M.-H. (2004) 'Romantic love and sex: their relationship and impacts on ad attitudes', *Psychology and Marketing*, 21 (1): 53–73.

Hughes, K. (2007) 'Shopping is the spirit of the silk route, not the online rut', *Guardian Comment and Debate*, 23 June: 30.

Ind, R. (1983) *Emberton*, London: Scolar Press.

Ito, M., Okabe, D. and Matsuda, M. (eds) (2006) *Personal, Portable, Pedestrian: Mobile Phones in Japanese Life*, Cambridge, MA: MIT Press.

Ives, S. (dir) (2005) *Las Vegas: An Unconventional History*, PBS.

Jackson, S. and Friedland, L. (1973) 'New lease of life for Hoover factory', *The Architect's Journal*, 27 January: 37–46.

Jackson, T. (2007) 'Supreme luxury', International Herald Tribune conference presentation, WGSN, Moscow: Ritz Carlton,

Jencks, C. (1979) *Bizarre Architecture*, London: Academy Editions.

Jencks, C. (2005) *The Iconic Building: The Power of Enigma*, London: Frances Lincoln.

Jiang, P. and Rosenbloom, B. (2005) 'Customer intention to return online: price perception, attribute-level performance, and satisfaction unfolding over time', *European Journal of Marketing*, 39 (1/2): 150–74.

Jones, M. A. (1999) 'Entertaining shopping experiences: an exploratory investigation', *Journal of Retailing and Consumer Services*, 6: 129–139.

Joseph, N. (1986) *Uniforms and Nonuniforms: Communications Through Clothing*, New York: Greenwood Press.

J.S. Journal (1991) *Rustington*, September: 9.

J.S. Journal (1991) *Hedge End*, December: 11.

Kavaratzis, M. (2004) 'From city marketing to city branding: towards a theoretical framework for developing city brands', *Place Branding*, 1 (1): 58–73.

Kelly, K. E. (2003) 'Architecture for sale(s)', *Harvard Design Magazine*, 17 (Fall/Winter): 1–6.

Kent A. M. (2003) '2D23D: Management and design perspectives on retail branding', *International Journal of Retail and Distribution Management*, 31 (3): 131–42.

Kiley, D. and Berner, R. (2005) 'Apparel makers go it alone', *Business Week*, 17 December.

Kingsnorth, P. (2001) 'Worth seeing', *The Ecologist*, 31 (5): 57.

Klein, N. (2004) *The Vatican to Vegas: A History of Special Effects*, New York: The New Press.

Klein, N. (2005) *No Logo*, London: Harper Perennial.

Kooijman, D. (1999) *Machine and Theatre. Design Concepts for Shop Buildings (Machine en theater. Ontwerpconcepten van winkelgebouwen)*, Rotterdam: 010 Publishers.

Kooijman, D. and Sierksma, R. (2005) 'Auto- of merkloyaliteit? De verkoop van auto's als belevenisindustrie' (Car loyalty or brand loyalty? Selling cars as experiences), *Vrijetijdstudies*, 23 (2): 37–49.

Kooijman, D. and Sierksma, R. (2007) 'Emotional driving. Cocooning in the urban realm'. Available online at: http://www.library.tudelft.nl/ws/search/publications/search/metadata/index.htm?docname=373189.

Kotler, P. (1974) 'Atmospherics as a marketing tool', *Journal of Retailing*, 49 (4): 48–64

Kozinets, R. V. (1999) 'E-tribalized marketing? The strategic implications of virtual communities of consumption', *European Management Journal*, 17 (3): 252–226.

Kozinets, R. V., Sherry J. F., DeBerry-Spence, B., Duhachek, A., Nuttavuthisit, K. and Storm, D. (2002) 'Themed flagship stores in the new millennium: theory, practice, prospects', *Journal of Retailing*, 78 (1): 17–29.

Lamacraft, J. (1998) *Retail Design – New Store Experiences*, London: Financial Times Retail and Consumer Publishing.

Lammiman, J. and Syrett, M. (2004) *Coolsearch:Keeping Your Organisation in Touch and on the Edge*, Capstone: Chichester.

Lancaster, B. (1995) *The Department Store: A Social History*, London: Leicester University Press.

Landry, C. (2000) *The Creative City: A Toolkit for Urban Innovators*, London: Earthscan Publications.

Lang, T. and Rayner, G. (eds) (2001) 'Why health is the key to the future of food and farming, joint submission to the policy commission on the future of farming and food', December. Available online at: www.ukpha.org.uk (accessed 3 August 2007).

'Las Vegas convention and visitors authority'. Available online at: http://www.lvcva.com/index.jsp (accessed 15 May 2007).

Lasch, C. (1984) *The Minimal Self. Psychic Survival in Troubled Times*, New York: Norton.

Laurier, E. (2001) 'Why people say where they are during mobile phone calls', *Environment and Planning D*, (19): 485–504.

Law, J. (2006) 'Cybertecture international', *Architectural Design*, 76 (5): 119–25.

Leach, N. (1999) *The Anaesthetics of Architecture*, Cambridge, MA: The MIT Press.

Leach, W. (1993) *Land of Desire: Merchants, Power and the Rise of a New American Culture*, New York: Vintage.

Leslie, T. (2005) 'The Pan Am terminal at Idlewild/Kennedy Airport and the transition from jet age to space age', *Design Issues*, 21 (1) Winter: 63–80.

Lewis-Barclay, O. (2005) 'Retail choice – firetrap flagship store, Covent Garden', *Marketing*, 23 February, London: 18.

Liedtka, J. and Mintzberg, H. (2006) 'Time for design', *Design Management Review*: 10–18.

Lindquist, J. D. (1974) 'Meaning of image: a survey of empirical and hypothetical evidence', *Journal of Retailing*, 50 (4): 29–38.

Lindstrom, M. (2003) *Brandchild*, London: Kogan Page.

Lion, E. (1976) *Shopping Centres Planning Development and Administration*, New York: Wiley.

Lloyd, D. (1999) *The Concise History of Ludlow*, Ludlow: Merlin Unwin.

London: A Combined Guidebook and Atlas (1936) London: Thomas Cook and Son.

London: The World's Largest City (1938) Edinburgh: A. Walker and Son.

London: What to See and Where to Stay (1930) The Residential Hotels and Caterers Association.

Losch, A. (1940) *The Economics of Location*, trans. by W. H. Woglam and W. F. Stolper (1954) New Haven, CT: Yale University.

Lowe, M. S. (2000) 'Britain's regional shopping centres: new urban forms', *Urban Studies*, 37 (2): 261–74.

Lowe, M. S. and Wrigley, N. (2000) 'Progress report: retail and the urban', *Urban Geography*, 21 (7): 640–53.

Lumpkin, L. (2006) Interview with Nicky Ryan, 8 February.

Lury, C. (1996) *Consumer Culture*, Cambridge: Polity.

Lury, C. (2004) *Brands: The Logos of the Global Economy*, London: Routledge.

Lynch, K. (1960) *The Image of the City*, Cambridge, MA: MIT Press.

Machleit, K. A. and Mantel, S. P. (2001) 'Emotional response and shopping satisfaction: moderating effects of shopper attributions', *Journal of Business Research*, 54: 97–106.

MacKeith, M. (1985) *Shopping arcades: a gazetteer of extant British arcades, 1817–1939*, London: Mansell.

Magrath, A. J. (2005) 'Managing in the age of design', *Across the Board*, 42 (5): 18–27.

Manhattanization Las Vegas (Las Vegas High Rise Condo Magazine – High Rise, Midrise, and Loft Projects). Available online at: http://www.manhattanization.com/ (accessed 30 July 2007).

Marchart, O. (1999) *Das Ende des Josephnisimus. Zur Politisierung der österreichischen Kulturpolitik*, Vienna: Edition Selene.

McGoldrick, P. J. and Thompson, M. G. (1992) 'The role of image in the attraction of the out of town mall', *The International Review of Retail, Distribution and Consumer Research*, 2 (1): 81–98.

McGuigan, J. (2003) 'The social construction of a cultural disaster: New Labour's millennium experience', *Cultural Studies*, 17 (5): 669–90.

McGuigan, J. and Gilmore, A. (2002) 'The Millennium Dome: sponsoring, meaning and visiting', *International Journal of Cultural Policy*, 8 (1): 1–20.

Marconi, J. (2005) *Creating the Marketing Experience*, Mason, OH: Thomson.

Marketing, (2004) *Marketing Design Awards: Retail Interiors*, 17 November: 21.

Markus, T. A. (1999) 'What do domes mean?', *Critical Quarterly*, 41 (4): 3–10.

Maronick, T. J. (2007) 'Speciality retail center's impact on downtown shopping, dining and entertainment', *International Journal of Retail and Distribution Management*, 35 (6): 556–68.

Martin, P. G. (1982) *Shopping Centre Management*, London: E and F. N. Spon.

Martineau, P. (1958) 'The personality of the retail store', *Harvard Business Review*, 36, January/February: 47–55.

Mehrabian, A. and Russell, J. A. (1974) *An Approach to Environmental Psychology*, Cambridge MA: MIT Press.

Meyhöfer, D. (2003) *Motortecture. Architektur für Automobilität, Design for Automobility*. Ludwigsburg: Avedition.

Meyrowitz, J. (1985) *No Sense of Place: The Impact of Electronic Media on Social Behavior*, New York: Oxford University Press.

Meyrowitz, J. (2005) 'The rise of glociality: new sense of place and identity in the global village', in K. Nyíri (ed.) *A Sense of Place: The Global and the Local in Mobile Communication*, Vienna: Passagen Verlag.

Mikunda, C. (2004) *Brand Lands, Hot Spots and Cool Spaces*, London: Kogan Page.

Miles, M. (2005) 'Interruptions: testing the rhetoric of culturally led urban development', *Urban Studies*, 42 (5/6): 889–911.

Miles, M. and Paddison, R. (2005) 'Introduction: the rise and rise of culture- led urban regeneration', *Urban Studies*, 42 (5/6): 833–9.

Miles, S. (2005) '"Our Tyne": iconic regeneration and the revitalisation of identity in Newcastle Gateshead', *Urban Studies*, 42 (5/6): 913–26.

Miller, M. (1981) *The Bon Marché: Bourgeois Culture and the Department Store, 1869–1920*, Princeton, NJ: Princeton University Press.

Mintel (1997) *Shopping Centres*, London: Mintel Market Intelligence.

Mintel (2004) *Luxury Brand Retailing*, London: Mintel Market Intelligence.

Mintel (2006) *Fashion Online*, London: Mintel Market Intelligence.

Mintel (2007) *Clothing Retailing UK*, London: Mintel Market Intelligence.

Mitchell, J. (2002) 'Fitness drive', *Retail Week*, 21 June: 26.

Moehring, E. (2002) 'Growth, services, and the political economy of gambling in Las Vegas', in H. Rothman and M. Davis (eds) *The Grit Beneath the Glitter: Tales from the Real Las Vegas*, Berkeley CA: University of California Press.

Monclus, F.-J. (2003) 'The Barcelona model: an original formula? From "reconstruction" to strategic urban projects (1979–2004)', *Planning Perspectives*, 18 (4): 399–421.

Montgomery, J. (2003) 'Cultural quarters as mechanisms for urban regeneration, part 1: conceptualising cultural quarters', *Planning Practice and Research*, 18 (3): 293–306.

Mooney, G. (2004) 'Cultural policy as urban transformation? Critical reflections on Glasgow, European city of culture 1990', *Local Economy*, 19 (4): 327–40.

Moore, C. M. (1995) 'From rags to riches – creating and benefiting from the fashion own-brand', *International Journal of Retail Distribution Management*, 23 (9): 19–28.

Moore, C. M. and Birtwistle, G. (2004) 'The Burberry business model: creating an international luxury fashion brand', *International Journal of Retail and Distribution Management*, 32 (8): 412–22.

Moore, C. M. and Birtwistle, G. (2005) 'The nature of parenting advantage in luxury fashion retailing – the case of Gucci Group NV', *International Journal of Retail and Distribution Management*, 33 (4): 256–70.

Moore, C. M. and Doherty, A. M. (2006) 'The international flagship stores of luxury fashion retailers', in T. Hines and M. Bruce (eds) *Fashion Marketing: Contemporary Issues*, Oxford: Butterworth Heinemann.

Moore, C. M., Fernie, J. and Burt, S. (2000), 'Brands without boundaries: the internationalisation of the designer retailer's brand', *European Journal of Marketing*, 34 (8): 919–37.

Moore, R. (1994) 'Sainsbury's takes wing', *Blueprint*, 20 February: 20.

Morris, N. (1998) 'Era of "sheds" to end', *Building Design*, 17 April: 9.

Morrison, K. A. (2003) *English Shops and Shopping*, London:Yale University Press.

Morton, H. V. (1937) *London: A Guide*, London: Methuen.

Muniz Jr, A. M. and O'Guinn, T. C. (2001) 'Brand community', *Journal of Consumer Research*, 27 March: 412–32.

Murray, J. H. (1999) *Hamlet on the Holodeck: The Future of Narrative in Cyberspace*, Cambridge, MA: MIT Press.

National Audit Office (2000) *Report*, 9 November.

Nava, M. (1996) 'Modernity's disavowal: women, the city and the department store', in M. Nava and A. O'Shea (eds) *Modern Times: Reflections on a Century of English Modernity*, London: Routledge.

Neal, L. (1932) *Retailing and the Public*, London: George Allen and Unwin.

Nesbit, M. (1992) 'In the absence of the Parisienne...', in B. Colomina (ed.) *Sexuality and Space*, Princeton, NJ: Princeton University Press

O'Brien, L. and Harris, F. (1991) *Retailing: Shopping, Society, Space*, London: David Fulton.

O'Callaghan, E. and O'Riordan, D. (2003) 'Retailing at the periphery: an analysis of Dublin's tertiary city centre shopping streets (1972–2002)', *International Journal of Retail and Distribution Management*, 31 (8): 389–400.

Olins, W. (1978) *The Corporate Personality: An Inquiry into the Nature of Corporate Identity*, London: Design Council.

Olins, W. (1989) *Corporate Identity*, London: Thames and Hudson.

Olins W. (1990), *Corporate Identity: Making Business Strategy Visible Through Design*, London: Thames and Hudson.

Olins, W. (2003) *Wally Olins on Brand*, London: Thames and Hudson.

Oliver, J. H. (2002) 'The similar eye: proxy life and public space in the MMORPG', in F. Mäyrä (ed.) *Proceedings of Computer Games and Digital Cultures Conference*, Tampere: Tampere University Press.

Olson P. (2005) 'Arnault's Louis Vuitton opens flagship store in China'. Available online at: www.forbes.com/2005/11/18/lvmh-vuitton-china (accessed 20 March 2006).

Olson, R. (2006) 'Second Life's first millionnaire', *Red Herring: The Business of Technology* (online magazine). Available online at: http://www.redherring.com/ (accessed 28 November 2006).

Österreichisches Zentrum für Kulturdokumentation, -forschung und -vermittlung (1992) *Darstellung und Analyse der österreichischen Kulturpolitik. Europaratstudie*, Vienna: Österreichischer Nationalbericht.

Parnass, 'Die Sammlung Leopold', tenth special edition of the Art magazine. Available online at: http://www. parnass.at. (accessed 10 October 2006).

Parnes, L. (1934) *Bauten des Einzelhandels*, Zurich: Orell Füssli.

Pedersen, S. B. (2004) 'Place branding: giving the region of Oresund a competitive edge', *Journal of Urban Technology*, 11 (1): 78–80.

Pegler, M. (2005), 'Brand imaging – a new look at retailing', *Retail Asia*, February, Singapore: Retail Asia Publishing.

Peñaloza, L. (1999) 'Just doing it: a visual ethnographic study of spectacular consumption at Niketown', *Consumption, Markets and Culture*, 2 (4): 337–465.

Peneder, R. (2005) 'State of the art in fashion shops and shopping', *Shop Aktuell 98*, Amstetten: Umsdasch.

Penley, C. (1991) 'Brownian motion: women, tactics, and technology', in C. Penley and A. Ross (eds) *Technoculture*, Minneapolis, MN: University of Minnesota Press.

Pevsner, N. (1976) *A History of Building Types*, London: Thames and Hudson.

Philips, D. (2004) 'Stately pleasure domes – nationhood, monarchy and industry: the celebration exhibition in Britain', *Leisure Studies*, 23 (2): 95–108.

Pine, J. B. and Gilmore, J. H. (1999) *The Experience Economy*, Boston, MA: Harvard Business School Press.

Pink, S. (2006) *Doing Visual Ethnography*, 2nd edn, London: Sage.

Plaza, B. (2000) 'Evaluating the influence of a large cultural artifact in the attraction of tourism: the Guggenheim Museum Bilbao case', *Urban Affairs Review*, 36 (2): 264–74.

Pleschberger, W. (1991) 'Staat und Kultur. Einige Überlegungen zur österreichischen Kulturförderung in rechtstheoretischer und rechtspolitischer Sicht', in: *Kultur. Kunst. Staat. Aufschwünge und Abgesänge zur Zukunft der Kulturförderung*, Vienna: Zukunfts- und Kulturwerkstätte (Hg.).

Pondy, L. R. and Mitroff, I. (1979) 'Beyond open systems of organizations', in B. M. Staw (ed.) *Research in Organizational Behaviour* (1), Greenwich, CT: JAI Press.

Pope, R. (2005) *Creativity, Theory, History, Practice*, London: Routledge.

Portman, J. and Riani, P. (1990) *John Portman*, Washington, DC: American Institute of Architects Press.

Poulain, R. (1931) *Boutiques*, Paris: Vincent Freal et Cie.

Pratt, A. C. (1997) 'Production values: from cultural industries to the governance of culture' in *Environment and Planning*, A29 (11): 1911–1918.

Pratt, M. G. and Barnett, C. K. (1997) 'Emotions and unlearning in Amway recruiting techniques: promoting change through 'safe' ambivalence', *Management Learning*, (28): 65–88.

Pratt, M. G. and Dutton, J. E. (2000) 'Owning up or opting out: the role of identities and emotions in issue ownership', in N. M. Ashkanasay, C. E. J. Hartel, and W. Zerbe (eds) *Emotions in Organizational Life*, Westport, CT: Quorum Books.

Pratt, M. G. and Foreman, P. (2000) 'Classifying managerial responses to multiple organizational identities', *Academy of Management Review*, 25 (1): 18–42.

Pratt, M. G. and Rafaeli, A. (1997) 'Organisational dress as a symbol of multilayered social identities', *Academy of Management Journal*, 40 (1) February: 9–45.

Pratt M. G. and Rafaeli, A. (2001) 'Symbols as a language of organizational relationships', *Research in Organizational Behaviour*, 23: 93–132.

Radice, V. (2002) 'Fashion 2002 – Luxury Unlimited', International Herald Tribune conference, presentation, Paris: George V Hotel.

Rafaeli, A. and Vilnai-Yavetz, I. (2004) 'Emotion as a connection of physical artifacts and organizations', *Organization Science*, 15 (6): 671–86.

Rafiq, M. and Fulford, H. (2005) 'Loyalty transfer from offline to online stores in the UK grocery industry', *International Journal of Retail & Distribution Management*, 33 (6): 444–60.

Rappaport, E. (2000) *Shopping for Pleasure: Women and the Making of London's West End*, Princeton, NJ: Princeton University Press.

Rasch, S., Manget, J. and Hauptkorn, B. (2005) *Die Vertikale Verlockung*, Munich: Boston Consulting Group.

Reilly, W. J. (1931) *The Law of Gravitation*, New York: Knickerbocker Press.

Resnick, A. S. (2004), 'Coach to open flagship store in Nagoya, Japan', *Coach Company Press Office*, 16 December, New York.

Reynolds, J. and Schiller, R. (1992) 'A new classification of shopping centres in great Britain using multiple branch numbers', *Journal of Property Research*, 9: 122–60.

Rheingold, H. (2002) *Smart Nobs: The Next Social Revolution*, Cambridge, MA: Basic Books.

Richards, G. (1999) 'European cultural tourism: patterns and prospects', in D. Dodd and A. van Hemel (eds) *Planning Cultural Tourism in Europe: a Presentation of Theories and Cases*, Amsterdam: Boekman Foundation/Ministry of Education, Culture and Science.

Riewoldt, O. (ed.) (2002) *Brandscaping – Worlds of Experience in Retail Design*, Berlin: Birkhauser.

Ritson, M. (2006) 'How Asprey lost its sparkle', *Marketing*, 4 May, London: 23.

Ritzer, G. and Stillman, T. (2001) 'The modern Las Vegas Casino-Hotel: the paradigmatic new means of consumption', *M@n@gement*, (4): 83–99.

Rogers, Y., Sharp, H. and Preece, J. (2007) *Interaction Design: Beyond Human–Computer Interaction*, Chichester: Wiley.

Roodhouse, S. (2001) 'The wheel of history – a relinquishing of city council control and the freedom to manage: Sheffield galleries and museums trust', *International Journal of Arts Management*, 3 (1): 78–86.

Roodhouse, S. and Mokre, M. (2004) 'The MuseumsQuartier, Vienna: An Austrian cultural experiment', *International Journal of Heritage Studies*, 10, Part 2: 193–208.

Ross, F. and Kent, A. M. (2004) 'An ethnographic photographic study of New York flagship stores and their websites utilizing an "experiential branding" conceptual framework for analysis', Eighth International conference of the European Association for Education and Research in Consumer Distribution London: University of the Arts, London, 30 June.

Rothman, H. (2000) *Devil's Bargains: Tourism in the Twentieth-Century American West*, Lawrence, KS: University Press of Kansas.

Rothman, H. (2002) *Neon Metropolis: How Las Vegas Started the Twenty-First Century*, New York: Routledge.

Rothman, H. (2006) Interview with Nicky Ryan, 8 February.

Rothman, H. and Davis, M. (eds) (2002) *The Grit Beneath the Glitter: Tales from the Real Las Vegas*, Berkeley, CA: University of California Press.

Routemaster (1998) *SK 6801*, St Albans: Pan Star.

Russell, J. S. (2002) 'Eden Project', *Architectural Record*, 190 (1): 93–5.

Ryan, J. (2005) 'Flags of convenience', *Retail Week*, 1 July.

Ryan, J. (2007) 'Nokia unveils London flagship plans', *Retail Week*, 31 August.

Rymaszewski, M., Au, W. J., Wallace, M., Winters, C., Ondrejka, C. and Batstone-Cunningham, B. (2007) *Second Life: The Official Guide*, Indianapolis, IN: Wiley.

Sainsbury (1997) *A Proposal for Greenwich Peninsular*, October, J. Sainsbury plc.

Saler, M. (1999) *The Avant-Garde in Inter-War England: Medieval Modernism and the London Underground*, New York and Oxford: Oxford University Press.

Samuel , R. (1994) 'Theatres of memory' (1), *Past and Present in Contemporary Culture*, London: Verso.

Saussure, F. D. (1983) *Course in General Linguistics*, trans. R. Harris, London: Duckworth.

Schmitt, B. and Simonsen, A. (1997) *Marketing Aesthetics: The Strategic Management of Brands*, New York: The Free Press.

Schulze, G. (2000) *Die Erlebnis-Gesellschaft. Kultursociologie der Gegenwart* (*The Experience Society. Cultural Sociology of Today*), Frankfurt am Main: Campus Verlag.

Schumacher, A. (1934) *Ladenbau*, Stuttgart: Julius Hoffmann.

Schwarz, D. (2006) 'Wynn's return a defining moment on the strip', *Las Vegas Business Press*, 9 January.

Schwarzer, M. (2005) 'Architecture and mass tourism', in J. Ockman and S. Frausto (eds.), *Architourism*, London: Prestel.

Second Report of the Greater London Regional Planning Committee (1933), March, London: Knapp, Drewett and Sons Ltd.

Sennett, R. (1977) *The Fall of Public Man*, London: Faber and Faber: 148.

Sennett, R. (1990) *The Conscience of the Eye. The Design and Social Life of Cities*, New York: W. W. Norton and Co.

Seth, A. and Randall, G. (1999) *The Grocers – The Rise and Rise of the Supermarket Chains*, London : Kogan Page.

Severin, V., Louvière, J. J. and Finn, A. (2001) 'The stability of retail shopping choices over time and across countries', *Journal of Retailing*, 77 (2): 185–202.

Shaw, C. and Ivens, J. (2002), *Building Great Consumer Experiences*, Basingstoke: Palgrave.

Sherman, E. and Smith, R. B. (1987) 'Mood states of shoppers and store image: promising interactions and possible behavioral effect', *Advances in Consumer Research*, 14 (1): 251–254.

Sherry Jr, J. F. (1987) 'Cereal monogamy: brand loyalty as secular ritual in consumer culture', 17th Annual Conference of the Association for Consumer Research, Toronto, Canada.

Sherwood, J. (2007) 'Why online fashion has not clicked for men', *Financial Times*, Weekend Style section, 19 May: 6.

SIRC (2006) 'Life online: the web in 2020'. A study by the Social Issues Research Centre, Oxford. Available online at: http://www.sirc.org/publik/web2020.shtml (accessed 17 December 2007).

Sirgy, M. J. and Cocksun, S. A. (1989) 'The store loyalty concept: dimensions and measurement', in S. A. Cocksun (ed.), *Retail Marketing Strategy*, New York: Quorum.

Sklair, L. (2005) 'The transnational capitalist class and contemporary architecture in globalizing cities', *International Journal of Urban and Regional Research*, 29: 485–500.

Sit, J., Merrilees, W. and Birch, D. (2003) 'Entertainment-seeking mall patrons: the missing segments', *International Journal of Retail and Distribution Management*, 31 (2): 80–94.

Smit, T. (2001) *Eden Project*, London: Bantam.

Smith, A. (2005) 'Conceptualizing image change: the reimaging of Barcelona', *Tourism Geographies*, 7: 398–423.

Smith, D. (2007) 'Another Eden is rising in the west', *The Observer*, 11 February: 25.

Smith, J. (2001) *Running Scared: The Life and Treacherous Times of Las Vegas Casino King Steve Wynn*, New York: Four Walls Eight Windows.

Smith, R. (2005) 'What effect Wynn Las Vegas? Experts wonder', *Gaming Wire*, 1 May.

Smith, R. B. and Sherman, E. (1993) 'Effects of store image and mood on consumer behavior: a theoretical and empirical analysis', *Advances in Consumer Research*, 20 (1): 631.

Smyth, H. (1994) *Marketing the City: The Role of Flagship Developments in Urban Regeneration,* London: E. & F. N. Spon.

Sorkin, M. (ed.) (1992) *Variations on a Theme Park: The New American City and the End of Public Space,* New York: The Noonday Press.

Sorkin, M. (1999) 'Gambling on the triumph of taste in Las Vegas', *Metropolis,* April: 59–61.

Spies, K., Hesse, F. and Loesch, K. (1997) 'Store atmosphere, mood and purchasing behavior', *International Journal of Research in Marketing,* 14: 1–17.

Staeheli, L. A. and Mitchell, D. (2006) 'USA's destiny? Regulating space and creating community in American shopping malls', *Urban Studies,* 43 (5/6): 977–92.

Stallabras, J. (1996) *Gargantua: Manufactured Mass Culture,* London: Verso.

Stein, J. (2005) 'Wynn's big bet', *Time Asia Magazine,* 27 June.

Stein, J. (2006) 'He didn't invent Las Vegas. He just makes it work', *TIME 100 Issue,* 8 May.

Strati, A. (1998) 'Organizational symbolism as a social construction; a perspective from the sociology of knowledge', *Human Relations,* 51 (11): 1379–402.

Stutz, H. (2005) 'Strip megaresort: Wynn creation opens', *Gaming Wire,* 28 April.

Sunday Telegraph (2007) 'We'd be daft to go to the US selling vests', 28 October: 5.

Sveningsson, S. and Alvesson, M. (2003) 'Managing managerial identities: organizational fragmentation, discourse and identity', *Human Relations,* 56 (10): 1163–93.

Svengingsson, S. and Alvesson, M. (2003) 'Managing managerial identities: organizational fragmentation, discourse and identity struggle', *Human Relations,* 56 (10): 1163–93.

Swarovski (2008) *Press Information Pack,* London.

Swyngedouw, E., Moulaert, F. and Rodriguez, A. (2002) 'Neoliberal urbanization in Europe: large scale urban development projects and the new urban policy', *Antipode,* Part 34: 542–77.

Szymanski, D. M. and Hise, R. T. (2000) 'E-satisfaction: an initial examination', *Journal of Retail,* 76 (3): 309–22.

Thomas, R. and Linstead, A. (2002) 'Losing the plot? Middle managers and identity', *Organization,* 9 (1): 71–93.

Thrift, J. (1997) 'What's in store for brands', *Marketing,* 27 February, London.

Tiemensma, L. (2007) 'The identity of fashion brands. Creating identity with retail design', Delft University of Technology, Master's Thesis. Available online at: http://www.library. tudelft.nl/ws/search/publications/index.htm (accessed 20 May 2007).

Tosh, G. (2005) 'Retail choice – warehouse flagship store Oxford Street', *Marketing,* 2 November: 12.

Tucker, J. (2003) *Retail Desire: Design, Display and Visual Merchandising,* Hove: RotoVision.

Turbayne, C. M. (1970) *The Myth of Metaphor,* Columbia, SC: University of South Carolina Press.

Turkle, S. (1995) *Life on the Screen: Identity in the Age of the Internet,* London: Weidenfeld and Nicolson.

Turley, L. W. and Milliman, R. E. (2000) 'Atmospheric effects on shopping behaviour: a review of the experimental evidence', *Journal of Business Research,* 49: 193–211.

Turley, L. W. and Chebat, J.-C. (2002) 'Linking retail strategy, atmospheric design and shopping behavior', *Journal of Marketing Management,* 18: 125–144.

Twitchell, J. (2002) *Living it Up: Our Love Affair with Luxury,* New York: Columbia University Press.

Urry, R. (2002) *The Tourist Gaze,* 2nd edn, London: Sage Publications.

Van der Grinten, E. F. (1980) *Shop Windows of the 19th Century in Western Cities (Negentiende-eeuwse winkelpuien in westerse steden),* Nijmegen: Radbout University.

Varley, R. and Rafiq, M. (2004) *Principles of Retail Management,* Basingstoke: Palgrave Macmillan.

Vegas Today and Tomorrow – The Future of Las Vegas. Available online at: http://www. vegastodayandtomorrow.com (accessed 20 May 2007).

Venturi, R., Scott Brown, D. and Izenour, S. (1998) *Learning from Las Vegas: The Forgotten Symbolism of Architectural Form*, London: MIT Press.

Virtual Brum (2003) *The New Bullring Shopping Centre*. Available online at: http://www. virtualbrum.co.uk/bullring03.htm (accessed 24 September 2007).

Voase R. (1997) 'The role of flagship cultural projects in urban regeneration: a case study and commentary', *Managing Leisure*, 2 (4): 230–41.

Vrechopoulos, A., O'Keefe, R.O., Doukidis, G. and Siomkos, G. (2004) 'Virtual store layout; an experimental comparison in the context of grocery retail', *Journal of Retailing*, 80 (1): 13–22.

Wallendorf, M. and Arnould, E. (1988) 'My favourite things: a cross-cultural inquiry into object attachment, possessiveness, and social linkage', *Journal of Consumer Research*, 14 (4): 531–47.

Walsh, C. (2003) 'Social meaning and social place in the shopping galleries of early modern London', in J. Benson and L. Ugolini (eds.), *A Nation of Shopkeepers: Five Centuries of British Retailing*, London: Tauris.

Ward, J. (2001) *Weimar Surfaces: Urban Visual Culture in 1920s Germany*, London: University of California Press.

Ward, P. and Davies, B. (2005) 'Exploring the connections between visual merchandising and retail branding: an application of facet theory', *International Journal of Retail and Distribution Management*, 33 (7): 505–13.

Warnaby, G., Bennison, D. and Davies, B. J. (2005) 'Marketing communications decisions in UK planned shopping centres', *Working paper 503/05*, University of Salford.

Weedon, C. (1987) *Feminist Practice and Poststructuralist Theory*, Oxford: Blackwell.

Weibel, P. (2001) 'Las Vegas the city: a place of consumption in the post industrial information society', in A. Farquharson (ed.) *The Magic Hour: The Convergence of Art and Las Vegas*, Ostfildern: Hatje Cantz.

Weiser, M. and Seely Brown, J. (1996) 'The coming age of calm technology', Xerox Parc Report. Available online at: http://www.cs.ucsb.edu/~ebelding/courses/284/w04/papers/calm.pdf (accessed 10 March 2007).

Westwood, B. and Westwood, N. (1937) *Smaller Retail Shops*, London: Architectural Press.

Westwood, B. and Westwood, N. (1952) *The Modern Shop*, London: Architectural Press.

White, M. (1999) 'MPs fear Dome cash shortfall', *The Guardian* (London): 9.

Wigley, M. (1995) *White Walls, Designer Dresses: The Fashioning of Modern Architecture*, Cambridge, MA: MIT Press.

Wilde, S. J., Kelly, S. J. and Scot, D. (2004) 'An exploratory investigation into e-tail image attributes important to repeat, internet savvy customers', *Journal of Retailing and Consumer Services*, 11 (3): 131–9.

Williams, B. (1994) *The Best Butter in the World: A History of Sainsbury's*, London: Ebury Press.

Williams, R. and Edge, D. (1996) 'The social shaping of technology', in W. H. Dutton (ed.) *Information and Communication Technologies*, Oxford: Oxford University Press.

Wilson, F. (1992) 'Language, technology, gender and power', *Human Relations*, 45 (9): 883–904.

Winograd, T. (ed.) (1995) *Bringing Design to Software*, Reading, MA: Addison Wesley.

Winship, J. (2000) 'Culture of restraint: the British chain store 1920–1939', in P. Jackson, M. Lowe, D. Miller and F. Mort (eds) *Commercial Cultures: Economies, Practices, Spaces*, Oxford: Berg.

Winstanley, M. (1983) *The Shopkeepers World 1830–1914*, Manchester: Manchester University Press.

Wittgenstein, L. (1958) *Philosophical Investigations*, trans. G. E. M. Anscombe, Oxford: Blackwell.

Wolfe, T. (1965) *The Kandy-Kolored Tangerine-Flake Streamline Baby*, New York: Farrar, Straus and Giroux.

Wolfingbarger, M. and Hilly, M. C. (2003) 'E-tailQ: dimensionalising, measuring and predicting e-tail quality', *Journal of Retailing*, 79 (3):183–98.

Worpole, K. (2000) *The Value of Architecture: Design, Economy and the Architectural Imagination*, London: RIBA.

Worsley, G. (2004) 'Review 2004: Architecture', *The Daily Telegraph*, 18 December.

Wright, J. (2007), quoted in Anon, 'Nokia secures its next flagship store in São Paulo', www.theretailbulletin.com (accessed 26 October 2007).

Wrigley, N., Warm, D. and Margetts, B. (2003) 'Deprivation, diet and food retail access: findings from the Leeds "food deserts" study', *Environment and Planning A*, 35: 151–88.

Wynne, D. (1992) *The Culture Industry: The Arts in Urban Regeneration*, Aldershot: Avebury.

Yang, A., Peterson, R. T. and Cai, S. (2003) 'Service quality dimensions of Internet retailing: an exploratory analysis', *Journal of Services Marketing*, 17 (7): 685–700.

Yerbury, F. R. (1928) *Modern European Buildings*, London: Victor Gollancz.

Yoo, C., Park, J. and MacUnnis, D. J. (1998) 'Effects of store characteristics and in-store emotional experiences on store attitude', *Journal of Business Research*, 42 (3): 253–263.

Young, R. A. (1985) 'Suburban growth poles', in J. A. Dawson, and J. D. Lord (eds) *Shopping Centre Development: Policies and Prospects*, London: Croom Helm.

Zalany, N. (1998) 'Discovering a flagship store'. Available online at: www.retailtrafficmag.com/mag/retail_discovering_flagship_store/index.html (accessed 25 October 2007).

Zola, E. (1998) *The Ladies' Paradise*, Oxford: Oxford University Press.

Zukin, S. (1995) *The Culture of Cities*, Oxford: Blackwell.

Index